The Elusiveness of Tolerance

UNC | COLLEGE OF ARTS AND SCIENCES
Germanic and Slavic Languages and Literatures

From 1949 to 2004, UNC Press and the UNC Department of Germanic & Slavic Languages and Literatures published the UNC Studies in the Germanic Languages and Literatures series. Monographs, anthologies, and critical editions in the series covered an array of topics including medieval and modern literature, theater, linguistics, philology, onomastics, and the history of ideas. Through the generous support of the National Endowment for the Humanities and the Andrew W. Mellon Foundation, books in the series have been reissued in new paperback and open access digital editions. For a complete list of books visit www.uncpress.org.

The Elusiveness of Tolerance

The "Jewish Question" From Lessing to the Napoleonic Wars

PETER R. ERSPAMER

UNC Studies in the Germanic Languages and Literatures
Number 117

Copyright © 1997

This work is licensed under a Creative Commons CC BY-NC-ND license. To view a copy of the license, visit http://creativecommons.org/licenses.

Suggested citation: Erspamer, Peter R. *The Elusiveness of Tolerance: The "Jewish Question" From Lessing to the Napoleonic Wars.* Chapel Hill: University of North Carolina Press, 1997. DOI: https://doi.org/10.5149/9781469656489_Erspamer

Library of Congress Cataloging-in-Publication Data
Names: Erspamer, Peter R.
Title: The elusiveness of tolerance : The "Jewish Question" from Lessing to the Napoleonic wars / by Peter R. Erspamer.
Other titles: University of North Carolina Studies in the Germanic Languages and Literatures ; no. 117.
Description: Chapel Hill : University of North Carolina Press, [1997] Series: University of North Carolina Studies in the Germanic Languages and Literatures. | Includes bibliographical references and index.
Identifiers: LCCN 96022248 | ISBN 978-1-4696-1464-9 (pbk: alk. paper) | ISBN 978-1-4696-5648-9 (ebook)
Subjects: Jews in literature. | Antisemitism in literature. | German literature — 18th century — History and criticism. | German literature — 19th century — History and criticism. | Religious tolerance — Germany. | Haskalah — Germany. | Antisemitism — Germany — History — 19th century.
Classification: LCC PT149.J4 E78 1997 | DCC 809/ .93352296

This book is affectionately inscribed to my mother, Jean McDonell Erspamer; my seven brothers, Dan, Dave, Gordy, Mike, Paul, Roy, and Marty; and to the memory of my father, Ernest Gordon Erspamer of Hurley, Wisconsin.

Contents

Acknowledgments	xi
1. Introduction	1
2. The Beginnings of the Tolerance Debate	32
3. Jewish Identity in a Changing World	64
4. Emancipatory Drama after Lessing	98
5. Myths of Ethnic Homogeneity: Anti-Semitic Literature after 1800	113
6. Concluding Remarks: Beyond the Tolerance Debate	151
Notes	157
References	177
Index	187

Acknowledgments

On occasion of this, my first book-length foray into that collective endeavor called scholarship, it gives me great pleasure to acknowledge those who have helped make it possible. An earlier version of this study was presented as a dissertation to the German Department of the University of Wisconsin–Madison in 1992. I would like to thank Klaus Berghahn for sharing his extensive knowledge of German Jewish Studies with me while he was guiding the project. I would like to thank Max Baeumer for the benefit of his advice during the process of the revision. Peter Pütz read an early draft of some of the chapters and made many helpful suggestions. The erudite critiques of the readers for the University of North Carolina Press were immensely helpful. A small section of this study has been accepted for publication under the title "Framing the 'Jewish Question' during the Enlightenment and Early Anti-Semitism in Its Aftermath" in *The Yale Handbook of Jewish Culture in Germany*, edited by Sander Gilman and Jack Zipes, forthcoming from Yale University Press. Some of the more arcane primary sources referred to in this study were procured for me from various libraries in Europe and the United States by the interlibrary loan staffs of the University of Bonn and the University of Missouri–Columbia. Monika Richarz of the Germania Judaica in Cologne gave me some useful tips on how to approach the logistical aspects of this project. Research for this study was financed by an exchange grant from the Rheinische-Friedrich-Wilhelms-Universität in Bonn, by a Fulbright Travel Grant, and a Fulbright Renewal Grant. I am also grateful for the generous support of the Lucius N. Littauer Foundation. Finally, I would like to thank Paul Roberge for accepting this study into the series, University of North Carolina Studies in the Germanic Languages and Literatures, and Brian MacDonald for his copyediting for the University of North Carolina Press. I would also like to thank my family, friends, colleagues, students, and teachers for random acts of kindness which have helped make the writing of this book an enjoyable experience.

Chetek, Wisconsin
1 September 1995

The Elusiveness of Tolerance

1. Introduction

Exposition of the Issues

Shortly after World War II, the historian Eva G. Reichmann reflected that "National Socialism, the political movement that brought about the catastrophe of the German Jews, did not suddenly spring into existence, but was the outcome of certain trends in the social development."[1] The political philosopher Hannah Arendt described anti-Semitism as a "furious reaction to emancipated and assimilated Jewry."[2] These observations that modern anti-Semitism was the result of a failed emancipation still hold true.[3] Emancipation was a progressive movement that failed to take root, in part because of its internal contradictions. These contradictions, which go to the heart of some of our fundamental conceptions as participants in Western society, need to be examined more closely. It is therefore instructive to examine the course of Jewish emancipation in Germany up until the development of a nationalistic anti-Semitism. In order to do this, the following study intends to analyze German literature thematizing Jewish emancipation and anti-Semitism from the years 1779 to 1815. I have chosen this time period because 1779 marks the publication of Gotthold Ephraim Lessing's emancipatory drama, *Nathan der Weise*, and 1815 marks the publication of Karl Borromäus Alexander Sessa's anti-Semitic drama, *Unser Verkehr*. The examination of three trends during this time frame—Christian Judeophobia, Jewish emancipation, and nationalistic anti-Semitism—reveals an awareness of the elusive nature of tolerance and of the formidable nature of authoritarian social constructs, as well as an increased knowledge of the battle among opposing social forces for linguistic control of even the most antiauthoritarian of ideologies and their rechanneling toward authoritarian ends.

The debate over whether Jews should be emancipated was largely carried out in the literary realm. Consequently, a large number of critics have concerned themselves with literature thematizing the "Jewish question."[4] My examination differs from most of the recent treatments of this topic in that I intend to analyze both imaginative literature and cultural documents relevant to tolerance and Jewish emancipation and to anti-Semitism in order to achieve a better understanding of the *ideological* content of these writings and of the historical process in which emancipatory concepts failed to find popularity with the broader public while anti-Semitism gradually became a mass movement. This investigation of attitudes of a dominant culture toward one of its minorities will be carried out within the context of an increasing awareness of the need for multicultural literacy. The fate of German Jewry is one of the most ominous repercussions of monoculturalist-ethnocentric ideologies, ideologies that can be dangerous and destructive in any land if they are permitted to multiply unchallenged and unchecked. The failures of the tolerance ideology and the successes of anti-Semitism in Germany are matters of international interest and relevance, because they are not without application to issues of contemporary importance. The moral relevance of this issue recedes into the background in most of the recent investigations of this topic. This study concentrates on discursive mechanisms that work against the empowerment of minorities and silence emancipatory discourses. As such, it brings previously unexplored aspects of the literary and historical reception of the "Jewish question" to the forefront.

Historical Background

The last quarter of the eighteenth century was a time of profound change. The political, social, and cultural emancipation of the bourgeoisie was underway. The revolutionary power of rationalistic thought found expression in declarations of human and civic rights, and in demands for constitutions and political freedom. Economic and social development lent the bourgeois movement its impact. A new optimism in progress pervaded Europe.[5]

Within the context of these changes came the question as to whether to leave Jews in their former condition as aliens or extend them full citizenship. This issue faced all Western countries that had abandoned the feudal structure for one in which all citizens were equal before the law.[6]

As Jacob Katz points out in *From Prejudice to Destruction* (1980), the granting of citizenship to the Jews should have depended on the states' relationships to the Christian Church and its institutions. To define the state as Christian would have meant automatic exclusion of the Jews from full citizenship. If the state was explicitly secular, no distinction ought to have been made between Jews and others.[7] The hegemony of Christianity was under sharp attack at this time and was subjected to persistent attempts to replace it with secular philosophies. In the meantime, pretexts for exclusion of the Jews without resort to religious arguments emerged.[8] The emancipation of the Jews was accompanied by stormy controversy. From 1780 on, the fitness of the Jews for citizenship was the subject of constant debate.[9]

The first concrete legal step in the direction of Jewish emancipation was undertaken by the Austrian emperor Joseph II, who issued the Edict of Toleration in 1781. The provisions of this edict included abolition of the yellow badges that Jews were forced to wear outside of the ghettos and the annulment of the dehumanizing body toll placed on Jews and their cattle. Other important provisions included granting Austrian Jews the right to send their children to elementary and secondary schools. Attendance at universities, which had never been forbidden, was now expressly allowed. Jews were allowed to frequent public places of amusement. Most dramatically, they were allowed to learn all trades and engage in wholesale business under the same conditions as Christian subjects and were permitted to establish factories.[10]

The Edict of Toleration did not go so far as to grant full emancipation to the Jews. They could neither join trade guilds nor become masters in their crafts, and acquisition of land was only allowed in Jewish communities. Public worship services were forbidden in Vienna and the number of Jewish residents was not supposed to increase.[11] Civic rights were forbidden them and they could not own printing presses for Hebrew books.[12]

Because of the Jews' newly acquired legal status, it was necessary to grant them family names. They were also made subject to military service. According to Alfred D. Low, Joseph II "wanted to have all Austrian subjects contribute to the welfare of the nation, without regard to nationality or religion." He viewed the economic diversification of the Jews as a means of making them more useful to the state.[13] Joseph II rejected every "pressure of the conscience as harmful" and maintained that religion was a matter of personal conviction. Joseph examined alleged shortcomings of Jews, such as their economic activity, and attributed these to harsh oppression. He believed that Jews had the capacity for moral improvement. Joseph's opening of agriculture to the Jews was done with the reasoning that they "should seize the hoe instead of the wallet."[14]

Joseph II attempted to promote the total assimilation of Jews to German culture. One means by which he hoped to attain this was through educating Jewish youth in German schools. School and study were seen as major avenues through which the Jews would be Germanized.[15] Joseph was, however, opposed to an increase in the Jewish population, because he was afraid it would delay the assimilation of the more educated Jews.[16]

Although Joseph's tolerance edict was regarded by many as a striking change for the better for the Jews living in his kingdom, it was in fact at best a restricted religious tolerance.[17] Joseph's reforms stopped short of granting full equality to Jews and it was clear that the "tolerated" were to remain second-class citizens. Bureaucratic chicanery often made it clear that the Jews were subjected to mere sufferance or forbearance and not to any modern standard of tolerance.[18] The tolerance was of limited range, because it had been granted by ruling powers who were convinced that they belonged to the sole true religion. Those who administered the reforms were equally convinced that they were religiously and morally superior.[19] Nonetheless, Joseph's reforms were regarded by many in the Jewish community as a substantial improvement in their condition. A sense of jubilation regarding the Edict of Toleration was expressed by the Jewish author Arenhof in his short play, *Einige jüdische Familienscenen* (1782).

In Prussia, conditions for Jews were less favorable than in Austria. Friedrich II had a more conservative Jewish policy than Joseph II. He generally did not feel any inclination to apply the tolerant and progressive religious principles he professed to Jews.[20] Much of this was due to the influence of Voltaire, who was a favored presence in Friedrich's court. In imitation of Voltaire, Friedrich mocked the putatively childish fables of religion and followed Voltaire's attacks on Judaism with enthusiasm.[21] Nevertheless, Friedrich on occasion indirectly advanced the progress of the German Jewry when it was in his interest to do so. His economic policy was to promote the development of industry and trade and to strengthen the middle class. Friedrich acted in accordance with the concepts of tolerance whenever he found the Jews to be useful instruments of his economic policy. Wealthy Jews enjoyed his support and benevolence, but poorer Jews lived in a state of oppression and abject misery.[22]

Under Friedrich's reign, a difference was made between regularly protected Jews and specially protected Jews. Regularly protected Jews ("ordentliche Schutzjuden") were allowed to pass the right of residency on to their eldest child, whereas specially protected Jews ("außerordentliche Schutzjuden") were allowed residency only for the lifetime of the holder of the letter of protection. Prussian Jews were not permitted to engage in crafts and agriculture. They could neither possess nor rent distilleries or breweries. Many areas of commerce were closed to them.[23]

A few very rich and enterprising Jews attained positions of influence, prestige, and privilege under Friedrich II. An order of October 29,

1757, specifying that only a Jew who established a factory would be eligible for a letter of protection drove Jews into manufacturing. Jews who established factories received public favors.[24]

Friedrich extended protection to Jews mainly for the development of trade, manufacturing, commerce, and goods. Jews were expressly forbidden to engage in agriculture. Friedrich used Jews as instruments of his mercantilist policy to his best advantage. Wealthy Jews who engaged in trade and industry could be used to help enrich the state treasury.[25] Such Jews were commonly referred to as "Court Jews" (*Hofjuden*).

The spirit of tolerance that was an important component of the Enlightenment manifested itself largely in the intellectual realm. In the house of Moses Mendelssohn, Jews and non-Jews met to hear lectures and discussions by Marcus Herz, Salomon Maimon, or Mendelssohn himself. Similar exchanges took place in the Jewish salons of Rahel Varnhagen, Henriette Herz, and Dorothea Mendelssohn Schlegel. In such environments, Jews and Gentiles socialized with one another and discussed the issues of the day and the latest intellectual fashions on an equal footing. These sorts of forums promoted goodwill toward the religious minority and increased the social status of certain individual Jews. These Jews were, however, widely regarded as exception Jews and not as typical of the Jewish masses. There was also a tendency to view them as probable candidates for conversion to Christianity and therefore subject to special treatment.

During 1790–91, the emancipation of the Jews was decreed by the newly installed French National Assembly. Real progress for German Jews did not come about until the Napoleonic incursions into Germany, which began in 1805. One of the phenomena accompanying Napoleon's dominion was the emancipation of Jews in states that were occupied or annexed by France.[26] In January 1808, Westphalia became the first German state to grant equal rights to Jews. It was ruled by Napoleon's brother Jerome, who was sympathetic toward the cause of Jewish emancipation. Frankfurt and Hamburg also liberated their Jews, and Lübeck and Bremen, where the residence of Jews had been prohibited, permitted their settlement.[27]

Prussia succumbed to French arms in 1806, and the liberation of the Jews followed in 1812. This emancipation was, however, not directly attributable to the French influence but followed a different model. Reinhard Rürup differentiates between two conceptions for Jewish emancipation: an enlightened state conception and a liberal revolutionary conception.[28] The French National Assembly on November 13, 1791, brought Jews immediate and unrestricted equal rights. The Prussian model placed the state in a pedagogical role: after a partial emancipation, which was to open up bourgeois society to the Jews, every additional step was to depend on the degree of assimilation or "normalization" that the Jews had reached.[29]

The Napoleonic liberation of the Jews offended the patriotism of many Germans, who sought liberation from "foreign tyranny."[30] Jews took part in a progressive economy and in a rationalistic movement that had promised their emancipation. They were seen as a threat to the feudal order by those who desired a return to the Middle Ages.[31] Many patriotic Germans maintained that the emancipation of the Jews could not be condoned because it began with French oppression.

Jews were rejected in this age of national fervor as being non-German. Furthermore, liberation of the Jews had been closely associated with the Enlightenment. With the new nationalism went a rejection of the Enlightenment, which was perceived as a French import. The new *Zeitgeist* made itself evident in the decline of the Jewish salons of Henriette Herz, Rahel Varnhagen, and Dorothea Schlegel. Many of the Gentile intellectuals who had been guests at the Jewish salons now frequented patriotic *Tischgesellschaften*. The diverse and cosmopolitan character of the salons gave way to clubs of a nationalistic, conservative, and exclusive character. The reactionary character of the national Romantic movement was coloring all sectors of society.

The broadest sectors of the Christian population had seen in Jewish emancipation the liberation of the pariah but not of themselves.[32] Monarchs and enlightened civil servants had recognized the usefulness of Jews in the development of trade and industry. Governmental borrowing from Jews was the beginning of credit as an important element in the economy of the state.[33] A small group of Jews became well-off through the new development. Such wealthy Jewish financiers received a privileged standing in bourgeois society.[34] In the meantime, debt-ridden farmers and unskilled laborers reacted with envy and fear as they witnessed the social ascent of members of a pariah caste. They felt they were being robbed and exploited by the Jewish parvenus.[35]

The lower nobility in Prussia and Bavaria also felt threatened by the Jews; some were in debt to Jewish financiers and felt that their honor and social standing were being endangered.[36] The net effect of these developments was a new nationalistic anti-Semitism that substantially repudiated the tolerance advanced by the Enlightenment.

We will return to these historical factors later in this chapter as we explore the public discourse underlying the transition from Jewish emancipation to anti-Semitism. Before we do so, however, I would like to examine some of the underlying causes of anti-Semitism as analyzed in recent research. For the purpose of this study, we will use the definition of anti-Semitism offered in the 1972 edition of the *Encyclopedia Judaica*: "Anti-Semitism, a term coined in 1879, . . . by the German agitator Wilhelm Marr to designate the then-current anti-Jewish campaigns in Europe. 'Anti-Semitism' soon came into general use as a term denoting all forms of hostility manifested toward the Jews throughout history."[37] In accordance with this definition, we will be using the term "anti-Semitism" to refer to Jew-hatred from all eras, including that prior to 1879. We will now proceed with a more detailed examination of the elements of anti-Semitism.

Elements of Anti-Semitism

One of the major efforts to explain anti-Semitism is derived from the premises of group sociology. A key concept is the notion of conflicting identities leading to group tensions. Almost all research in this area has its basis in the early twentieth-century work of the American sociologist William Graham Sumner, who distinguished between ingroups and outgroups.[38]

The ingroup (also called the we-group) is the group with which the subject identifies, with which she or he feels a sense of belonging. The outgroup (also called the others-group) consists of all the people not belonging to the specific ingroup. Relations between ingroups and outgroups are often characterized by emotional polarizations and by the judgment of all values according to the conception of one's own group. The greater the degree of adherence to one's own group, the greater the degree of hostility toward others. Hostility and xenophobia are derived from the alien characteristics of strangers.[39]

Ingroup identification fulfills important psychological needs: the feeling of belonging to a group, of sharing community goals, and identifying shared values.[40] But it quickly leads to ethnocentrism, which may be resorted to in order to foster a more coherent group identification and bolster the self-esteem of the group.[41] Werner Bergmann in his 1988 study, "Group Theory and Ethnic Relations," explains the psychological and sociological functions of ethnocentrism: "It strengthens the homogeneity of the group, making internal communication, decision processes, and friendly relations easier, it raises the level of motivation and persistence in the pursuit of group goals."[42] The impact on intergroup relations, however, can be devastating: "Increased integration in one's own group is matched by decreased adaptability and flexibility, and by increased combativeness toward other groups."[43] Taking refuge in stereotypes and group conformity makes an individual feel "safer." Prejudice is often an inescapable element in the psychological economy of people with strong group identifications. In his 1948 study, *Anti-Semite and Jew*, Jean-Paul Sartre applies this problem to the situation of the Jews: by treating the Jew as an "inferior and pernicious" being, ethnocentric individuals affirm the feeling of belonging to an "elite." The anti-Semites find the existence of the Jew absolutely necessary. Otherwise, asks Sartre, to whom would they feel superior?[44]

The status of a stigmatized outgroup tends to perpetuate the structure of the dominant group. The minority becomes a "negative reference group" defining the unity of the ingroup. The existence of a pariah caste fosters identification of the lower classes of society with the dominant group by giving the lower classes a sense of common status with the ruling classes. A pariah caste is by definition below the lowest caste or class and thereby raises the ranking of all strata of the dominant group.[45]

Viewing Jews as outsiders and aliens provides what Theodore Isaac Rubin describes in *Anti-Semitism: A Disease of the Mind* (1990) as an artificial source of "belonging and being insiders with attachment to the main group. This reinforcement of identification with the national majority becomes necessary during attacks of inadequacy and disruptions of dependency feelings."[46] This artificial sense of being an "insider" is provided by isolating the Jews from the dominant group and viewing them as outsiders. Jews are thought of as being a homogeneous group that is categorically different from the dominant group. The outgroup is thought of as being a homogeneous group that is categorically different from the dominant group. There is little ability to distinguish between individual members of that group.[47]

As such, the failure of a large group to accept ingroup values creates tension and hostility. This manifests itself in the ethnocentric individual as a feeling of being threatened, of being persecuted by the outgroup.[48] According to Theodor W. Adorno, Elke Frenkel-Brunswick, Daniel J. Levenson, and R. Nevitt Sanford in the distinguished study *The Authoritarian Personality* (1950), the ethnocentrist views the outgroup with a "sense of contraidentification, of basic conflict, of mutual exclusiveness, of violation of primary values."[49] The ingroup values are viewed as being an incontrovertible truth and any sign of nonconformity is viewed as oppositional and subversive.[50]

The outgroups provide unwanted competition for members of the ingroup, because they are generally groups of low status who are striving to improve their position in society. The ingroups feel that they are superior in "morality, ability, and general development" to the more subordinate groups. They therefore believe that they ought to be superior in power and status, and when they sense that their status is undermined or threatened, they perceive that they are being victimized or persecuted. Attempts by marginalized groups to upgrade their status are viewed as threats to the ingroup rather than as efforts to attain equality and mutual interaction.[51]

These general principles of group relations must be considered within the historical context of the situation of the Jews in the late eighteenth and early nineteenth centuries. A major source of group antagonism emerged because the Jews preserved their coherence as a group longer than could have been expected at the time of emancipation.[52]

The character of the Jewish community before emancipation was essentially national and religious. Emancipation was granted under the assumption that segregation would cease and religion would become a totally secondary concern.[53] Despite a significant alleviation of the social barriers separating Jew and Gentile and the insignificance of the remaining religious differences, the character of the Jews as a distinct population group remained.[54]

The Jews in Germany had conserved their medieval way of life until the beginning of emancipation. They lived in religious, cultural, legal, and social separation. Segregation contributed to the development and preservation of Jewish identity.[55] Practically all Jews in the ghetto adhered to Jewish cultural values. The intensity of Jewish identity was frequently condemned by Gentiles as either stubbornness or arrogance. The contempt was often mutual. When their liberation from the ghettos came about, masses of Jews were unprepared for their new situation.[56]

Along every step of their transition toward emancipation, parts of the Jewish tradition were abandoned: national peculiarities of language and clothing, segregation, and separate law became the first to go. Mitigation and adaptation of religious precepts ensued. In the end, all that remained was a nominal adherence to the Jewish community. However, the numerical strength of German Jews and the depth of Jewish feeling at the time they were emancipated led them to retain a specific identity.[57]

Tradition safeguards the coherence of the minority group, and the evaporation of its segregating power is very gradual. The group character of the minority persists as does the resistance to acceptance of an "alien" group. Jews therefore continued to constitute a separate group after their emancipation.[58]

Many observers emphasize the role of external factors, such as the prejudice of the Gentile majority, in perpetuating Jewish identity. Rubin points out that Jews were not in a position to be individualistic:

"Outside discrimination pressures virtually guaranteed group identification, group cohesiveness, group cooperation, and a consequent very powerful subcultural value system."[59] Sartre also feels that Jewish identity is to a large extent externally imposed: "What is it, then, that serves to keep a semblance of unity in the Jewish community? . . . it is because they have in common the situation of a Jew, that is, they live in a community which takes them for Jews."[60]

Although the pressures of the dominant group were certainly a significant factor in the maintenance of a Jewish identity, it would be an oversimplification to ignore the internal factors in the Jewish community that perpetuated a sense of Jewish identity. Reichmann examines the impact of Jewish immigration on the maintenance of Jewish identity. She notes that "Jewish history is a record of perpetual migration." Until the middle of the seventeenth century, Jewish migration flowed mostly from west to east. With the year 1648, this direction was reversed. During this period of westward migration, eastern European Jews were distinguished from the Jewish community to which they came by a lower standard of living. Economic hardship and the desire to escape persecution caused their migration. Contact between eastern European Jews and existing Jewish communities slackened the pace of assimilation. Immigration of unassimilated Jews "helped revive the Jewish ethos which had been commencing to fade among the old settlers." New settlers exercised a Judaizing influence on their more assimilated fellow Jews. This aroused anti-Jewish feeling, which resulted in a further strengthening of Jewish identity.[61]

The coexistence of divergent groups often creates an objective social problem. The contact of one social group with another tends to create hostility between them. The identification of individuals with a group satisfies many psychological needs, but may tend to make them less tolerant of outgroups. The impulse of individuals is to preserve the homogeneity of their group. They experience a sensation of challenge when brought into contact with another group.[62]

I would like to return briefly to Helen Fein's point that the existence of a pariah caste fosters identification of the lower classes of society with the dominant group. The lower classes are given a sense of common status with the ruling classes.[63] This situation creates a peculiar and contradictory phenomenon: while the ethnocentrists fear the impact of an increase in "power" on the part of the outgroup, they tend to be blindly subservient to the power of the ruling classes in their ingroup.[64] Such subservience tends to reinforce their sense of group identity at the price of repressing any rebellious or antiauthoritarian impulses they may have.

Governments learned how to exploit this phenomenon for their own ends. Anti-Semitism serves a purpose for the ruling powers in that it acts as a diversion. The oppressed masses are enraged, but they do not know where to direct their anger. Anti-Semitism acts as a vent. The rage of the masses is diverted onto those who cannot defend or protect themselves.[65]

As Otto Fenichel explains, people are in conflict between a rebellious tendency and a respect for authority. Anti-Semitism gives them the means for satisfying both contradictory tendencies at the same time: the rebellious tendency through destructive actions against defenseless people, and the respectful tendency through obedient action at the command of the ruling powers.[66]

Anti-Semitism channels revolutionary drives toward the destruction of certain people rather than institutions.[67] Deceiving the masses about the origins of their frustrations permits a deflection of their reactive hatred and aggressions from their rulers to the Jews.[68] The feeling of being victimized manifests itself as a hostility that can be directed against outgroups without fear of retaliation. Despite the assertion that the Jews are powerful, the knowledge of their relative weakness makes them suitable as scapegoats. Toward the truly powerful groups, the ethnically prejudiced are likely to suppress hostility and exhibit submission.[69]

The anti-Semite's feeling of belonging to the privileged group is a highly tentative one, because of the struggle against one's own marginal situation: "It is as a defense against the possibility of being grouped with the outcast and underdog that he [the anti-Semite] rigidly has to assert his identification with the privileged groups."[70]

Christianity can be a potent source of ingroup identification, leading to an automatic exclusion of the "other." In their 1966 study on *Christian Beliefs and Anti-Semitism*, Charles Y. Glock and Rodney Stark are convinced of the existence of a causal link between anti-Semitism and Christian orthodoxy. They define Christian orthodoxy as a "commitment to a literal interpretation of traditional Christian dogma."[71] Christian orthodoxy is characterized by a phenomenon known as particularism. Particularism is a belief that only one's own religion is legitimate: "A particularist outlook discredits all persons whose religious status lies beyond the boundaries of what is seen as the 'true' faith."[72] Particularism is a sort of ingroup identification accompanied by the characteristic rejection of outgroups. Christianity claims universal application and is a very specific, theologically detailed religion. These are conditions that lend themselves to particularism.[73]

Christian particularism produces two sorts of responses to religious outsiders. On the one hand, it promotes missionary zeal: the faith is open to all. When others reject the call to convert, the hostility latent in particularism is activated.[74] Particularism is a significant source of religious hostility toward Jews. They are resented because they remain outside the "true" faith.[75]

According to Adorno and his colleagues, whether or not religion contributes to prejudice depends on what functions it fulfills for the individual. It can represent an "effort toward belonging to a privileged group and the explicit acceptance of a set of conventionalized mores and rules of behavior prevalent in a majority group."[76] Alternatively, religion can represent "a system of more internalized, genuine experiences and values." If the former is the case, "religion tends to assume the function of an external authority deciding what is good and bad, thus relieving the individual from making his own decisions."[77] When religion functions as an agent of social conformity, it lends itself to "subservience, overadjustment, and ingroup loyalty as an ideology which covers up hatred against the disbeliever, the dissenter, the Jew."[78] The danger exists that people achieve social adjustment through obedience and subordination.[79] This leads to an overt rigidity of conscience that is intolerant toward difference.

Many unprejudiced individuals may share religious principles similar to those held by anti-Semites. But they would tend to be more flexible in their insistence on such principles and less disturbed by "value-violators."[80]

Persons who are blindly subservient toward religious precepts do not have such precepts sufficiently integrated into their psychological makeup. An exaggerated and inflexible obedience toward such precepts causes considerable repression. This in turn creates pent-up hostility, unleashed upon those who do not follow the same religious precepts. They feel that others "are getting away with something." They are therefore very antagonistic toward those who do not share their religious beliefs.[81]

The emancipation of the Jews occurred in an environment of widespread Christian particularism. Although orthodox Christian belief was increasingly being challenged by the adherents of Enlightenment and tolerance, the Enlightenment was to remain a minority discourse. As we will see when we examine the writings of Goeze and Tralles (Chapter 2), blind subservience to Christianity was a social norm during the period under consideration.

In examining the issue as to why the Jew is so prone to be used as a scapegoat, many scholars have turned to psychoanalytic interpretations of anti-Semitism. The most recent study of this nature is Rubin's *Anti-Semitism: A Disease of the Mind* (1990), but the most valuable research into this area continues to be that done in the 1940s and 1950s by such luminaries of social psychology as Max Horkheimer, Theodor W. Adorno, Ernst Simmel, Otto Fenichel, and Bruno Bettelheim. The most common of these psychoanalytic approaches to explaining anti-Semitism is the theory of false projection. Adorno points to the readiness of the ethnocentrists to condemn the minority on moral grounds: they are driven to see immoral attributes in the minorities regardless of whether these immoral attributes really exist. This is a device for countering both their own inhibited tendencies and relieving themselves of feelings of guilt for their own failings. The individual's own unacceptable impulses and failures are projected upon marginalized individuals or groups who are then rejected.[82] When individuals blame the outgroup for their failures, "such behavior is the consequence of a lack of ego strength and of adequate controls which favor irrational discharge and evasion rather than rational action."[83] Self-love prevents prejudiced individuals from accepting their own failures and taking responsibility for their own immoral impulses, so they ascribe responsibility for these to members of the outgroup.[84]

Authoritarian submission and authoritarian aggression are paradoxically linked, and both tend to manifest themselves in the same individual.[85] *Submission* to an authority is quite different from *acceptance* of an authority, whereby the individual exercises a high degree of autonomy. For example, when individuals accept religious teachings because they fear damnation or societal disapproval and not because they consider them absolute standards of behavior, they are unlikely to internalize these moral precepts.[86] The intolerant person feels deprived and feelings of deprivation create interethnic and interreligious hostility. Through submission to outside authority, intolerant individuals have had to accept a number of externally imposed restrictions on the satisfaction of their needs. This leads to an inability to integrate conscience with personal desires. They therefore harbor strong underlying aggressive impulses. The outlet for this aggression is through displacement of hostility onto outgroups.[87]

False projection is a defensive and self-delusional process. Impulses coming from the subjective realm of the individuals' psyche, which they dare not identify as originating from themselves, are attributed to the objective outer world. Violent persons see their victim as their persecutor. The most powerful nations have seen the weakest neighbors as an insufferable threat before they attack them. The rationalization is both a stratagem and a compulsion. The disturbance lies in the lack of differentiation between real and imaginary input into projected material.[88] Ethnocentric persons need prejudice as an outlet for a hostility that threatens the integration of their personalities. They are unwilling to submit their intolerant beliefs to reality testing, because they unconsciously fear the loss of an important psychic outlet.[89]

The paranoids only perceive the outside world as it conforms to their purposes. They recreate everything according to their own image of it. Ideas that have no relation to reality become fixated. Projection consists of the transfer of tabooed impulses of the subject onto the object.[90] Inner psychic phenomena are perceived as if they were external and alien to the ego.[91]

Otto Fenichel discusses specifically how false projection can lead to anti-Semitism. Projection is one means of defense against strivings of one's unconscious. It consists of seeing in others that which one does not wish to become conscious of in oneself.[92] Everybody struggles with repressed instincts that continue to exist in the unconscious. Such instincts may include murderous tendencies and sexual impulses, especially those considered low or "dirty." The lust to kill, the love of dirt, and tabooed or forbidden sexual impulses are things people try to keep hidden in their unconsciousness.[93]

These impulses are uncanny because each of us has felt such impulses and later repressed them. The subject finds murder and incest strange and unsettling. A person or race that is in any way uncanny is viewed as being capable of murder or incest.[94] The "strangeness" of the Jews is, according to Fenichel, grounded in the obstinacy with which they have resisted assimilation and clung to their own identity.[95] This strangeness was reinforced by the ghetto system, which "excluded the Jews artificially from full participation in the cultural life of the host nations," and by "the stubborn acceptance of the ghetto system by the Jews themselves."[96] Jews retained their peculiarities. Their clothes and everyday language were those of an entirely different period. They wore clothes resembling those of their European hosts during the Middle Ages and spoke Yiddish, a restructured form of medieval German, which sounded archaic to members of the host culture.

Jews are strange or uncanny, and one's own subconscious is also uncanny, so Jews are particularly vulnerable to selection as scapegoats or "displacement substitutes." Anti-Semites displace their own unwanted impulses onto the Jews, whom they recreate according to their own image of them. Projection is a psychological defense mechanism against recognition of one's own guilt.

Anti-Semitism is a personality disturbance that provides the individual with certain gains. Prejudice, according to Ernst Simmel, gives the anti-Semite "a feeling of ego inflation, of superiority, for he belongs to a community of supposedly superior values, the community of the non-Jews."[97] According to Sartre, the anti-Semite "wants his personality to melt suddenly and be carried away by the collective torrent."[98] Through attaching themselves to a pathological mass movement, disturbed individuals can find a temporary sort of pseudoadaptation to a distorted reality.[99]

No examination of anti-Semitism would be complete without examining the economic factors involved. The economic motivations for anti-Semitism are multifarious and complicated. Perhaps one of the most important causes of prejudice was the participation of the Jews in the credit industry. The stereotype of the Jew as usurer gripped the popular imagination, making its most indelible mark in William Shakespeare's *The Merchant of Venice* (1596). Lending money for interest was banned by the Third Lateran Council of 1179 as violating Christian religious precepts and was therefore officially permissible only for Jews. The Jews were frequently barred from trade by their Christian competitors and were prohibited by law from engaging in agriculture, craftsmanship, and most other trades. They therefore seized the opportunities for a legal monopoly created by the Christian prohibition on moneylending.[100] Of course, Christians also engaged in moneylending despite the prohibition, but they were subjected to religious sanctions such as exclusion from communion, confession, and absolution and were later subjected to persecution as heretics.[101] Christian moneylenders needed to be more circumspect about their money circulation activities than Jews and therefore it was the Jew who became a synecdoche for moneylending.

The popular image of the Jews as moneylenders caused them to meet with resistance and it brought forth hatred. Religious denunciations of the Jewish usurers aroused the animosity of the Christian debtors.[102] The public resented the relatively high returns that came about through moneylending: an allegedly immoral occupation, involving little labor, yielded profits such as the artisan or peasant could never hope to attain.[103] As moneylenders, Jews entered increasingly into relations with the popular masses, and these relations worsened steadily. Dire distress forced peasants and artisans to borrow from the Jewish usurer. In some extreme cases, they even had to pawn their working tools. They saw the Jew as the direct cause of their ruin.[104]

The other occupation with which the Jew came to be identified in the popular imagination fom the Middle Ages onward was that of the itinerant peddler. The strong concentration of Jews in itinerant peddling reinforced the widely believed stereotype that they were natural traders. They were contrasted with "honest workers" such as artisans and farmers. The high proportion of Jews in "unestablished" professions lent popularity to the saga of the "Wandering Jew."[105]

The preemancipatory concentration of the Jews in moneylending and petty trade led to a disproportionate Jewish concentration in commerce and finance on a grander scale beginning in the eighteenth century.[106] Commerce and finance were relatively new to the realm of economics and did not enjoy the respectability of the more established occupations of agriculture and craftsmanship, which Jews had been prohibited from engaging in.

The middleman's entry into the economic scene was accompanied by a certain stigma. There was a feeling that commerce is unproductive, that it increased the prices of articles without adding to their value.[107] According to Horkheimer and Adorno, the role of the Jews as middlemen led to their scapegoating. The producers used the middlemen to hide their mastery over the production.[108]

In precapitalistic epochs, despotism and exploitation were less subtle and more easily identifiable than under capitalism. The despots were directly repressive. Not only was the work left to the underlings, but work was declared a disgrace—which it always was to the despot. The mercantilism of the absolute monarch eventually evolved into that of the large manufacturer. Production thereby became respectable. The belief prevailed that work did no harm. Manufacturers considered themselves to be workers while in reality they remained the "takers," the exploiters. The factory owner competes for the profits commensurate with his capital. He "takes" not only through the market, but at the source: as a functionary of his class, he ensures that he gets his "share" from the work of his people. The worker must deliver as much as possible. By virtue of the possession of machines and materials, the manufacturer is able to force others to produce. The economic work of the capitalist, by justifying his profit as the producer's wages, conceals the exploitative nature of the economic system. Only when the worker begins to buy does he realize how little purchasing power he has. He blames this on the middleman.[109]

The Jew was thereby blamed for the injustices of the entire system. The factory owner had his debtors: the workers in his factory. He needed Jews as middlemen: they protected him against the masses. The masses had to foot the bills for progress. The Jews were the colonizers of progress. They were the representatives of big city, bourgeois, and industrial conditions. They brought capitalistic conditions to the country and drew upon themselves the hatred of those who had to suffer from capitalism's inception. For the sake of economic progress, Jews were a thorn in the side of handworkers and farmers, whose social position was lowered through capitalism.[110]

The growth of capitalism led to an increasingly competitive society, in which the dominant group felt threatened by the efforts of the minority to advance socially by improving its financial status. Léon Poliakov points to the "tenacity of preconceived ideas about a congenital and quasi-biological aptitude on the part of Jews for business and for making money."[111]

Keen competition between Jewish and Christian merchants was the source of much resentment against the Jews. Wherever Jews appeared as business competitors, complaints arose that Christian traders suffered as a consequence.[112] The differing cultures and customs of Christians and Jews were reflected in different commercial practices.[113]

Jews frequently ignored the commercial etiquette agreed upon by the Christian guilds; that was in part a logical consequence of their exclusion from the guilds. Underlying this conflict were differing outlooks on economic life. The Christians adhered to the view that producer and trader should receive sufficient compensation for their needs. The guilds agreed upon many measures that promoted a minimizing of competition. For example, each person's activity was to be limited to a set locality.[114]

For the Jews, obtaining profit was the ultimate goal of all commercial activity. They relentlessly looked after business interests.[115] Money was viewed as an avenue toward gaining greater prestige and social acceptance. The insecurity of the Jews' political and social status created in them a hunger for wealth.[116] Because the Jewish community had to fear pogroms, expulsion, and severely discriminatory taxation, Jews "tended to become attached to money because this was one of the few means of wealth which they could own and which was easy to carry."[117]

Jews could trade in all types of merchandise, whereas Christians were confined by law to one type of business.[118] German guilds complained about this sort of diversification, which ignored the demarcation of all economic activities into separate categories.[119] Jewish traders frequently undersold Christian peddlers. Not being bound by the regulations of the guilds, they were able to reduce the cost of production. They frequently sold goods of inferior quality that did not conform to the guild standards.[120] They also traded in old, damaged, and renovated goods.[121]

Jewish trade soon became very popular because of low prices which defied all competition. Christians could not undersell them because they were bound by guild regulations regarding a "just price." The lower standard of living to which Jews had become accustomed meant that they could afford to lower prices because they had fewer expenses.[122] The frequent expulsion of the Jews led to their having international connections, which proved to be an advantage in trade. The

Jews' precarious status also induced them to take risks unheard of for Christian merchants. Jews were also alleged to have sold merchandise of dubious origin, such as stolen goods or war plunder.[123]

The Jews' exclusion from the institutions of the dominant society, such as guilds, led them to ignore the precepts and conventions of that dominant society. This fostered competition and created intergroup antagonisms.

Economically motivated antagonisms were also created by the employment of Court Jews as financial intermediaries between the ruling classes and the masses. Jews were historically sought out by the ruling classes on the basis of their economic utility.[124] To the monarchs, Jews "were either a source of revenue or a vehicle of economic development in the areas of foreign trade, money and credit, and later, manufacturing industry."[125] Jews were dependent upon their monarch, who considered them "a pliable instrument of government policies and an important source of money income."[126] In some regions, the upper nobility shared in the power of the government. In such cases, the nobility enjoyed the economic convenience and financial services of the Jews on the same basis as the monarchs.[127]

The Court Jews also had many clients among the gentry. They acted as middlemen for the sale of the gentry's agricultural surplus and supplied the gentry with manufactured goods on terms more favorable than those offered by Gentile merchants. The Jews also served as a source of credit for "the money-hungry, debt-ridden gentry."[128] Like the nobility, the gentry utilized the Jews as intermediaries in dealing with the peasants for such functions as employment and income opportunities. They thereby became involved as the gentry's agent in the economic exploitation of the peasantry and became scapegoats for the wrath of the peasants.[129]

The Jews raised money from the peasants through lending money. The proceeds were in turn lent to the monarchs, nobility, and representative members of the emerging bourgeoisie, who needed vast amounts of capital. The beginning of credit as an important element in the economy of the state had its basis in governmental moneylending from Jews.[130] Jews fulfilled a stigmatized but widely sought after social function. They were condemned for taking part in "unproductive activities," without taking account of the fact that they were forced into such activities by a prohibition on practicing most established trades and professions.[131]

Jews participated in an economic function by which they came to be defined. They were the middlemen between the nobility and the peasantry. Each class of society that came into conflict with the ruling powers became anti-Semitic because the only social group that seemed to represent the ruling powers was the Jews.[132]

There was an intense irony in the emergence of economic anti-Semitism because only a small minority of Jews participated in the economic activities to which Gentiles objected. The Court Jews were the economically strongest element among the German Jewry while the itinerant peddlers were among the socially and economically weakest members of the Jewish community. It was these two groups who had the most contact with Gentiles through the centuries and who most influenced the Christian image of Judaism. They did not, however, represent the majority of the German Jewry who lived a self-contained existence within the ghettos and "lived completely within the mold of tradition."[133]

Religion, Nationalism, and Public Discourse

Sociologists have established that ethnocentrism comes about through the coexistence of two or more groups with conflicting identities. An important question to be examined is how identity is established. One central component of identity establishment is linguistic in character. Therefore I would like to examine some of the discourse theories promulgated by Michel Foucault and by Mikhail M. Bakhtin and his circle.

The formation of ingroup identification rests upon the recognition of certain fundamental assumptions whose acceptance is a prerequisite for inclusion in the main group. These fundamental assumptions are known as consensus formations. The acceptance of consensus formations automatically inhibits the emergence of other discursive formations that fall outside the parameters of the society's fundamental assumptions. Consensus formations not only provide a positive function in terms of affirming identity, but they fulfill a negative function by confining whatever opposes their principles of construction.[134]

The mechanisms that protect the consensus formation from being assailed by oppositional or noncompatible discourses are known as rules of exclusion. Rules of exclusion are limitations on permissible discourse, and their transgression results in formidable resistance, if not social sanctions.[135] Rules of exclusion set parameters on permissible discourse. Through forbidding or restricting expression about certain subjects, the discursive realm is directly restricted. The discursive realm can be less directly restricted through permitting only certain types of people to speak of certain subjects, although the end effect may be similar. When only a certain group of people is permitted to discuss a certain subject, it is more than likely a group that has been indoctrinated to limit its realm of inquiry to exclude certain aspects deemed objectionable. One example of this sort of phenomenon is the attempt of clergy in the eighteenth century to claim an exclusive right to discuss theological questions and exclude philosophers and secular writers from involvement in that area. This issue gave rise to Immanuel Kant's treatise *Der Streit der Fakultäten* (1798) as well as the famous Lessing-Goeze controversy (see Chapter 2).

The consensus formation is negatively defined through the presence of more interrelated rules of exclusion. Linguistic formations of this sort consist of an inventory of socially permissible expressions. Underlying such formations is a broad set of ideological assumptions. Because consensus formations are one of a society's major unifying factors, they are an indispensable mechanism for the formation of a group identity. The price of nonacceptance of the consensus formation is exclusion from or marginalization by the ingroup.

However, consensus formations are always being renegotiated. This is made possible through the employment of "subversive" or ambiguous discursive strategies. Such a strategy may consist of taking socially permissible speech and trying to employ it in a devious manner or trying to infuse it with new meaning. This is an example of what the Russian critic and Bakhtin disciple V. N. Voloshinov (writing in 1929) calls the ideological struggle for control of the sign. Because of the precarious relationship between signifier and signified, sign and meaning, different social interests compete for linguistic control over the sign. This malleability of language is an essential element for the use of language as an agent of social change. It is in the interest of the ruling powers to impart a universal, unalterable character to the linguistic sign so that it cannot be subversively employed; social progress depends on a multifaceted, constantly evolving language.[136]

The concept of the ideological struggle for linguistic control of the sign becomes clearer when a specific example is examined. Take the concept of "tolerance," for instance. Let us examine this definition from Walter Brugger's *Philosophical Dictionary* of 1967:

> The necessity of tolerance in modern society is based on the freedom of the person, to whom it belongs from personal insight, to judge for himself in the questions of truth and falsity, and about what is morally good or evil; it is also based on the incontrovertible fact of man's almost universal capacity to err. Therefore tolerance is demanded by justice which requires that each one receive what is his due.... The individual has no right to embrace

error as error, but he does have a right to his own convictions which flow from his experience; in this situation error must sometimes be respected, since there is no other way to protect this particular right.[137]

Certain ideological assumptions underlie this definition: it imputes an egalitarian, all-encompassing quality to tolerance with its emphasis on freedom of conviction and permissiveness in matters of belief. Such a definition would tend to make tolerance incompatible with religious particularism of any kind. Compare this definition of tolerance with the following definition, which was taken from a German theological dictionary of 1965:

> Der Begriff Toleranz (tolérance, toleration) wird in Europa seit der 2. Hälfte des 16. Jahrhunderts mit der Bedeutung "Konzession," "Erlaubnis" verwendet im Zusammenhang mit der Religionsfreiheit jener Untertanen, die nicht der Religion des Fürsten oder des Staates angehören. . . . "Die Religion" ist allein die wahre, von Gott offenbarte, und als einzige Heilsmittlerin gestaltete Religion. . . . Diesen Prinzipien folgend, "erachtet es die Kirche für unerlaubt, die verschiedenen Kulte auf die gleiche rechtliche Stufe zu stellen wie die wahre Religion." . . . In einer solchen Sicht fällt die Frage, welche Freiheit anderen Religionen, Konfessionen und Kulten außer der wahren Religion zugebilligt werden könne, mit der Frage der Duldung eines Übels in der Gesellschaft zusammen. . . . Vor allem im Verhältnis der religiösen Gruppen und der Einzelmenschen ist eine bloße Toleranz zu überbieten durch christliche Bruderliebe, die keineswegs Indifferenz der Wahrheitsfrage gegenüber besagt, sondern dem Mitmenschen gerade auch das Geschenk der vollen Wahrheit wünscht.[138]

Note the differing ideological accent of this definition: instead of equating tolerance with freedom of conviction, this description seeks to semantically narrow tolerance to a sense of "concession" or "permission." The egalitarian underpinnings of the Brugger definition are missing: tolerance is reduced to a notion of "sufferance of evil" and, as such, does not connote an equality of worth or unrestricted freedom of belief. Whereas the Brugger definition precludes religious particularism, the definition from the theological dictionary actively promotes it. Here is a clear example of two different social concerns trying to infuse the key concept of "tolerance" with radically different ideological content. This evidences a continuing struggle between religious and secular forces to gain control over language. The first definition of tolerance cited is a modern one, the second is a more traditional one. This demonstrates that forces for social change exert pressure for changes in the ideological content of language.

Through these contrasting definitions of "tolerance," we see how the linguistic sign can be the locus of social struggle. According to Voloshinov, everything ideological possesses meaning and manifests itself as a sign: "Without signs, there is no ideology." A sign reflects and refracts another reality. Wherever a sign is present, ideology is present: "Everything ideological possesses semiotic value." Signs are a product of "the process of interaction between one individual consciousness and another."[139] Every sign has the purpose of promoting social interaction between human beings possessing separate consciousnesses. This in turn has an impact on the relationship between sign and existence. There is a "dialectical refraction of the existence of the sign."[140] As Voloshinov explains, "Existence reflected in the sign is not merely reflected but *refracted* . . . by an intersecting of differently oriented social interests within the same sign community."[141] Differently oriented accents intersect in every ideological sign, and that is why we are able to get such differing definitions of tolerance. One way of circumventing rules of exclusion is to infuse signs permitted by the ruling powers with a new and subversive meaning.

However, manipulating the elusive qualities of language is not a cure-all for the restrictive impact of rules of exclusion. According to Manfred Frank, "The order of discourse is a net of mechanisms of repression."[142] Rules of exclusion do more than limit speech, they limit thought, too. Limits on permissible discourse limit our ability to apprehend or conceptualize the world. A language is a body of rules that has the potential to authorize an infinite number of performances. The field of discursive events, on the other hand, is a finite grouping that is limited to the linguistic sequences that already have been formulated.[143] Social conditions inevitably provoke rebellious impulses, but the language to express those impulses may be undeveloped due to the finiteness of established discourse and the repressive limitations on language. This puts the subject on a subconscious quest for an unnamed signified. We may be altogether unable to define our desires, but they live on in our subconscious. This tends to make us receptive to discourse that may appear to approximate the unnamed signified we are searching for, even if it is only remotely related to the original impulse.

The formulation of notions that go against the established discursive order may themselves appear in a distorted or refracted medium. The repression of impulses that lie outside of the domain of socially permissible expression leads to the creation of a substitute formation.[144] The forbidden idea is replaced with a displacement substitute, often by displacement onto something entirely different.[145] Displacement substitutes may manifest themselves in different individuals in paradoxically different manners. The rejection of a consensus formation may lead certain individuals to reduce their degree of identification with the ingroup. This could manifest itself in a heightened sympathy for an outgroup, which is really a symbolic distancing of oneself from the dominant group. This is made evident by the tendencies in literature to idealize the outgroup, such as in the "Noble Savage" theme prevalent from the Renaissance to Romanticism, as well as in the portrayal of Jews by Lessing and by authors on the periphery of the Enlightenment who imitated him. In the latter instance, rejection of the consensus formation of Christianity in its dominant form could not be overtly expressed and manifested itself in the displacement substitute of pariah identification. The use of the noble Jew as a symbol for the rejection of orthodox Christianity had a positive effect in promoting the emancipation of the Jews, demonstrating that the effects of displacement substitution need not be negative.

The preceding scenario presupposes, however, a willingness on the part of the individual to loosen the bonds that tie him to his ingroup. This necessitates an independent personality and an antiauthoritarian frame of mind, which leads to such a positive identification of rebellious impulses. The inability, however, to define rebellious impulses may lead to their identification in negative terms. The quest for an undefined signified may make people more susceptible to anti-Semitic propaganda. Powerless minorities may become a vent for their pent-up rebelliousness. They could repress their initial discomfort with society through an intensified ingroup identification and sublimate their discontent through a punitive attitude toward the "outsiders."

The repression of forbidden impulses may take radically different forms depending on the chain of substitutions employed to satisfy the impulse. The closeness of the substitute formation to the original impulse is dependent on the ability of individuals to diagnose the causes of their dissatisfaction. This is in turn dependent on the range of discourses available to them and the extent to which they have mastered these discourses. Although strategies exist to modify consensus formations, the modification process is indirect and complicated and may become thwarted in the long run.

Nonetheless, this is a necessary process for the fomentation of social progress. Consensus formations constitute the fundamental codes of a given group: they govern "its language, its schemes of perception, its exchanges, its techniques, its values, and the hierarchy of its practices."[146]

When a group imperceptibly begins to deviate from the empirical orders prescribed by its consensus formations, it institutes a gradual separation from them and frees itself sufficiently to discover that the order established by the consensus formations is not the only possible one.[147] Codes of language, perception, and practice thereby come to be criticized and are rendered partially invalid.[148]

Such change must be renegotiated within the complex and vaguely defined parameters of the discursive order. As Foucault notes, "Taboos, barriers, thresholds and limits are deliberately disposed in order to master and control the great proliferation of discourse."[149] The production of discourse is "controlled, selected, organized, and redistributed according to a certain number of procedures whose role is to avert its powers and dangers."[150] An individual or group of individuals seeking to subvert or modify the discursive order tries to establish a resemblance between the marginalized discursive formation and the dominant discourse; to promote a sense of sameness, to establish a sense of identity with the marginalized object. The writer thereby tries to promote a sense of sympathy with the marginalized object.[151] The appeal to sympathy is a double-edged sword. It may bring objectionable discourse into the parameters of the permissible, but in so doing it has the tendency to modify or compromise the "otherness" of the marginalized discourse. What comes into effect is the "co-option" of the oppositional discourse. It is assimilated into the dominant discourse in a diluted form, which is less threatening to the linguistic unity/identity of the larger group. There were numerous attempts to co-opt the tolerance discourse amounting to a dilution of its critical potential, some examples of which we will be exploring.

We will attempt to place the literature thematizing the "Jewish question" within the context of the eighteenth and early nineteenth centuries to analyze its relation to the consensus formations and corresponding rules of exclusion: to see whether the rules of exclusion are promoted, accommodated, resisted, or subverted.

The proponents of religious tolerance and Jewish emancipation had to contend with two formidable consensus formations: traditional Christianity and, after 1800, German nationalism. Christianity in the eighteenth century was a very particularistic doctrine and had the broad support of the masses. Although the Enlightenment as a reform movement had influence on some church figures, it generally met with considerable resistance.

One example of the power of the church can be found in the case of Christian von Wolff, a professor at the University of Halle. Wolff was an early advocate of Natural Religion, the notion of moral principles separated from religious dogma. He opposed the concept of revealed religion, a step bound to ignite controversy. But the move that culminated in his ouster was his decision in 1723 to teach the writings of Confucius. Theologians at the university filed a petition against Wolff with King Friedrich Wilhelm I. They argued that Wolff's instruction was a threat to public morals. Wolff taught in Marburg after his dismissal and was only called back to Halle after the ascent of Friedrich II.[152]

The incident illustrates the rigidity of the linguistic code: the seemingly innocent act of imparting an awareness of the existence of a different religious tradition transgressed social taboos. The confrontation with differing cultural values was viewed as a threat: it encouraged individuals to realize that there was an alternative way of viewing the world and therefore called upon them to put their own assumptions into question. Such a phenomenon is a challenge to the overriding group identity of a society. The society does more than work to make such modes of thought unacceptable; it has a strong interest in making them entirely inconceivable, in order to maintain the existing social fabric.

The dominant order of discourse did not, however, go unchallenged. By the 1770s, the Enlightenment Wolff had helped bring into being was at its peak. Although it remained a minority discourse, the Enlightenment mounted a substantial and influential challenge to the conventions of orthodox Christianity. Secularization was becoming a fact of life. This led to the proliferation of alternative modes of thought, such as Deism and Natural Religion. The discourses promoting Deism and Natural Religion and those promoting Jewish emancipation were compatible and, to a large degree, mutually supportive. Most of the adherents of Christian heterodox discourses demanded tolerance for themselves and, for consistency's sake, advocated tolerance toward Jews as well.[153]

Advocates of emancipation pointed to the principles of Enlightenment: rationalism, humanism, and universalism. Rationalism was the acknowledgment of reason as the highest authority, and reason did not permit an individual's status to be based on religious tenets, which were by nature irrational. Humanism demanded respect for the human element in every person, including the Jew. Universalism held that the rights of human beings should be determined by universal criteria. Rationalism sought to "subvert the fundamentals of theological thought and reject the conclusions based on it."[154] Hallmarks of the rationalistic approach included the "spirit of criticism, the willingness and the ability to examine natural and historical phenomena with detached human understanding."[155]

The secularization brought about by the Enlightenment led to resistance not only from the older orthodox circles of Christianity but from new mystical currents of the time as well.[156] A new movement within Christianity arose, which was known as Pietism. This supranaturalistic ideology emphasized mystical and biblical premises. Large portions of the old dogmas fell by the wayside and the proponents of this movement extolled the divinity of Christ and inspiration of the Bible. The strong Pietist movement played a major role in preserving Christianity from the influence of the Enlightenment. It popularized a predominantly conservative position toward the heritage of the church and provided a counterweight to the Enlightenment's attempts to weaken the hegemony of Christianity.[157] A mystical conception of Christianity was used to attack rationalism and reassert Christianity as a consensus formation. A glance at Pietistic literature, such as Pfranger's drama *Der Mönch vom Libanon* (1782), reveals that the Pietists, to the extent that they advocated tolerance at all, viewed tolerance as a sufferance of evil and did not conceive of it as a foundation for the emancipation of the Jews.

Another current of opposition to the notion of Jewish emancipation came from within the ranks of the rationalists themselves. Some advocates of the Enlightenment, particularly in its early phases, promoted an antireligious attitude that developed a particularistic dynamic of its own: an inability to tolerate religious attitudes of any sort. The proponents of this position attacked Judaism as being just as egregious as orthodox Christianity in terms of being a barrier to social progress. This attitude made possible the maintenance of earlier stereotypes and prejudices against the Jews. The most prominent proponent of this sort of position was the French Enlightener Voltaire. The language Voltaire uses to attack the Jews is largely the discourse of Christian Judeophobia, so even while he tries to break away from orthodox Christianity, he is hopelessly entrapped within at least one of its tenets. The rationalistic anticlerical Judeophobia, ironic as it seems, was rooted in the Christian Judeophobia.[158]

Rationalism had a dialectical impact on Jewish emancipation. As Jacob Katz points out: "On the one hand, the criticism of Christianity removed the justification of discrimination against the Jews on the grounds of Christian doctrine; on the other hand, it provided new weapons to the opponents of the Jews by casting aspersions on their religious heritage."[159]

Contrary to the proponents of emancipation, the enlightened opponents of Jewish emancipation did not make religion solely responsible for anti-Semitic attitudes, but brought other factors such as ethnic extraction or "historical identity" into play. Such opponents of emancipation did not attribute the special religiocultural and socioeconomic profile of the Jewish minority to one thousand years of oppression. Instead of arguing historically, they argued in terms of the existence of an original special character of the Jewish nation. Such people promoted the notion of an incorrigible or unchangeable Jewish national character.[160]

Although some rationalistic factions promoted their own brand of anti-Semitism, the overall importance of the Enlightenment in furthering the cause of Jewish emancipation should not be underestimated. The mutual supportiveness of the discourses promoting Deism and Natural Religion and that promoting emancipation of the Jews has been noted by Alfred D. Low[161] and Jacob Katz who point to a close relationship between Jewish emancipation and the increasing secularization, which manifested itself in Natural Religion.[162] Jewish emancipation and the secularizing processes of which Natural Religion was a part were virtually symbiotic discourses. In his *Nathan der Weise* (1779), Lessing promoted Jewish emancipation in part to voice his views on Natural Religion. But emancipation of the Jews was dependent on the secularization brought about by the discourse promoting Natural Religion. The tolerance precepts within the Enlightenment spelled the emergence of an alternative discourse, which, had it met a wider breadth of acceptance, could have fundamentally altered the primary discursive codes of the society out of which it emerged. In mounting a challenge to the linguistic hegemony of Christianity, an alternative possibility of apprehending the world emerged. Not surprisingly, this alternative discourse was viewed as a threat by those with an interest in maintaining the contemporary social structure and the linguistic status quo.

Although the Enlightenment influenced public opinion, it never won mastery over it. Although the theoretical aim of the Enlightenment was to spread learning among the ignorant, it was based "almost too exclusively on foreign patterns and was too intellectual for the great mass of people."[163] Attempts to curtail the Enlightenment and maintain the prior discursive order were pervasive and effective. The most visible outward sign of this is the passage of the Wöllner religious edicts in 1788. These edicts criticized the Enlightenment as having brought about "zügellose Freiheit, Glaubenslosigkeit, Sittenverderben." In 1793, Friedrich Nicolai had to move publication of the *Berliner Monatsschrift* to Kiel and Hamburg in an attempt to circumvent these edicts. The

Wöllner religious edicts led to the successful prosecution of the theologian Johann Heinrich Schulz and of Immanuel Kant, who was suspended from his teaching post for a year.[164]

Friedrich Wilhelm II was a proponent of the new mystical currents emanating out of Christianity and had an antipathy toward the Enlightenment. Under his leadership, the powers of the state mounted a counterattack against the Enlightenment. Not only did the emergence of Christian mysticism work against the Enlightenment, but so did the developments in France and the initial enthusiasm of many Enlighteners for the French Revolution.

Enlightened proponents of bourgeois emancipation and empowerment were originally enthusiastic about the French Revolution and desired the realization of revolutionary precepts in the German territories. The French Revolution served as a model for those advocating the overthrow of political systems which were not legitimized by the people.[165] A sort of German patriotism of cosmopolitan underpinnings developed, in which German intellectuals demanded decisive democratic reforms for the German regions.[166] A Francophile model for a future German state decreased in popularity after the Jacobins took power in France. After Napoleon took power, pro-French feeling was marginalized and closeted.

The Napoleonic dominion brought the opponents of Enlightenment, rationalism, and emancipation to the forefront. The group identity of the Gentile majority was redefined through a new consensus formation: that of German nationalism. The German nationalism that emerged at the beginning of the nineteenth century raised the state to the highest political ideal. Nationalism was closely related to another political phenomenon: conservatism. Both originated with the "political Romantics." The broader movement of political Romanticism had its origins in the patriotic resistance against the occupation through the expansionistic French.[167]

The struggle against Napoleon's dominion and the subsequent backlash against everything French manifested itself in Romantic conservatism, regionalism, and concepts of German "Volkstum." The new nationalism emphasized the ideal of German unity. The nationalistic "freedom fighters" appropriated an idealized conception of the Middle Ages under Teutonic emperors from the Germanic past, supplanting the earlier concept of German unity and patriotism based on the French revolutionary concept. They wanted to overcome the territorial splintering and political weakness of Germany. They were therefore quite receptive to newfound postulates of national sovereignty. The human rights postulates of the western European Enlightenment, however, were considered by many adherents of the German national movement as being too rationalistic and individualistic. Against such conceptions, which were considered abstract and inimical to the German spirit, many patriots preferred the backward-oriented utopia of a Germanic *Volksgemeinschaft*.[168]

The emergence of this German nationalism had a negative impact on Jewish emancipation. Anti-Semitism reemerged in new terms: the basis of contempt was translated from theological to national grounds.[169] According to Rosemary R. Ruether, "The Jew in the modern state became the representative of the 'outsider' to nationalist identity."[170] Eva Reichmann has observed that anti-Semites "reproached the Jews on the ground that their maintenance of international Jewish ties could not be combined with truly 'national' feelings toward Germany."[171]

After the Congress of Vienna, there was a movement to restore the prerevolutionary status quo. This entailed a movement to strip Jews of any rights they had achieved during the Napoleonic occupations.[172] The denial of rights to Jews was grounded in their having un-Germanic character traits with which they were imbued regardless of their specific religious beliefs.[173] The emancipation of the Jews appeared as an obsolete remnant of French dominion because the associations between its principles and maxims of the French Revolution were universally evident.[174]

A major factor at this time was the heightened national consciousness of the Germans. This was rooted in the continuation of German disunity well into the epoch of the European national states.[175] The national question received "an unhealthy predominance over the social and political questions which in other countries in the nineteenth century moved into the foreground of public affairs."[176] During the Wars of Liberation, the whole concept of liberty received a purely nationalist coloring. Instead of freedom meaning freedom of the individual, it came to mean freedom from the external enemy.[177]

Reichmann points to the philosophical significance of the reactionary outlook. It amounted to a repudiation of Western civilization and manifested itself in political Romanticism, which became a powerful breeding ground for anti-Semitism.[178] Since the Romantics "could not rejoice in any present national existence, they looked to the distant past for German glory. . . . They revelled in dreams of the old imperial splendor and the once so mighty Catholic Church."[179] Nationalistic contemporaries held that because Jews "are irrevocably and definitely excluded from the German past as well as from the German race, they do not belong to the German nation and cannot do so in the future."[180]

Added to this was the influence of conservative philosophy, which advanced the view that individuals are inherently unequal before the law and therefore the law could not be severed from the *Volksgeist*.

Emancipation of the Jews had been based on their demand for equal rights. Those who opposed an artificial interference with law's natural evolution, which could only emanate from the *Volksgeist*, were natural antagonists to the Jews.[181] The renunciation of reason became a consensus formation in its own right. Romantic ideas spread through the populace with startling speed. A tradition of legal exclusiveness emerged, in the face of which the "Rights of Man" was viewed as an outdated concept.[182]

Nationalism emerged as a new consensus formation, which had a substantial marginalizing influence on the critical discourses of the Enlightenment. Advocates of Jewish emancipation once again found their ideas subjected to powerful social resistance. The Christian heterodoxies of Deism and Natural Religion, which had contributed to an environment in which Jewish emancipation would be possible, were submerged by a new Catholicizing mysticism associated with Romanticism. The antiauthoritarian discourses of Enlightenment and rationalism were now countered by the emergence of a new authoritarian discursive order. The new nationalism, like the orthodox Christianity of the previous generation, followed its own brand of exclusiveness and particularism.

According to both Christian rationalist and Christian Romantic theories, Judaism was to be no longer regarded as a religion. A new order of discourse defined Judaism in national, quasi-racial terms. According to Ruether, "Judaism was said to be, not a religion, but the laws of a nation. The antithesis of Judaism and Christianity was translated into an antithesis between Jews and Europeans, or Jews and Germans."[183] The new authoritarian order was, if anything, more inimical to the humanistic spirit of the Enlightenment and its tolerance precepts than the orthodox Christianity that the tolerance debate had attempted to modify.

One of the factors contributing to the rise of nationalism as an authoritarian consensus formation was, ironically enough, the partial success of the Enlightenment as a secularizing force. While the Enlightened influences modified the use of Christianity as an irrationalistic underpinning, it did not lead to a popular internalization of rationalism as an ideological concept. Nationalism was to a large extent a substitute formation for religion: one irrationalistic ideological underpinning was substituted for another. According to Koppel S. Pinson, the individual could "no longer find the support which he craved solely in his Christian religion but was forced to seek a secular outlet for his enthusiasm and his feeling of social kinship. The outlet was provided by the national group."[184] The feeling of belonging to a national group supplied the individual with support, sustenance, and a raison d'être.

This emergence of German nationalism was anathema to the ideals of the Enlightenment: "The intellectual climate conducive to the growth of a spirit of nationalism has always drawn upon irrationalism, anti-intellectualism, and emotional mysticism."[185] Nationalism depends on sentiment and emotional stimulation rather than on any appeal to rationalism.[186] Nationalism functions as a secularized religion, creating its own dynamic of particularism and ingroup identification. As such, it creates it own reasons for rejection of the "Other."

We will next undertake an in-depth examination of both the strengths and the contradictions of the tolerance ideology and attempt to determine why it did not take root in the German consciousness. We will begin our examination with the main progenitor of the Tolerance Debate, Gotthold Ephraim Lessing.

2. The Beginnings of the Tolerance Debate

Lessing's Struggle with the Christian Traditionalists

Whoever attempts to examine Gotthold Ephraim Lessing's *Nathan der Weise* (1779) in all its richness must also come to grips with its internal contradictions.[1] Like all works of art, Lessing's work has its conceptual fissures, which are largely a result of the historical circumstances under which he lived. Like all great works of art, it also has its philosophical triumphs. We can only come to a true understanding of the work by viewing it through a dialectizing optic and taking cognizance of both its conceptual fissures and philosophical triumphs.

The Lessing-Goeze dispute is too well known to need a full recounting here. Suffice it to say that when Lessing published fragments from the work of the Deistic popular philosopher Hermann Samuel Reimarus in his *Von der Duldung der Deisten: Fragmente des Ungenannten* (1774), it set off a bitter theological dispute between Lessing and Johann Melchior Goeze, a prominent Hamburg pastor. That this dispute was the inspiration for *Nathan der Weise* has long since been established in the annals of Lessing scholarship. What previous scholarship has not examined, however, is the extent to which the play was a reaction specifically to anti-Semitic comments made by Goeze.

The Lessing-Goeze debate was more than likely an exacerbation of a mutual theological antagonism between Lessing and Goeze that predated the release of Reimarus's fragments. Goeze, who was an avowed Judeophobe, was very likely familiar with Lessing's earlier emancipatory play *Die Juden* (1749) and would have disapproved of its message. Furthermore, Goeze was openly hostile toward Lessing's intellectual friendship with the Jewish philosopher Moses Mendelssohn. Lessing, for his part, was surely aware of Goeze's anti-Semitic pronouncements such as the following Judeophobic critique of Mendelssohn in the pamphlet *Ein Predigt gegen fremde Religions-Verwandte* (1771):

> Der jüdische Gelehrte hat sich, so viel mir bekannt geworden, bisher noch nicht öffentlich als ein angreifender Feind und Lästerer unsers Erlösers, und seiner allerheiligsten Religion bewiesen. Indessen ist er bey aller seiner übrigen Geschicklichkeit ein Jude, und seine abgegbne [sic] Erklärungen zeigen genugsam, wie er im Herzen gegen Jesum and gegen seine Lehre gesinnet sey. Die

übertriebenen Lobsprüche und Schmeicheleyen, mit welchen er von Christen, von Gelehrten, von Gottesgelehrten beehrt worden, sind daher unwidersprechlich der Ehre unseres Erlösers nachtheilig, und können mit den Gesinnungen, welche wahre Christen gegen denselben haben müssen, nimmermehr bestehen; sie machen die ganz ohnedem schon so stolze Nation der Juden noch stolzer und sind ebenso starke Hindernisse ihrer Bekehrung, als die offenbaren Aergernisse, die ihnen von unserer Seite gegeben werden.[2]

Goeze's diatribe was directed just as much against Lessing as it was against Mendelssohn, because Goeze attacks Mendelssohn's public promoters from the Christian community and Lessing was one of the people most responsible for making Mendelssohn known to non-Jewish intellectual circles. Goeze's anti-Semitism was based on traditional Lutheran teachings about Judaism, which posited a dichotomy between good Jews who accepted Christ and converted and bad Jews whose refusal to accept Christ led them to destructive acts.[3]

Goeze's pronouncements during the Lessing-Goeze debate were also not devoid of anti-Semitism. He attempted to denigrate Reimarus's Deism by equating it with Judaism:

Noch ein Wort von den Fragmenten überhaupt. Sie sind keine bescheidene Einwürfe gegen die christliche Religion, sondern die *lauteste Lästerung* desselben. Ihre Wirkungen sind in unseren gegenwärtigen Zeiten schon sehr betrübt, und werden noch schröcklicher werden. Den Juden wird insonderheit das letzte Fragment sehr willkommen sein, und ihnen zur Bestärkung in ihrem Unglauben, und in ihrer feindseligen Gesinnung gegen Jesum und seine Religion, bessere Dienste tun als ihr Toldos Jeschu.[4]

By "Toldos Jeschu," Goeze means the *Toledot Yeshu* (or "Life of Jesus"), a medieval Hebrew-language work that tried to deny that Christianity had any spiritual meaning. Christ is portrayed as a magician who is divested of his magical power by Jewish sages.[5] Although the work was started in the tenth century A.D., it was kept alive and added to throughout the Crusades.

The Crusades, largely directed against the Moslems, were also marked by pogroms against Jews. Massacres of the Jews began in Rouen, France, in the eleventh century. In 1096, there were pogroms in the Rhineland cities of present-day Germany. In Mainz, Jews tried to fight back and were overcome, leading to a tidal wave of killings and forced conversions.[6] Goeze's invocation of Jewish criticism against Christianity during the Crusades inspired Lessing to set his own drama during the Crusades.

As W. Daniel Wilson points out, Lessing wanted to pick a time for his play that did not reflect well on Christianity. He is also correct in asserting that the ideology of the Crusades was still alive and well in the eighteenth century.[7] Lessing reflected on the goodness of the Jews as a means of showing the ethnocentrism of the European Christians.[8] He did so by constructing his Jewish protagonist after the character and personality of the noble Moses Mendelssohn. Because Goeze had exploited anti-Semitism as a device to incite both his readership and the ruling powers against Reimarus and Lessing, Lessing decided to use a positive portrayal of Jews in order to respond to Goeze.

The equation of Christian dissidence with Judaism originating from Goeze's pen was co-opted by Lessing. This was an easy step for Lessing not only because of his friendship with Mendelssohn, but also because of his earlier drama, *Die Juden*. However, Goeze directly inspired Lessing to place *Nathan* in the twelfth century rather than the eighteenth century through his comparison of the Reimarus fragments with the *Toledot Yeshu*. In constructing the figure of Nathan in reply to Goeze's anti-Semitic criticism equating Christian dissidents with Jews, Lessing casts Nathan as a binary opposition between Jew and Christian dissident.

Lessing expresses his dissent from his Christian ingroup by identifying with a representative of a pariah caste. By so doing, he is able to signal his distancing of himself from the intolerant excesses of his Christian ingroup. He stops short, however, of an unconditional embrace of the outgroup. His pariah is an idealization, a man of wealth and noble character, an "exception Jew."

Through his portrayal of Nathan, Lessing advanced the notion that Christianity was not a sine qua non for strength of character. The character of Nathan is contrasted with that of the Christian patriarch of Jerusalem. In the figure of the patriarch, Lessing parodied Goeze's contention that orthodox Christianity was the only path of spiritual well-being. The patriarch responds to Nathan's rescue of the infant Recha and his raising her as a Jewess with the following words: "Besser / es wäre hier im Elend umgekommen / Als daß zu seinem ewigen Verderben / Es gerettet wird" (4.2).[9]

Through the figure of the patriarch, Lessing asserts the inhumanity of the position that Christianity is the sole acceptable point of view. He contrasts the intolerance of the believer with the tolerance of the nonbeliever. Nathan's tolerant outlook is maintained despite the fact that his wife and children were killed in a pogrom by Jew-hating Christians. By portraying the non-Christian as morally superior to the Christians, Lessing tries to assail a formidable tenet of the discursive order and relegate it to a position of historical obsolescence. Nathan follows a dialogic ideology, while the patriarch is absolutely monologic in his worldview.

While Nathan the Jew is largely a substitute formation for Christian dissidence, this should not be taken as an indication that Lessing was not interested in bettering the social conditions of the Jews. Hans Mayer rightly credits Lessing with having established Jewish emancipation as an unconditional component of the Enlightenment. Nathan, while holding religion to be accidental and interchangeable, is nonetheless connected with the Jewish experience through the pogrom of which he tells.[10] As we have already discussed, such pogroms were a major part of the Jewish experience during the Crusades. Helmut Jenzsch's contention that Lessing is not concerned with fighting prejudices against Jews is not accurate.[11]

Christian dissidents had long since recognized that Jewish emancipation was a logical consequence and component of their own arguments on behalf of religious tolerance.[12] At the same time, German Jews received *Nathan* positively because it encouraged them in their struggle against bigotry. George L. Mosse describes the drama as a "Magna Charta" of German Jewry. Jews related positively to Nathan's wisdom and the allowance for diversity of religious outlook.[13] There were Jews in the ghettos who memorized the entire *Nathan der Weise*. No other German author has been so frequently translated into Hebrew as Lessing.[14]

This leads me back to my observation that Nathan is cast as a binary opposition between Jew and Christian dissident. Benjamin Bennett points to the dialectical nature of Nathan's position as both Jew and non-Jew: "The Jew is detached from his religion intellectually, by his awareness of its imperfection, its lack of absolute validity, but at the same time, he still resolutely belongs to it."[15] The portrayal of Nathan as both Jew and dissident for the Christian Enlightenment is a conceptual fissure in the text—one that is grounded in the hybrid origin of the play in its intent to attack both Goeze's anti-Deistic stance and his anti-Semitism.

Other internal contradictions are present in the portrayal of Nathan: he is both a father and a nonfather.[16] This contradictory status forces limitations upon him. He can postulate that religious, familial, and political connections and privileges are social trappings but he cannot transcend them.[17] Occident and Orient are united in the final family scene: Saladin and Sittah, Recha and the templar. But Nathan is related to nobody: he remains outside the family circle.[18] As Bennett points out, "Something is wrong with this family of mankind if the wisest of all, the man whose wisdom makes it possible in the first place, is excluded."[19] The tragic dimension of Nathan lies in the equation of tolerance with outsiderness. Nathan feels a group identity with nobody: he feels ties neither to other Jews nor to the larger interfaith family of Saladin. He distances himself from any notion of a group identity with other Jews when he asks the templar: "Sind / Wir unser Volk?" (2.5).[20]

In addition to being cast as a binary opposition between Jew and Christian dissident, Nathan is also portrayed as a binary opposition between "father" and "outsider." Although he is not Recha's biological father, he is a parent par excellence. Not blood ties or incidental manifestation of homogeneity, but virtue is the bond that ties the enlightened person to his fellow human beings.[21] Nathan tries to coax Recha out of her dreaminess, because such dreaminess motivates inaction on her part. Such an incapacity for action prevents people from taking a role in the larger community. They do not respond to the mortal needs of others or react to the interdependencies that are a natural part of human existence.[22]

There is an irony in the text: Nathan the outsider is raising his daughter so that she will take her place within a larger group setting. She becomes more sensitive to the potential needs of others, and therefore more suited to play a positive role within a larger group context. This group context is of broader scope than an ingroup, however. It is nothing less than a multicultural circle, representing a utopian condition. Wilfried Barner describes *Nathan* as promoting a utopian conception of a harmonious social order.[23] Nathan is aware that someday Recha will leave him for a broader family setting: the Jew's daughter must cease to be a Jewess and join a larger circle of humanity. This assimilationist tendency undercuts Lessing's tolerance motif.

Nathan finds himself in a situation like that of Moses in the Old Testament: he leads his people (not only Recha, but also Curd, Saladin, and Sittah) to the border of the utopia/promised land, but he cannot enter it himself. The universal utopia is at the same time strangely exclusive. He cannot cease to be a Jew, so he must be excluded from this broader circle of humanity. He is further isolated when his daughter surrenders her Jewishness, to enter the broader utopian family.

Lessing's emancipatory discourse is a mediated discourse: his demands for an improvement in the human condition are filtered through a bourgeois consciousness. He strives to promote an overall identification with humanity that transcends ingroup identifications, but he fails to overcome the effects of his own group identifications. Lessing succeeded in distancing himself from his Christian ingroup but largely replaced this sort of affiliation with an identification with the emerging bourgeois class of which he was a part. This condition is reflected in his writing. In *Nathan der Weise*, Nathan's absence of specifically Jewish qualities was a strategic maneuver on Lessing's part to make the drama more palatable to a bourgeois audience.[24] Other concessions to bourgeois values are also made. As in his earlier drama *Die Juden*, Lessing made the assimilation of the Jewish outsiders dependent on two preconditions: education and property.[25] This principle is expressed by Lessing in *Nathan der Weise* in terms of the interchangeability between "der Weise" and "der Reiche," practically making them equivalent signifieds. Nathan is representative of a citizen who thinks about his own economic advantage: he personifies the bourgeois desire to ascend socially through money.[26]

Nathan's wealth is of commercial origin and is positively valuated: the bourgeois can give generously, because he is always earning.[27] The productivity and security of the middle-class merchant is contrasted with the desperate situation of the feudal ruler: Saladin is portrayed as an aristocratic spendthrift who is incompetent at handling money.[28] Saladin's humanity and moral virtue are subject to the limitations of the material conditions and the economic realities that drive the society.[29] Lack of money impedes the ruler from doing good. The pursuit of material interests is viewed as playing a positive role in the society. Nathan's wealth is the justified result of his wisdom: it is at once an expression and confirmation of that wisdom.[30]

In writing from a nascent middle-class perspective, Lessing forms a close association between morals and business. In the course of doing this, Lessing attempts to subvert the negative associations of the connection between "trade" and "Jew" by combining the concept of trade with the bourgeois value system.[31] The trade concept is bound up with positive associations and takes on a bourgeois rather than "Jewish" signification. Through this strategy, Lessing points the way toward Jewish emancipation: assimilation into bourgeois society. This was destined to become the pathway for Jews seeking equal rights. In no small measure due to the encouragement of middle-class writers, the Jews emulated the bourgeoisie: under the guise of emancipation, they conformed to bourgeois values and so came to epitomize the bourgeoisie.[32] This pathway toward Jewish emancipation would later draw the wrath of those who sought the restoration of feudal society.

Lessing and other middle-class writers sought to relax the fetters of the feudal state and the Christian Church both for their own benefit and for the benefit of the minorities with which they had come to sympathize. In the process of sympathizing/identifying with religious and social pariahs such as the Jews, they came to conceptualize and portray the Jews in terms of an image to which they themselves could relate. This played an influential role in rendering the Jews more similar to themselves: in opening the door to assimilation, one means of rapprochement with the nonidentical became available. But through this process, the "otherness" of the nonidentical was substantially compromised.

On the other hand, the attempts of Enlightened authors to change the status of stigmatized outgroups comprised a frontal assault on the feudal aristocracy. As discussed in Chapter 1, the ruling classes exploited anti-Semitism in an attempt to foster identification of the lower classes with the aristocracy. Through the existence of a pariah group, even socially marginal people felt a sense of common status with the dominant group. By attempting to improve the social image of the pariah, Lessing is taking an action that would lessen the almost universal identification with the ruling powers, and thereby benefit the middle class as well as the Jews. In struggling for the interests of the bourgeoisie, the Enlighteners did their utmost to discourage identification with the ruling classes.

Lessing takes a stance in favor of the toleration of nonconformist individuals as well as non-Christian religious minorities. The religious guardianship of the state was under attack. The goal was to turn belief into a strictly private concern and to transform the state into a secular organization.[33] The ultimate goal was to redefine the organization of society. In the case of Nathan and Saladin, the issue of religious affiliation atrophies as a basis of interaction between ruler and subject.[34] No longer is the nonconformist to be subjugated or oppressed on the basis of his religious belief but to be given credit for his valuable contributions to the welfare of the state. Although no examination of *Nathan der Weise* would be complete without a glance at the contradictions between authorial intention and textual performance and the conceptual fissures that characterize all texts, this should not be taken as a minimizing of the critical importance of Lessing's drama. Lessing raised issues that could only have been raised within a literary context, spurring lively debate on both the question of Jewish emancipation and the question of religious freedom in general.

Accordingly, it is also necessary that we read the text in the light of its philosophical and artistic triumphs. The Ring Parable is surely one of the text's most triumphal moments in terms of Lessing's efforts to combat the Crusade ideology. This is so because it is one of the few parts of the play where Lessing's criticisms of both anti-Semitism and anti-Deism comfortably coexist in a general plea for religious freedom. During the 1950s and 1960s, scholarship by Stuart Atkins and Heinz Politzer saw the Ring Parable as a straightforward rationalistic criticism promoting tolerance but that view has been greatly amplified by more contemporary scholars.

According to Politzer, the three sons are bound up in a competition for a confirmation of legitimacy to be brought about by the exclusive endorsement of their father. The desired endorsement does not come about for any of them, so that they are forced to regard one another as equals and work together. Politzer sees the theme of the parable as being that humankind can no longer afford the illusion of a God-given endorsement granting exclusive legitimacy to a single ingroup at the expense of all outgroups. Rather, the various groups must attain the ability to work together and solve problems in a "this-worldly" fashion.[35] Stuart Atkins similarly argues that Lessing uses the Ring Parable to attack the notion of ingroup loyalty altogether. Nathan rejects Saladin's premise that one single religion constitutes the ideal prescription for belief.[36]

Both Politzer's and Atkins's interpretations are relatively straightforward and uncomplicated. However, Rüdiger Zymner, writing in 1992, comes up with a new twist to the Ring Parable. In the judge's speech, he speaks not about three rings but about four: about the possibly lost original ring and the three false rings of the sons. The rings of the sons must all be false according to the judge, because none of the rings has the miraculous power of the original.[37]

Zymner points out that the ring contained an opal and opals cannot be reproduced or falsified. He indicates how unbelievable it would be for there to be a double reproduction of an opal showing 100 colors. The artist in the Ring Parable presents the father with three rings among which the original cannot be discovered. This leads to a question whether the original ring is among the three. When there are three opals that are completely alike, none of them can be the correct opal of the father. They must be three completely identical forgeries. The artist cheated the father and the three sons and kept the original ring.[38]

If the artist kept the original ring, then this must have specific implications. The artist must be in possession of the absolute truth regarding true religion. However, he only makes it available through his representations, which are subject to a multiplicity of interpretations. If the artist is the sole possessor of truth, then truth must be interpreted out of the artist's representations. Therefore, truth, like art, cannot be reduced to a single configurative meaning. Hence, everyone must read their own meaning out of the rings.

Such hermeneutic implications to the Ring Parable are explored by Robert S. Leventhal in his 1988 essay, "The Parable As Performance." According to Leventhal, it is "the power endowed through faith and belief that determines the actual power of the ring." Between differing religions, there are major historical and cultural differences. At the same time, "there is a deeper, fundamental commonality that unites these traditions and makes coexistence possible."[39]

The origin of religion is indeterminate and accordingly, no religion can claim truth on the basis of its origin. Orthodox Christians claimed the unique legitimacy of their religion on the basis of the Bible and their belief that it had been divinely revealed, a claim to origin which had been problematized by the eighteenth-century Deists. Nathan presents to Saladin the problematical nature of tradition, cultural transmission, and belief: "In human history, there can be no certainty in the anagogical sense. . . . In *Nathan*, the Parable achieves only formal closure; the actual judgment or ultimate sense is deferred."[40]

Leventhal points to the problematic nature of tradition in terms of continuing it to future generations and how later generations are to interpret it. He sees the Ring Parable as problematizing monologism: "there is no clear heir to the inheritance, the crisis of the one supposedly true version." He also points to the problematic nature of deciding between three equally pious religions and three equally plausible interpretations of secular history. Original intention cannot be demonstrated and leaves the interpreter with manifold readings. The only solution is to recognize a multiplicity of positions/interpretations.[41]

A single definitive reading of history—religious or otherwise—has become suspect. Differing interpretations of history must be viewed as legitimate: human beings must enter into dialogue with one another. The judge in the Ring Parable defers judgment until a period thousands of years into the future, beyond human history. The judge himself discredits belief in any absolute judgment. Religions are therefore emancipated from the hegemony of the past.[42]

Because there is no single universal message, the hermeneutic activity is turned over to the readers, who are confronted with the possibility that other readings of religious history besides their own are legitimate.[43] Benjamin Bennett examines Nathan's ironic wisdom. Nathan advocates the position that one should be true to the religion of one's fathers and at the same time recognize that absolute certainty about the truth of one's belief is impossible.[44]

Lessing's Ring Parable is an attempt to dialogize his society by making the central concerns of the members of that society subject to differing individual readings, to a diverse number of interpretations. Accordingly it was a fit response to the tyrannical monologism of Pastor Goeze, with his anti-Semitism and anti-Deism. Lessing's critical discourse was not safely within the realm of contemporary rules of exclusion. As Hans Friedrich Wessels points out, Lessing was afraid the play would be banned. The authorities viewed his work with distrust. Lessing stopped selling subscriptions because he wanted to bring the work before the reading public in as inconspicuous a manner as possible. He tried to avoid a collision with the Viennese authorities by rejecting 200 subscriptions from Vienna.[45] *Nathan der Weise* was banned in Frankfurt am Main after the authorities there cited "den scandeleusesten Inhalt im Rücksicht der Religion."[46] The work also occasioned controversy in Dresden: Simon Friedrich Olbrecht, city clerk of Dresden, complained about "unterschiedene, der christlichen Religion sehr anstößige Stellen" and recommended censorship.[47] Further evidence of a desire not to overtly court controversy is to be seen in Lessing's reluctance to have the play performed, a reluctance that was shared by his friend, the popular philosopher Georg Christoph Lichtenberg, and by the director of the Berlin Theater, Johann Jakob Engel, who feared the wrath of the censors.[48] Wessels explains the relative paucity of reviews of the play in the eighteenth-century literary journals by explaining that the journals did not want to be drawn into the controversy surrounding the Reimarus fragments. Particularly noteworthy is the failure of Friedrich Nicolai to review the work in his *Allgemeine deutsche Bibliothek*. He feared he would have to deal with possible censorship if he commented on the work. Nicolai's concession to the perceived restrictions of his times strained his friendship with Lessing.[49]

Wessels mounts a comprehensive investigation of the reception of *Nathan*, noting that the polarization of the reception followed the lines of the Lessing-Goeze dispute. One journal, for example, described Nathan as "die bitterste Satire gegen christliche Religion,"[50] while another defended the piece as "das bleibendste Denkmal von den Fortschritten unsers Zeitalters in der Kenntnis des wahren Gehalts unsrer und andrer Religionen, und . . . das bleibenste Denkmal von der Freimüthigkeit im Untersuchen und Prüfen solcher Gegenstände."[51]

Orthodox Christian reception to Lessing's play was typified by Balthasar Ludwig Tralles. In addition to being one of Lessing's most bitter critics, Tralles was a renowned physician whose Latin-language tracts on medicine and science are still studied by medical scholars today. His tract, *Zufällige alt-deutsche und christliche Betrachtungen über Herrn Gotthold Ephraim Lessings neues dramatisches Gedicht "Nathan der Weise"* (1779), is a reaffirmation of Christianity as a consensus formation. Orthodox Christian values and ideology are presented as an absolute a priori with which everyone must agree in order to attain the minimum level of acceptability in the society. As such, Tralles's writing is both a confirmation and a documentation of the rules of exclusion in effect in the eighteenth century. Tralles's conviction that Christian institutions are above criticism is communicated through an expression of shock and horror over the content of Lessing's play. In authoritarian fashion, Tralles seeks the "utopian" condition of absolute monologue.[52]

As a purveyor of "official discourse," Tralles resists communication by attempting to compel his opponent to restrict himself to those linguistic formations which correspond to Tralles's own.[53] The emotional nature of Tralles's polemic is evidenced in his portrayal of *Nathan* as a mockery of Christian religion. The work was written in a serious, philosophical discourse and is devoid of any satirical intent. In Lessing's own words: "Es wird nichts weniger als ein satirisches Stück um den Kampfplatz mit Hohngelächter zu verlassen. Es wird ein so rührendes Stück, als ich nur immer gemacht habe."[54] Tralles's presentation of the piece as a mockery of Christianity is an attempt to appeal to the wounded pride of members of the Christian ingroup. Solidarity with other Christians is the basis from which he attempts to reaffirm Christianity as a consensus formation and suppress Natural Religion as a critical discourse.

Tralles attempts to portray Christians as being threatened by Lessing's critical discourse and thereby to unify Christians against it. He maintains that all Christians have a duty to oppose Lessing's criticism. He recognizes the political implications of Lessing's attempt to break the stronghold of orthodox Christianity and portrays the Enlightener's criticism as a threat to the social order. He explicitly agrees with Lessing's character, the patriarch, that lack of formal belief is dangerous to society.

For Tralles, Christianity is an important ideological anchor preserving the status quo. Whoever criticizes Christianity endangers the entire social order and, from Tralles's viewpoint, is not to be tolerated. By presenting Lessing's position as dangerous to society, Tralles attempts to mobilize the conservative social forces toward suppression of a critical discourse that pointed the way toward social change.

Tralles attempts to suppress the critical rationalism of the Enlightenment by promoting a Christian mysticism: "Der Saame der Vernunft, wenn er auch noch rein ist, trägt keine Frucht, welche die ganze Seele sättigt und nähret." Tralles's advocacy of a Christian-oriented irrationalism manifests itself in an attack on the rationalistic elements in Lessing's text. He is particularly offended by the scene in which Nathan conveys to Recha that her rescuer is not an angel but a normal man. He describes it as "eine artige und feine Spötterey über die Wunder." Tralles maintains that the rescue should have been presented as a manifestation of divine providence and that Recha's reaction should have been praised rather than condemned as "andächtige Schwärmereyen."[55]

Tralles condemns Natural Religion and its rationalistic component. He maintains that the irrational component of orthodox Christianity makes it superior to Natural Religion. He condemns the critical nature of Natural Religion. In so doing, he wants to promote a public that is obedient, subservient, and uncritical. He wishes to put a stop to the unleashing of critical discourses within the public sphere. By making Christianity unassailable and by strengthening the rules of exclusion that protect it, the critical possibilities of the public sphere are diminished. A public incapable of criticizing the church will also be incapable of criticizing the state.

The major element of Lessing's critical discourse is that of tolerance. Tralles responds to the tolerance critique by maintaining that Christianity itself is tolerant. He points to the ability of orthodox Christians to tolerate other orthodox Christians from varying Protestant and Catholic sects. Tralles's linguistic strategy is that of a semantic narrowing of the tolerance concept. Religious minorities and dissidents are excluded from any notion of tolerance whatsoever; it is to be restricted to orthodox followers of differing Christian sects. He tries to attack the tolerance ideology through the semiotic redefinition of one of its key concepts, making the sign a locus for social struggle. Furthermore, he defines those who fail to fit within the narrow framework of orthodox Christianity as being intolerant, as being oppressors of Christians. He tries to do away with Lessing's critical discourse by refracting some of its key concepts from his conservative ideological perspective.

He states that nonbelief is the sole form of religious oppression and that it does more harm than ever was done by fire and sword. Implicit within this pronouncement is a notion that the carnage of the Crusades was justified, while criticism of such intolerance is oppressive. By equating criticism of Christianity with oppression of Christians, Tralles attempts to impart new meanings to the concepts of tolerance and oppression in such a way that contemporary rules of exclusion are upheld. This is an example of the ideological struggle for linguistic control of the sign. Tralles, an advocate of the interests of the ruling class, attempts to undermine a critical discourse through a linguistic redefinition of some of its key concepts in order to make it harmless and uncritical.

Tralles condemns Lessing for maintaining that it should be a matter of indifference whether someone is a Christian or Jew. He maintains that Judaism is an inferior culture: Tralles feels that Jewish children are routinely raised in an environment of ignorance. He accuses them of being a culture of swindlers who are both unhygienic and immoral. He tries to further incite hatred against the Jews by incriminating them for their refusal to accept the Trinity. He feels that this refusal constitutes a defamation of Christ.

Tralles's religious anti-Semitism was part of the dominant discourse of his time. He characterized the firm resistance with which society met the demand for religious tolerance. In asserting Christian doctrines as incontrovertible facts of scientific dimensions, Tralles pursues his wish for a condition of monologue.

He does this by maintaining the moral inferiority of anyone who does not take his stance as absolute truth, including the Jews; and he wishes to silence their advocates. It is therefore not surprising that Tralles would not approve of the message of the Ring Parable: "Man untersuche nunmehr auf allen diesen Probiersteinen den jüdischen, türkischen und christlichen Glauben. Man muß mit Vorurtheilen ganz umnebelt und völlig blind seyn, oder seyn wollen, wenn man die offenbarsten und vortrefflichsten des letzten von den zwei nicht einsehen, erkennen und zusehen will."[56] In a noteworthy semantic reversal, Tralles asserts that it is not the orthodox Christians who are prejudiced, but the people who fail to accept the premises of orthodox Christianity. For Tralles to blame the Jews' refusal to convert on Jewish prejudice is a classic instance of blaming the victim. He projects his own prejudice onto the outgroup.

Tralles cannot accept a notion of religion directed toward moral principles alone but insists on a strict obedience toward the dogmatic and mystical side of religion. These elements are, however, grounded in irrationalism and thereby directed toward encouraging an uncritical social conformity. Such religious principles were effective underpinnings for maintenance of the absolutist state, because they hindered the possibility that criticism of the church would serve as a precedent for criticism of the state.

Tralles advocates the homogenization of cultural life under a conservative traditionalistic vision of Christianity. Tralles does not recognize Lessing as having the right to speak: he wishes to abolish Lessing's possibilities for entering into critical dialogue altogether. The goal of his argumentation is not critical dialogue, but the upholding and the triumph of the dominant discourse at any price.[57] For Tralles to have entered into a critical dialogue with Lessing would have entailed a risk: he might have come to new insights that would have forced him to modify his relationship with his ingroup.

One representative of orthodox Christianity who was initially influenced by Lessing's demands for tolerance toward religious dissidents was the Lutheran pastor Johann Georg Pfranger. The release of the *Wolfenbüttler Fragmente* and of *Nathan der Weise* unleashed in him doubts about Christianity.[58] Pfranger, however, resisted this critical discourse and attempted to bring his beliefs back into line with the dominant discourse of orthodox Christianity.[59] For Pfranger, the prospect of being cut off from the ingroup was a dangerous one: he feared loss of the perceived advantages of group identification with Christianity, such as eternal salvation. Pfranger's friend, Johann Ernst Berger, explained that Pfranger wrote his play *Der Mönch vom Libanon* (1782) with the goal, "manche Aengstliche zu beruhigen und zu zeigen, was das Christenthum auf so manchen witzigen und scheinbaren Einwurf des Lessingischen Dramas antworten könnte."[60]

Pfranger's work is an attempt to take Lessing's critical discourse and co-opt it within the dominant discourse: to bring it within the parameters of rules of exclusion promoting the linguistic hegemony of Christianity.

Pfranger portrays Saladin on his deathbed, greatly in need of spiritual support as well as medical attention. He faces death with the fear of divine punishment for earlier acts of violence. As such, Nathan is unable to help him. Nathan's philosophy of the relativity of religious belief is parodied by Pfranger as sophistry: "Was einem Wahrheit ist, das gilt dem andern / Für Irthum."[61] Saladin criticizes Nathan's relativistic stance as inadequate: "Nimm dich in Acht mit deiner Weisheit, Nathan, / Daß sie nicht deiner Tugend unvermerkt / Den Hals bricht."[62] A rationalistic stance is criticized as being dangerous: it threatens the virtue of the individual. Saladin expresses the viewpoint that religious faith is a source of comfort: "O Nathan! / Für Menschen, die so sind, wie wir, für die / Das Forschen nach der Wahrheit Angst, die Tugend / Hier Zweifel und dort Stolz gebiehrt, ist Glaube / Ein köstlich Ding!"[63] Pfranger criticizes Lessing's Ring Parable, which he views as an evasive maneuver to conceal the truth of the Christian religion. He has Saladin admonish Nathan: "Verschwende nicht / Auf solche Mährchen, die du selbst nicht glaubst. . . . Glaube mir / Du weichst nur so der Wahrheit künstlich aus."[64]

Saladin, through his speeches, promotes conservative ideologemes.[65] He portrays religion as the sine qua non of virtue and as an irreplaceable response to human needs. He expresses sentiments against the rationalistic drive of the Enlightenment. In sleep, he has a vision that he will that very day be in paradise. Nathan, the rationalist, tries to convince the sultan that this is not a premonition, but merely a dream, to which he responds: "[Ein Traum], der mir lieber ist, / Als die Weisheit dieser Welt. O! mache mir meine Freude nicht zu Wasser! Laß mich träumen / bin vielleicht der erste nicht, / Der wenn er schläft, am klügsten denkt."[66] Pfranger expresses the view that the rationalistic critique of religion drives many human beings to despair: it is a destruction of a dreamlike bliss. He feels that people are happier and more virtuous when they are under the influence of religion.

Natural Religion is portrayed as a misguided effort that only destroys humankind's major source of comfort: revealed religion. As such, Natural Religion threatens human well-being. By portraying Natural Religion as a cause for unhappiness, Pfranger is trying to relegate it to the status of a marginalized discourse. He thereby reaffirms the linguistic and social hegemony of orthodox Christianity.

Pfranger rejects the premise that Natural Religion is more tolerant than orthodox Christianity. He maintains that tolerance is a cornerstone of Christianity. Tolerance is represented through the character of the Christian monk of Lebanon, whose reputation as a man of tolerance is known far and wide: "Auch dort galt ihm / Christ, Jud', und Muselmann, so sehr er selbst / Ein Christ ist, nur nach ihrem wahren Werth: / Und wo es Hülfe durfte waren alle / Die Nächsten ihm. Unaufgefordert spricht / Er wenig von Religion."[67] Through the character of the monk of Lebanon, Pfranger tries to differentiate Christianity from the viewpoint represented by Lessing's patriarch of Jerusalem. His reaction toward Nathan's adoption of the Christian-born Recha is positive: "Dort . . . wirds ihm Gott vergelten, wo / Die guten Thaten alle Gott vergilt."[68]

Pfranger portrays the monk's tolerance as being firmly grounded in Christian teachings. The problem of differing religions is developed in the following exchange between Saladin and the monk:

> Saladin: Nun sind wir anderen denn / Verdammt? Was sagst du?
> Mönch: Das, o Sultan, zu / Entscheiden hat mich Christus nicht gelehrt. / Gott, Gott allein kan wissen, was die Hölle / Verdient hat, was des Himmels fähig ist. / Uns ist ausdrücklich untersagt zu richten, / Zu lieben nicht, dieß ist Befehl.[69]

However, Pfranger's assertion of tolerance is not without its internal contradictions. He establishes a hierarchy of "superior" and "inferior" religions. The ambivalence of Pfranger's tolerance notion is revealed in the following statement made by the monk: "Kein Volk ist in der Welt, in dessen Glauben / Nicht etwas Wahres sey, und wär es nichts, / Als das: es ist ein Gott! Schon Grund, als sein / Geschöpf ihm treu zu seyn. Je weiter dieser Gedank entwickelt ist, um desto besser / Ist die Religion."[70]

The notion of tolerance embodied in the statement that all religions have something true about them is modified by the statement that some religions are better than others. The contradiction between tolerance and hierarchization of religion is also expressed in an exchange between the monk and Recha. Pfranger initially expresses tolerance for the Jews:

> Recha: Wie? / o meynst du, guter Vater, daß auch wol / In deinem Paradies ein Judenmädchen / Ihr Plätzchen finden könnte? glaubst du das? / In allem Ernst?
> Mönch: Ein frommes Judenmädchen? / Warum denn nicht?[71]

However, Pfranger makes it clear that this tolerance should not be regarded as a qualitative equality between Christianity and Judaism when the monk endeavors to convert Recha to Christianity:

> Recha: Aber selig / Kan auch die Jüdin werden; Dann: Wozu noch Christin erst?
> Mönch: So? Könnten wir nicht auch / Als Thiere glücklich seyn? Wozu erst Menschen? / Gieb dir die Antwort selbst![72]

It is a strange notion of tolerance to argue that the difference between Christian and Jew is as great as the difference between human and animal. A major internal contradiction emerges in the text in that Pfranger wants to adhere to two mutually exclusive positions: he wants to embrace tolerance while maintaining his religious particularism. As such, he views tolerance as a temporary forbearance of an inferior point of view and as a mere prelude for conversion to the "superior" religion. This represents a substantial modification of Lessing's position that Christianity and Judaism are qualitatively equal. Lessing promotes a modern concept of tolerance as an acknowledgment of equality, whereas Pfranger wants to promote tolerance in its traditional Christian conception as a tentative sufferance of the inferior. Both authors grapple for linguistic control of what was a very important signifier: Lessing seeking to define it broadly and Pfranger seeking the most narrow possible definition of tolerance.

Pfranger grounds the supposed superiority of Christianity over Judaism in the greater degree of mystification that Christianity has undergone. The monk describes Judaism as being more earthbound, Christianity as being more heavenly: "Moses / Gab seinen Wundern durch die Hoffnung des / Verheißnen Landes ein Gewicht, das leichter / Ihm Glauben schaffen konnte. / Was denn Christus? / Nichts, nichts, was Menschen reizt: im Gegentheil / Verläugnung alles Irdischen, und Leiden; / Zuletzt schmachvoller Tod war seiner ersten Bekenner los."[73]

Pfranger appeals to mystical and ascetic elements as proof of the superiority of Christianity. Religion can be viewed as being composed of two elements: the ethical and the mystical. The followers of Natural Religion wished to deemphasize the mystical element in favor of the ethical. Pfranger and Tralles both defend the mystical as being an essential element of Christianity. Pfranger privileges Christianity over Judaism because of the greater degree of mystification in Christianity. Interestingly, the Jewish philosopher Moses Mendelssohn viewed that situation as being in Judaism's favor. For him, the fact that Judaism was more earthbound than Christianity meant that it was better grounded in reason. The "heavenly" orientation of Christianity was viewed by Mendelssohn as being an overmystification, an attempt to make something as routine as religion seem more exotic or more exciting. The mystical rhetoric of orthodox Christianity and its close connection to Christian mythology is to be seen in the following statement by the monk:

> O Nathan! Nathan! / Und aller Menschen Seelen, aller Leben / Für alle Ewigkeit hin zu retten, / Durch einen blut'gen Tod, ein willigs Opfer, / Für aller Menschen Sünden dem Gerechten / Sich darzustellen: das ist mehr, ist mehr, / Als Menschenkräfte leisten können! höher, / Als alle Grenzen des Verstandes zu / Umfassen es vermögen! ist wohl werth, / Der ersten ew'gen Thaten Gottes eine / zu seyn![74]

Pfranger's mysticism has affinities with Tralles's mysticism. By promoting a mystical antirationalism, Pfranger is attempting to promote a broader public incapable of thinking critically in matters of religion. An obedience toward the institutions of the church is promoted, with the implication that obedience toward the institutions of the state is also desirable.

Wessels points to the change of function that Nathan undergoes in Pfranger's piece. Instead of being a merchant, he is a treasurer for the sultan. He goes from being a representative of the emerging middle class to being a fixture of the feudal order.[75] Nathan is thereby no longer an ideologeme for bourgeois values. The original Nathan is a model of middle-class diligence and a symbol of the bourgeois desire to ascend socially through money. In Pfranger's version, Nathan is stripped of this affirmation of bourgeois values. He is thereby made harmless as a critical ideologeme representing the bourgeoisie. Whereas Lessing seeks to promote middle-class sympathy with the Jew by portraying Nathan as a quintessential bourgeois, Pfranger attacks Nathan as a symbol for middle-class identification by casting him as a servant of the aristocracy. He thereby promotes an outmoded image of the Jews: for centuries, they were middlemen between nobility and peasantry. Many of the bourgeoisie believed that the Jews stood in the way of industrialization and capitalization.[76] By encouraging this viewpoint, Pfranger works to weaken the impulse toward accepting Jews into mainstream bourgeois society.

Nathan is also made harmless as a critic of orthodox religion. Perhaps the most blatant example of this is when he shuns his critical rationalism and allows himself to be persuaded by the monk's Christian mysticism: "Du sprichst beredter Mönch, für deinen Glauben, / Als deine Patriarchen. Dachten alle, / Die ihn bekennen, so, wie du dann wär' / Unglaube freilich Sünd', und Freude wärs, / Ein Christ zu seyn."[77] Nathan repudiates not only his own Enlightened rationalism and his leanings toward Natural Religion, but also Lessing's criticism of Goeze by substituting the monk for the patriarch as representative of orthodox Christianity.

Whereas Tralles's linguistic strategy toward Lessing's critical discourse is one of condemnation and open repression, Pfranger pursues more subtle methods. He wishes to modify Lessing's criticism and thereby bring it into the linguistic realm permitted by contemporary rules of exclusion. He thereby attempts to make Lessing's criticism harmless.

For example, while purporting to favor tolerance, Pfranger maintains that Judaism is a more primitive and less developed religion than Christianity. This is a substantial modification of Lessing's position that both religions are fully equal. Lessing wishes to reduce religion to moral and ethical principles, and discard mystical elements that promote irrationalism and uncritical obedience toward institutions. Pfranger wishes to preserve this mysticism and uncritical obedience, maintaining that it better promotes virtuous behavior and human happiness.

Pfranger contradicts his avowal of tolerance by displaying open prejudice toward Moslems. He portrays Islam as being a fundamentally violent religion. The monk of Lebanon tells a story in which he compares Christianity to an iron plow, which helps the farmer to harvest good fruit. He notes that thinkers from other religious directions, such as Deism and Natural Religion, reshaped the plow, so that it was no longer able to help the farmer provide nourishment. The monk is asked what the Moslems did to the plow. He responds: "so wisse: Dies fand ein hitz'ger Kopf und dachte: Ha! / Das Ding ist scharf; ist gut zum Hauen! und Verwandelte die Pflugschar in ein Schwerdt / Er zog damit von Land zu Land, und hieb / Und mordete; und rief bei jedem Schlag: Seht, Thoren, da! dies ist Religion!"[78] In portraying Islam as a fundamentally and uniquely violent religion, Pfranger casts a blind eye toward numerous Christian battles and conquests of the sword, and implicitly endorses the Crusade ideology.

Jazid and Abdullah are portrayed by Pfranger as dangerous fanatics. They poison Saladin and pin the blame on the monk, so that Jazid may be restored to his previous role as the sultan's physician.

Even Saladin is not portrayed in a particularly positive light. His spiritual crisis comes about as a result of his having murdered and plundered in his role as sultan. At the end of the play, he rejects the monk's entreaties not to punish Abdallah through death. Abdallah saves himself by portraying himself as an earlier victim of the sultan's oppression, and Saladin dies through the shock of self-recognition. Forgiveness, which purportedly would have saved Saladin, is portrayed as a uniquely Christian trait. Pfranger portrays Christianity as an ethically principled religion, while maintaining that Islam is totally lacking in such principles. As such, he reveals a prejudiced attitude toward Islam. This is an example of the anti-Islamic prejudice that the cultural critic Edward W. Said calls Orientalism.[79]

Pfranger further reveals his Christian particularism through his subversion of Lessing's recognition scene in which most of Lessing's characters find they belong to the same family. In Pfranger's recognition scene, the monk reveals to the dying Saladin that he is Saladin's long-lost brother, Assad. The monk has become a saintly man through renouncing Islam and converting to Christianity. Pfranger thereby adopts an element from Lessing that promotes the notion of the differing religions having equal worth and rewrites it in order to promote his own belief that Christianity is a superior religion. The Lutheran clergyman answers the statement of Lessing's Nathan to the templar that "Wir haben beide / Uns unser Volk nicht auserlesen" (2.5)[80] by having his protagonist voluntarily embrace Christianity. Religion is a matter of choice, and the morally superior person will select Christianity.

Pfranger attempts to bring Lessing's critical discourse of tolerance into the parameters of contemporary rules of exclusion by accepting it in theory while rejecting it in practice. As an orthodox Christian, Pfranger is unable to accept Lessing's principle of religious relativism, without which true tolerance is impossible. Whereas Tralles attempts to combat the tolerance discourse through open rejection, Pfranger's standpoint is much more complicated and ambivalent. He wants to combine the tolerance discourse with orthodox Christianity. In so doing, he weakens the tolerance discourse and renders it impotent by presenting internal contradictions, of which he himself is not aware.

Another example of Pfranger's attempt to try to modify Lessing's critical discourse lies in his revision of Lessing's portrayal of the "other" as oppressed. Lessing develops this theme through having Nathan tell the very emotional story of how his wife and seven children were murdered in a Christian pogrom. Pfranger revises this critical discourse by portraying the oppression of the Christian by the "other." Two Moslems plot against the saintly monk, and succeed in having him thrown into prison. The monk maintains his dignity and humanity through assertion of a Christian asceticism: "Auch Leiden sind oft Lohn, / Wo uns die Freude nur das Herz verderben / Und für das bessre Leben nicht ersprießlich / seyn würde."[81]

By portraying the monk as taking his undeserved punishment so meekly and without bitterness, Pfranger is attempting to promote an "us-identification" with Christianity. Instead of portraying the majority group oppressing a minority group, Pfranger shows how narrow-minded fanatics from a minority group persecute an exemplary member of the majority group. As does Tralles, Pfranger seeks to promote an ingroup identification with Christianity. Tolerance toward outgroups is for Pfranger at most a pretext to attempt to persuade them to join the ingroup.

Wessels indicates that *Der Mönch vom Libanon* promotes a restoration of feudal society, including a close relationship between church and state. The promotion and furtherance of an irrefutable, truth-preserving religion is functionally bound with the structure of society.[82]

Both Tralles and Pfranger attempt to quash the critical and antiauthoritarian discourse unleashed by Lessing and to reaffirm orthodox Christianity as an authoritarian consensus formation. Both emphasize the mystical content of Christianity and point to its superiority over other religions. Both purport to believe in tolerance, but neither wishes to eschew their Christian particularism and as such they attempt to promote very narrow definitions of tolerance. Tralles believes in tolerance only toward other Christian sects, whereas Pfranger believes in a patronizing sort of tolerance toward adherents of other religions as a strategic first step toward converting them to Christianity. He clearly portrays Judaism as a backward religion and Islam as an unacceptable religious belief.

Der Mönch vom Libanon is a "Kontrafraktur" to *Nathan der Weise*. Nathan, the compelling protagonist of Lessing's drama, is rewritten as a minor character and as something of a sophistic gadfly in Pfranger's revision. The friar, a minor character in the original, becomes Pfranger's hero: the ever noble Monk of Lebanon. Whereas *Nathan* protests against the oppression of religious minorities, *Der Mönch* portrays minorities as being backward and, in some cases, a threat to the religious majority. Lessing is a rationalist and Pfranger is a mysticist. Pfranger advocates maintenance of the feudal order, while Lessing pushes for empowerment of the middle class.

Lessing assails the feudal order by asserting identification with the pariah and therefore weakens the case for people to assert their identification with the dominant society by differentiating themselves from the socially marginalized. For Pfranger to avow his loyalty to the feudal apparatus, it becomes necessary for him to overtly differentiate himself from the outgroups. He defines himself in opposition to the minority in order to assert his identification with the religious and social status quo.

Pfranger's play was generally regarded as a tendentious minister's work. The older Goethe was especially dismissive of the work, equating it in quality with such works as Friedrich Nicolai's Goethe parody *Die Freuden des jungen Werthers* (1776) and Pustkuchen's falsification of *Wilhelm Meister's Wanderjahre*.[83] In religious circles, interest in *Der Mönch* was maintained over a century after the play's publication, however. In a sermon in 1881, the Lutheran pastor Eugen Borgius compared *Nathan der Weise* with *Der Mönch vom Libanon*. His comparison was, predictably, to Lessing's detriment. He accused Lessing of having portrayed Christianity as having been an inferior religion to Judaism and Islam.[84] Borgius maintains the attitude that all goodness stems from Christianity, and, to the extent that any goodness can be attributed to Jews or Moslems, it comes about because they have subconsciously absorbed Christian teachings.[85]

There is an intriguing parallel between the messages of Lessing and Pfranger and their relations to the dramatic conventions of their time. Pfranger wishes to deliver a very conservative message and turns to a historically obsolete paradigm to deliver that message: *Der Mönch vom Libanon* is based on the model of the martyr dramas of the seventeenth century and earlier.[86]

Martyr dramas promote the sacrifice of self in the service of the Christian faith. They do so by espousing such virtues as magnanimity, fortitude, and submission to providence.[87] Magnanimity is portrayed by Pfranger in terms of the monk's loftiness of spirit that enables him to bear severe hardship calmly, disdaining anger and the desire for revenge. He goes to a cell in a dungeon calmly and without protest and upon his release pleads that punishment not be exacted upon the men who framed him.

The monk is also portrayed as a man of fortitude: when Nathan and Recha visit him in prison, he shows neither concern for his own well-being nor bitterness over his undeserved fate, but bears adversity in a dignified manner. Submission to providence is also espoused in Pfranger's drama. Divine providence is portrayed as something in which humankind can have blind faith. The monk is willing to accept the death that appears to be his fate, but his innocence and moral goodness are proved and he is rewarded by being rescued from prison and restored to a position of trust.

Another motif appearing in *Der Mönch vom Libanon* typical of the martyr drama is that of the mediator. The monk plays the role of mediator between Saladin and the world of Christianity. Through mediation to help the ruler resolve existential problems, that ruler comes to experience the "truth" of the Christian religion.[88] The previous mediator, Nathan, with his non-Christian point of view, is unsuccessful in providing comfort or solace.

Another common motif from the martyr drama that finds its way into Pfranger's play is that of the converted tyrant. Saladin is plagued by the realization of crimes he has inflicted upon others but, through his last-minute conversion to Christianity, is able to face death with spiritual comfort.

Pfranger's revival of elements from the outmoded paradigm of the martyr drama represents nothing less than a rejection of the Enlightenment. His choice of genre is a reflection of his conservative intent: he rejects not only the new religious ideas emanating out of the bourgeoisie, but their literary tastes and conventions as well. He thereby acts in strict opposition to Lessing's dramaturgical intentions. According to Ruth Klüger: "Lessing wollte einen neuen Dramentyp entwickeln, eine Art Anti-Märtyrerstück, untragisch, ohne Gewalttätigkeit und Erotik."[89]

Whereas Pfranger uses an antiquated dramatic convention, Lessing, who wishes to deliver a very nontraditional message, cannot find a dramatic convention to accommodate his artistic needs and is forced to utilize an innovative *genre môyen*, which does not readily fall into the traditional categories of comedy and tragedy but combines elements of both.

Schiller was disturbed by Lessing's failure to adhere to established theatrical conventions, but Lessing's deviations are consistent with his expressed aesthetic philosophy. He believed that artists should not be unduly bound by rules and aesthetic conventions, but should follow the inclinations of their own genius. In so doing, he felt, they often fulfill the spirit of the rules more effectively than they would through a mere technical adherence to them.

Lessing cannot make Nathan his spokesperson for tolerance either by portraying him in a state of hopeless collapse or by portraying him in terms of a ridiculous differentiation from the norms.[90] He therefore rejects both traditional tragedy and comedy as aesthetic models. Like the authors of tragedies, Lessing wanted to write a "touching play." Like the authors of comedies, Lessing wanted to provide a happy ending, so that he could signify his utopian intent. The comic elements of the play are couched in a quiet laughter that does not detract from the serious message.[91] Nathan's superior humor, the good-natured sarcasm of the dervish, and the dry humor of the friar all underscore the attempted combination of the "touching" elements with the comical.[92] There is a serious message underlying the quiet and gentle humor of the following exchange:

> Klosterbruder: Nathan! Nathan! / Ihr seid ein Christ!—Bei Gott, Ihr seid ein Christ! / Ein beßrer Christ war nie!
> Nathan: Wohl uns! Denn was / Mich Euch zum Christen macht, das macht Euch mir / Zum Juden! (4.7)[93]

The hatred of the patriarch disrupts the comic elements of the play, however, while Nathan's recounting of the death of his wife and children is an element of pure tragedy.[94] The good and tenderhearted people who prevail in the main action of the play, however, are antithetical to the spirit of a truly tragic conflict.[95]

Pfranger and Lessing provide examples of differing dramaturgical strategies: Pfranger, who seeks to restore and preserve the rules of exclusion protecting the dogmatic side of Christianity, is a dramaturgical antiquarian who wishes to promote a modified form of the martyr drama. Lessing, who wants to assail the same rules of exclusion Pfranger attempts to protect, is a dramaturgical innovator who desires to unite a new dramaturgical form with a very nontraditional message.

The aesthetic strategies of Lessing and Pfranger are closely bound to their notions of tolerance: Lessing aspires to broaden the conventional notion of tolerance, to unite it with concepts of equality without transgressing the rules of exclusion, and, in so doing, he seeks a new literary form with which he can have better control over the literary and linguistic sign. Pfranger endeavors to semantically narrow the conception of tolerance and, in so doing, wishes to utilize more traditional literary forms.

Why is Lessing's drama, the promotion of a minority discourse, still performed on the stage, whereas Pfranger's drama, an avowal of the dominant discourse of his time, is relegated to obscurity? The reason surely lies in the relative aesthetic merit of the two plays. The promoters of tolerance were fortunate to have someone of Lessing's artistry as an advocate of their viewpoint.

Pfranger's communicative efficacy, on the other hand, is substantially compromised through the sheer sentimentality of his text. One example is the implausible joy with which Saladin meets his own death: "Du hast mir mein Ende fröhlich— / hast meinen Lieben— meinen Sterbetag— / Zum Freudenfest gemacht—Gott sey gelobt!— Lebt wohl—lebt ewig wohl."[96] Sittah responds to this expression of celebration: "Gott! Gott! er stirbt."[97] For her, Saladin's death is anything but the "Freudenfest" he considers it to be. Another example is to be seen in the way in which Pfranger has Saladin reject Nathan's Ring Parable:

> Nathan: Kennst du / Nicht deinen Nathan mehr, mein Saladin?
> Saladin: Geh, Jude! geh, betrogener Wucherer, / Mit deiner Waare! sie ist falsch: verkauf sie / Den Narren! geh!—Was weinst du? was verlangst du?
> Nathan: Das ist erschrecklich!
> Saladin: Schrecklich? was? habe ich sie umgebracht? Verlangst du deine Kinder / Von mir?
> Nathan: Gott! Gott![98]

To put an ethnic slur in the mouth of Saladin is an unwarranted falsification of Lessing. Nathan is referred to in terms of the artless oxymoron of the "cheated usurer" who should sell his "false wares" (i.e., his Enlightened philosophy) to fools. Nathan is horrified by this denigration of his philosophy.

Saladin responds by indicating that it is not the denigration of Nathan's philosophy that is horrible, but the slaughter of his children—for which Saladin can bear no responsibility. Pfranger thereby attempts to argue that the rejection of the Jews is not to be equated with the horror of the pogroms. It is unconvincing to the point of ridiculousness that Nathan would be so "horrified" by the rejection of his philosophy. What has become of the unruffled dignity of Lessing's character? Nathan has become recast into Pfranger's image of the Jew, but Pfranger's image has less verisimilitude than even the noble "exception Jew" portrayed by Lessing.

Prussian Officialdom and the Case for Jewish Emancipation

Although our examination of the Christian reaction to Lessing's *Nathan der Weise* gives some idea of the determined opposition the tolerance motif was to face, the fact cannot be ignored that Lessing's work was to have a major impact on other pro-Jewish emancipators. The publication of Lessing's play was a major factor influencing Moses Mendelssohn to take a more active role in promoting the rights of his Jewish coreligionists.[99] In addition to his own emancipatory writings, one of Mendelssohn's most important actions in this regard was to prevail upon his friend, Christian Wilhelm von Dohm, to write *Über die bürgerliche Verbesserung der Juden* (1781–83).[100] Dohm's book helped shape the debate over Jewish emancipation for the next century.[101]

The purpose of Dohm's tract was to investigate the moral and political conditions of the Jews. The writing of the tract was motivated by a concern over the unhappy situation of the Jews. Dohm points to the oppressive conditions under which Jews were forced to live, which he viewed as an anachronistic remnant of the inhumane prejudices of earlier years. He maintained that the Jewish people had been ruined because the state had denied them their rights. Dohm argues from a pragmatic and utilitarian point of view: granting the Jews civil rights would increase the number of good citizens. Dohm sets out to investigate the issue as to how the Jews can become more useful to the state.

Dohm sees a bitter irony in the policies of the Prussian state. On the one hand, an increase in the populace is viewed as being desirable for the common good, even to the extent of seeking settlers from other countries. On the other hand, there are pervasive attempts to prevent the Jews from increasing their population. He indicts specific policies that have such an impact: banning the right to residence or demanding large sums of money for that right. He points out that the right to residency can only be passed on to the eldest son; for daughters, the right to residency is contingent upon a fortuitous marriage. Because such policies cause the separation of families, Jewish parents are seldom allowed to live among their grown children.

Dohm's biggest indictment is the fact that most occupations are closed to the Jews. Even trade, practically the only avenue left open, has restrictions to assure that the profit of the Jew is extremely small and permits only the most miserable sort of existence.

In defending the Jewish religion, Dohm argues that it is totally compatible with Christian coexistence and has no principles that stand in conflict with justice or the love of one's neighbor. The major precept of the Jews, the law of Moses, is honored by the Christians as well. The Jews hold their religious tradition for the first and most complete and only hold it all the more dear because they have been oppressed for following it.

Dohm maintains that society is capable of absorbing many diverse elements. Division through religion is not the only division in civil society. All manner of divisions into smaller subgroups exists. Every group has its own rules and prejudices and allows special benefits for its own circle. Dohm points to the division between noblemen, burghers, and peasants, between city dwellers and land dwellers. He asserts that the great and noble task of the government is to unify the inevitable divergence of standpoints, allowing every subgroup its pride and its identity. Nevertheless all these divergent groups are united into a common larger entity. The nobleman, the farmer, the scholar, the handworker, the Christian, and the Jew: all are *citizens*.

Including the Jews in this larger common entity would benefit society as a whole. Jews are human beings more than they are Jews, and it would be inconceivable for them not to love a state in which they could freely accumulate property and enjoy the same rights as other citizens, where their taxes would not be greater than those of other citizens, and where they could hope for honor and respect. They would naturally bond with people with whom they share the same rights and the same duties. More just circumstances for the Jew would turn him into the most patriotic of citizens.

Dohm points out that members of other religious groups have sometimes come into conflict with the state. The beliefs of Quakers and Mennonites appear to contain teachings that are inimical to the interests of the state because of their pacifist inclinations. Nevertheless, there are Quakers and Mennonites in all German states, where they have been accepted as good and useful citizens. Catholics also have exclusive attitudes that they regard as necessary for their eternal salvation and they are committed to converting others to their belief, yet they are regarded as patriotic citizens in most countries.

The Jews are not prevented from being good citizens by their religion, as soon as the government will give the rights which will enable them to establish good citizenship. In contradiction to Lessing's portrayal of the noble Jew, Dohm is emphatic about regarding Jews as people who have the *potential* to become good citizens if their social circumstances are improved. Dohm maintains that Jews are more morally deficient than other peoples; they commit a greater number of illegal acts than the Christians: their character is more oriented toward usury and deception in trade, and their religious prejudices are divisive and asocial. Dohm does not condemn Jews for what he regards as their failings, but feels that these are the inevitable results of the oppressive situation in which Jews find themselves. These adverse conditions are the responsibility of Christians, who for centuries persecuted and restricted the Jews.[102]

Lessing portrays Nathan as someone whose profession as a tradesman contributes to his ennoblement. Through his commercial activity, he attains great wealth which assists him in doing good for others.

Dohm's view of the Jewish tradesman diverges considerably from Lessing's idealized portrayal. Dohm maintains that Jews tend toward cheating and deception because of their involvement in trade. He asserts that trade seduces a person toward such actions more than other sorts of livelihood.

Dohm explains that Jews have no regard for the laws, because they are so harshly oppressed under them. The state tolerates them only insofar as it can extort excessive taxes from them. The Jew cannot help but hate a nation that provides so much proof of its own hatred.

The Jews have been forced for centuries to live only from trade. The love of profit is more active among Jews than Christians, because it is their only means of subsistence. Usury and unjust profit must be considered by them to be more permissible, because all branches of their trade have such substantial taxes imposed upon them. Contrary to Lessing, Dohm argues that restricting Jews to trade has been detrimental to their moral character and political acceptance.

Most of Dohm's recommendations for resolving the "Jewish question" are enrooted in the notion that Jews should be occupationally diversified and discouraged from indulging in trade or in anything involved with the profit motive. His first recommendation is that the fullest freedom of occupation and means of sustenance be granted to Jews. This would help to make the Jews be more useful and happier members of society. Dohm proposes that the government guide Jews away from their preoccupation with trade and alleviate the influence of trade on them. He believes that Jews should be encouraged to take up handwork.

Dohm also advocates that farming be opened to the Jews in the interest of equal rights. But Dohm maintains that the government should be cautious about encouraging Jews to take up agriculture because of its similarities to trade and its dependence upon speculation and profit. He does not wish to see the Jews become large landowners but does advocate permitting them to farm small plots of land themselves.

Dohm further advocates that every art and science should be open to the Jews. He does not, however, advocate that Jews be permitted access to public office. He feels that Jews are currently in a morally inferior position, and that permitting them to become public officials is against the public interest.

Dohm next concerns himself with education, particularly moral education and enlightenment, which can make the coming generations of Jews persons who will be better integrated into society. He also maintains that Jews should become better acquainted with the sciences. Jewish parents should therefore be allowed to send their children to

Christian schools. Dohm advocates that even Jewish children who get most of their education from Jewish schools take some of their classes from Christian schools to bind them with the outer society. All of these reforms are in one direction. According to David Sorkin, "Emancipation was conceived as a reciprocal process in which Jews were to refashion themselves in exchange for rights."[103]

Along with moral improvement of the Jews, Dohm points out that it is also necessary that Christians make a sincere effort to lessen their prejudices against their Jewish fellow citizens. From earliest childhood, they should be taught to treat the Jews as brothers and sisters and fellow human beings who worship God in another manner, which pleases God just as much when the religious precepts are followed in the correct way. The spirit of human love and true Christianity should lead to the remembrance of the Good Samaritan and the belief that representatives of all peoples who do good are pleasing to God. Dohm's argumentation in this section reveals the influence of Lessing's Ring Parable: he advocates the viewpoint that the content of the religious precepts, not the form of the religious dogmas and mythologies, gives religion its relevance.

Dohm does not view the differing religious culture as being the primary cause of the ostracism of the Jewish outgroup but attributes this to the economic activity of the Jews, an argument that was later to be echoed in anti-Semitic circles. However, unlike the anti-Semites, Dohm points to the lack of voluntariness in Jews' concentration on trade: they were forced into their economic role by the Christians and it is the responsibility of Christians to help them out of this role. Contrary to most earlier interpretations of the "Jewish question," Dohm does not attribute adverse social conditions to the Jewish character or the unalterable character of the Jews.[104]

The writing of this tract was an act of boldness: Dohm hesitated to publish his work in Berlin. He feared the displeasure of the Berlin censor because of the political opinions expressed therein. At the same time, he feared to publish the work outside of Prussia, because of the religious opinions expressed therein.[105] The book posed a touchy challenge to several consensus formations. Dohm was subjected to harsh attacks from theological circles, whose members objected to his promotion of governmental indifference toward the religious convictions of the citizenry.[106]

Nonetheless, Dohm's tract had an impact of epoch-making proportions. It awakened broad interest in Germany and inspired a large amount of literature in reaction to it. The "Jewish question" reached the forefront of public discussion.[107] Franz Reuss gives a comprehensive overview of the literature written in reaction to Dohm's tract, and we will not repeat his work here. We will, however, take a closer look at Heinrich Friedrich von Diez's little-known but highly relevant tract, *Ueber Juden: An Herrn Kriegsrath Dohm in Berlin* (1783). Diez was a Prussian public official and was at one time Prussian ambassador to Turkey. Diez differs from Dohm in that he goes even further than Dohm does: Whereas Dohm recommends transitional steps in the emancipation of the Jews (particularly barring Jews from public office), Diez demands unconditional full emancipation.[108] Although Diez has largely been forgotten, he is well worthy of study today because he was one of the first Gentile thinkers to call for unconditional emancipation of the Jews in his lucid exposition of the "Jewish question" from a Deistic point of view.

Diez condemns the pressure placed upon the Jews to convert to Christianity. He sees a bitter irony in the wish to force Jews to abandon their own beliefs and take up the religious beliefs of their oppressors. He exposes the fallacy of the claim that it is only done to make them happier for the next life. They, whose religion is among the oldest, would be forced to convert to a more recent religion. It was insane to believe that they would appreciate the teachings of those who made them objects of hatred and vilification. His arguments anticipate those made later by Sartre, who argued that Jewish identity is largely externally imposed through the oppression and the defensive posture it generates.

The Jews are neither subjects, who live as "children" of the state under its laws, nor strangers who are subject to laws of humanity and hospitality. They have in effect been outlawed and made *vogelfrei*, so that crimes can be committed against them with impunity.

Spite, mockery, and oppression are the lot of the Jew. Jews were placed in a position where they had to fear everything and bear everything. They came to consider misery to be a condition of life that could not be separated from it. They knew the teachings that were the ground for their oppression and secured themselves all the more firmly to their faith, as it became more difficult to adhere to it. Among the would-be converters, they always remained the unconverted.

Diez, a follower of Deism and Natural Religion, briefly describes his own religious principles. He is an opponent of positive religion, because he feels it can only reign at the cost of humanity. He is, however, convinced that the Jews can only save their adherence to humanity in the face of oppression through faithfulness to their religious principles. Jews are so humiliated and dehumanized that their religious principles are their only hold on life.

Diez maintains that it is a disgrace for barbarism and superstition to dominate for so long, and hatred against Jews is one of the oldest of superstitions. Nonbelievers, long since pushed aside by both Jews and Christians, do not deny that both religions profess mutual love instead of oppression, because the one evolved out of the other. Even the more enlightened Christians disapprove of a hatred of which their God of Love could not approve.

Diez examines the contention that Jewish religion contains much that goes against the spirit of contemporary values and customs. He contends that people have prevented Jews from reconciling their religion with the intellectual currents of later centuries by isolating them from the mainstream. It is unfortunate that it was decided to integrate the Jews into civil society only after their conversion to Christianity. This inhumane policy promoted Jewish isolation by barring Jews from taking part in the continual redefinition of the dominant society.

Jewish trade practices alienated many people and contributed to a situation in which Jews led an existence separate from that of the Gentile masses. They felt no motivation to imitate the customs, practices, and principles of the dominant culture. This had the impact of further binding individual Jews to their people, who provided the only outlet for friendship and community. Their frame of orientation, the Jewish religion, became ever more precious to them the more they were pressured to give it up.

Diez argues that the reformation of the Jews will not occur so long as public policy continues to make them martyrs and champions of their own religion. The first step toward breaking this vicious cycle is for princes and governments to make Judaism an officially sanctioned religion. That will alleviate the blind zeal with which Jews cling to their religion. In time, Diez maintains, Jews will discover for themselves that "new truths are better than old errors." In order to make human beings more similar to one another, one must only give them the opportunity to influence one another undisturbed. Dialogue, and not a coerced monologue, is the route to social betterment.

Diez's ultimate goal is to supersede religion altogether. He feels, however, that while it is possible to increase the presence of religious convictions, one can never forcibly reduce them. Diez contends that it is astounding that more than eighteen centuries are necessary to bring Christianity into proportion with other religions, with bourgeois society, and with reason. He states that it can readily be predicted that Judaism will reform itself more quickly and bring itself more in line with the dominant pulse of society if the Jews are granted civil rights.

Diez next addresses the issue of what is to become of Jews if they cease to be Jews. Christians imagine that they will convert to Christianity. Diez maintains that it is an error to believe that abandoning

Judaism will lead to Catholicism or Protestantism. Jews are destined to convert to Natural Religion or to rationalistic moral teachings. Diez is promoting an assimilation concept in which both Christians and Jews give up the dogmatic underpinnings of their religions and meet on the common ground of Natural Religion. But he feels that this should occur in a natural, uncoerced manner. Neither states nor laws can make something be regarded as the truth, if the subject regards it as an error. No religious dissenter should be punished, but rather the person who cannot tolerate the dissenter.

Dohm and Diez both advocate the granting of civil rights to the Jews. But they diagnose the problems of Gentile-Jewish relations differently. For Dohm, the existence of a "Jewish problem" lies in the economic activity of the Jews, which he attributes to harsh oppression. He feels that the problematical nature of Christian-Jewish relations can be solved by enabling the Jews to diversify their means of livelihood, particularly through involvement in handwork, and by the government actively taking a role in encouraging them to do so. Dohm feels that the government-enforced concentration in trade has morally corrupted the Jews and that the "Jewish question" is primarily an economic question. He actively encourages the Jews to maintain separate religious institutions and feels that this provides no conflict with the interests of society.

For Diez, on the other hand, the "Jewish question" is not a primarily economic question, but a religious question. The ultimate solution lies in a Christian-Jewish consensus on a plane that is neither Christian nor Jewish, but based on the principles of Natural Religion. Diez is, to an even greater extent than Dohm, an advocate of assimilation. By allowing the dominant group and the Jewish outgroup the legal basis for equality, they would eventually find common ground with one another. Like Lessing, Diez uses the issue of the "Jewish question" to assail orthodox Christianity as a consensus formation. Part of the reason why Diez's pamphlet remained so obscure in the aftermath of the wide attention granted Dohm is that it assails rules of exclusion in a manner in which Dohm's pamphlet does not.

Both Dohm and Diez diverge from Lessing in seeing a need for the Jewish people to improve themselves. Lessing's Nathan is the most exemplary of human beings and, as a representative of a brutally repressed and downtrodden group, is idealized and ennobled, a fact that was later to be exploited by anti-Semitic travestiers. Lessing, as a dramatist, is trying to promote religious tolerance in a more affective manner, whereas Dohm and Diez are trying to appeal to people on a more cerebral level.

Although Lessing's fictional incarnation of his ideal for the Jewish

Beginnings of the Tolerance Debate 63

people in the figure of Nathan may be removed from either Dohm's programmatic or Diez's philosophical approach, interesting parallels do exist. Nathan's noble character is made possible by his superior wealth and education. Dohm advocates equality of educational and economic opportunity for the Jews, because he regards their shortcomings as a people to be due to economic privation. Dohm advocates the abolition of special taxes on the Jews, which would improve their economic status. Increasing the occupational opportunities for Jews will better them both materially and morally. Lessing grounds Nathan's tolerance for other peoples in Nathan's adherence to Natural Religion and opposition to positive religion. Diez advocates an adherence to Natural Religion on the part of both Jews and Christians as a step toward creating a society that is better able to serve the needs of both groups. It is conceivable that Lessing's fictional work laid the groundwork for both political tracts.

Diez's tract also had some similarity to certain tracts of the Haskalah or Jewish Enlightenment. We will consider some of these tracts in the next chapter.

3. Jewish Identity in a Changing World

The Heterogeneity of German Jewry

During the time period under consideration, the German Jews did not constitute a monolith, but were increasingly divided between three distinct groups, which sometimes came into conflict with one another: orthodox Jews or traditionalists; adherents of the *Haskalah* or Jewish Enlightenment, who were known as *Maskilim* and who tended to be reform-minded and vigorously promoted emancipation; and converted Jews or *Taufjuden*, who converted to Christianity in order to escape discrimination and persecution.

We will take an in-depth look at the Maskilim and the Taufjuden, but first I would like to devote a few words to the orthodox Jews. The representatives of orthodox Jewry were very reserved in their attitude toward emancipation, at least until the middle of the nineteenth century. Orthodox Jews were very sensitive in regard to defending the integrity of their religion against threats from the surrounding culture.[1] In the Jewish ghetto, there had been a unified culture centered around orthodox Judaism until the end of the eighteenth century. Its inner substance was Jewish religiosity: this was not reduced to faith, but determined the entire societal existence.[2]

Orthodox Jews observed the Torah (the five books of Moses) and wished to retain the old laws despite the changing social conditions of the Jews. Orthodox Jews rarely took part in German political movements. Their leaders cared little about equality for the Jews; they wished to retain Jewish structures of social organization as they were. They did not want to give up laws and customs that they viewed as holy.[3]

Orthodox Jews were fearful of such signs of change as external conformity to the dominant culture in manners and dress, education, changes in livelihood, and the giving up of any concept of Jewish nationhood. The Jewish orthodoxy was an impediment to emancipation, because they feared that the outward advantages it offered would come at the sacrifice of their own culture.[4]

Orthodox Jews saw themselves as foreigners and a nation in exile still waiting for the redemption of the Messiah.[5] According to Steven M. Lowenstein, "In the middle of the eighteenth century, the communal officials tried to deal with signs of cultural modernity with traditional methods, including the use of coercion against innovators." In

1746, a man named Gerson Bleichröder was expelled from Berlin by the Jewish communal officials for having a German book.[6]

After the death of Moses Mendelssohn in 1786, the power and influence of the orthodoxy among the Jewish community decreased sharply.[7] The distinction between reformers and orthodoxy was becoming more pronounced. By the early nineteenth century, the Berlin Jewry was predominately nonorthodox.[8] Lowenstein notes, however, that orthodox Jews were less touched by the *Taufepidemie* between 1780 and 1830 than their opponents among the Haskalah.[9]

Because the bulk of the German-language literature thematizing the "Jewish question" was written by the Maskilim and the converted Jews, we will devote the rest of this chapter to them,[10] including the most famous of the Maskilim, Moses Mendelssohn.

Building the Temple of Reason: The Religious Writings of Moses Mendelssohn

The contradictions of the tolerance teaching of the Enlightenment are perhaps nowhere so apparent as in the case of Moses Mendelssohn, easily the single most distinguished figure of the Haskalah. Although he remained a committed Jew in a society in which Jews were seriously disadvantaged, he became a renowned and highly respected figure. His social circle included the likes of Wieland and Herder and he counted Lessing and Friedrich Nicolai among his closest friends. His house held great drawing power for contemporary intellectuals. Jews and Gentiles came into contact as if there were no social barriers between them. Jewish scholars from Mendelssohn's circle such as Marcus Herz and Salomon Maimon lectured on philosophy before non-Jewish audiences. However, the Christian society that interacted with them was at best a "semineutral" society. Jews were permitted to philosophize about abstract problems but were excluded from demanding practical and political solutions to social problems.[11]

Mendelssohn is considered to have been the first Jew to have produced important writings in the German language. Alexander Altmann regards Mendelssohn's rise to fame and acceptance among educated society as evidence of a more liberal *Zeitgeist*: "The humanistic outlook of the Enlightenment had prepared the ground for a greater willingness to treat an individual Jew on his merits."[12] Hannah Arendt, however, argues that Mendelssohn's connections with non-Jewish society were the same sort of ties that had bound Christian and Jewish scholars together in all centuries of European history. One component of the new humanism was the desire to establish intimacy with all types of human beings. Because Jews were an oppressed people, they held a certain exotic appeal. Arendt writes about Mendelssohn: "his exceptional social status and freedom had something to do with the fact that he still belonged to 'the lowliest inhabitants of the (Prussian king's) domain.'"[13] Both Altmann and Arendt agree that Mendelssohn enjoyed a situation vastly superior to that of most of his people. Yet Mendelssohn was to suffer the effects of discrimination and religious bigotry all his life.

In eighteenth-century Germany, Jews were subject to nearly every career restriction. Moneylending and retail trade were practically the only careers left open to them. They lived in segregated ghettos, which were notorious for their impoverished conditions. The parishes were led primarily by Polish rabbis who were not fluent in German, had no desire to become so, and discouraged their parishioners from learning German.[14] In the meantime, those Jews who sought contact with non-Jewish society were expected to be something special. Arendt explains: "What non-Jewish society demanded was that the newcomer be as 'educated' as itself, and that although he not behave like an 'ordinary Jew,' he be and produce something out of the ordinary, since, after all, he was a Jew."[15]

Moses Mendelssohn was born in Dessau, Germany, in 1729. His father, a schoolteacher and village scribe, arranged for Moses to receive tutoring in Hebrew language and scripture from the local rabbi, David Fränkel. Fränkel was transferred to the Berlin parish in 1743 and the fourteen-year-old Mendelssohn accompanied him. When Mendelssohn arrived in Berlin, he belonged to the category of Jews that had absolutely no rights and could be deported at any time. He was allowed to enter Berlin only because the Jewish parish agreed to support him.[16]

In Berlin, Mendelssohn began teaching himself how to read and write German, which was at that time strictly forbidden. Mendelssohn was obliged to keep his studies secret for fear of being expelled from Berlin by the Jewish authorities and had to teach himself almost entirely without systematic aid from others.[17] He succeeded in teaching himself to read and write German, Latin, French, and English and sought contact with the few cultured Jews in Berlin at that time. One of these, Aron Emerich Gumpertz, introduced Mendelssohn to Gotthold Ephraim Lessing. Lessing and Mendelssohn became fast friends and Lessing arranged for the publication of Mendelssohn's philosophical writings.

Mendelssohn grew up in Berlin and obtained a job as a private teacher for the children of Isaak Bernhard, a Jewish silk manufacturer. After Bernhard's children were grown, Mendelssohn became a bookkeeper and subsequently manager in Bernhard's silk factory. Mendelssohn was tolerated in Berlin only because he was in the employ of Bernhard, an "ordentlicher Schutzjude." At the age of thirty-two, Mendelssohn became engaged to Fromet Gugenheim and found it advisable to apply for his own letter of protection. He found this to be a distasteful process. "Es thut mir weh, daß ich um das Recht der Existenz erst bitten soll, welches das Recht eines jeden Menschen ist," he wrote to the marquis d'Argens, a French philosopher and protégé of Friedrich II.[18] Nonetheless, Mendelssohn wrote a letter to Friedrich requesting the right to settle in Berlin for both himself and his descendants. The first application was ignored and Mendelssohn attempted again, this time supplementing the request with a letter from d'Argens extolling his philosophical accomplishments. Friedrich finally granted Mendelssohn the status of "außerordentlicher Schutzjude," that is, Mendelssohn was permitted to settle in Berlin for his lifetime, but was not permitted to pass his residency on to his descendants.[19]

In the meantime, Mendelssohn's reputation as a philosopher was bolstered by a 1763 prize from the Royal Academy in Berlin. Mendelssohn's essay "Über die Evidenz der metaphysischen Wissenschaften" was accepted as the best of the thirty entries, while Immanuel Kant received honorable mention.[20]

Mendelssohn's growing fame brought him under increasing pressure from Christian circles to undergo baptism. Such people undoubtedly respected Mendelssohn, but regarded him as an exception Jew and were not willing to accord Judaism equal status with Christianity. Mendelssohn eschewed such a thought as conversion for assimilation's sake as opportunism:

> Wenn die bürgerliche Vereinigung [der Juden mit den Christen] unter keiner anderen Bedingung zu erhalten, als wenn wir von dem Gesetz abweichen, das wir für uns für verbindlich halten, so müssen wir lieber auf bürgerliche Vereinigung verzichten. . . . Von dem Gesetze können wir mit gutem Gewissen nicht weichen, und was nützen euch Mitbürger ohne Gewissen?[21]

An example of the pressure to convert that Mendelssohn encountered was Johann Kaspar Lavater's challenge to Mendelssohn to either refute Christianity or convert. Mendelssohn responded with a plea for religious tolerance. He rejected the challenge to refute Christianity. As a member of a religious minority, he did not want to offend members of the religious majority.[22] Mendelssohn was well aware of the rules of exclusion surrounding Christianity and his own marginalized status in the society.

In 1771, members of the Royal Academy in Berlin recommended that Mendelssohn be appointed to teach at the academy.[23] King Friedrich II refused to ratify the appointment and the nomination was subsequently withdrawn. Despite Friedrich's promotion of the rights of other religious minorities, he held a strong antipathy toward the Jews. Because of this sentiment, the forty-year-old Mendelssohn, long since distinguished in intellectual circles, was forced to continue managing a silk factory in order to support himself. This was undoubtedly a crushing disappointment for Mendelssohn. The words Horkheimer and Adorno used to describe the Jewish situation in general apply also to Mendelssohn: "Der Handel war nicht sein Beruf, er war sein Schicksal."[24]

Dohm wrote his *Über die bürgerliche Verbesserung der Juden* at Mendelssohn's behest. Mendelssohn arranged for the second printing of Dohm's tract (1782) to be accompanied by Menasseh ben Israel's *Vindiciae Judaeorum* (originally published in 1655) and by Mendelssohn's preface to that work. *Vindiciae Judaeorum* was a seventeenth-century tract arguing for the readmission of Jews to England. Mendelssohn arranged to have his friend Marcus Herz translate the work from the original English because it effectively refuted many timeworn prejudices, and Mendelssohn wanted people to see the historical roots of anti-Semitism, an area Dohm had not covered.[25]

In his preface, Mendelssohn examines the origins and causes of bigotry. He discusses the means in which prejudices against the Jews seem to emerge every century in a different form: "In jenen abergläubischen Zeiten waren es Heiligthümer, die wir aus Muthwillen schänden, Crucifixe, die wir durchstechen und bluten machen; Kinder, die wir heimlich beschneiden, und zur Augenweide zerfetzen; Christenblut, das wir zur Osterfeyer brauchen, Brunnen, die wir vergiften, usw."[26] Now that such stories no longer make the desired impression, the Jews are themselves accused of the superstition and foolishness that has characterized their accusers. A number of undesirable characteristics are falsely projected upon them: Jews are accused of being lawless, of having a lack of moral values, of having an insuitability for scholarly endeavor, and a general lack of usefulness to society. These prejudices have completely excluded Jews from meaningful participation in their society.

The conventional wisdom for dealing with the Jewish problem has been to try to get the Jews to convert to Christianity. Due to their refusal to convert, Jews came to be regarded as a social burden. The zeal to convert the Jews disappeared and was replaced by sheer neglect. Now, says Mendelssohn, Jews are kept away from science and scholarship and all other useful endeavors. They are prohibited access to an education and their lack of education is cited as a reason for their further oppression: "Man bindet uns die Hände und macht uns zum Vorwurfe, daß wir sie nicht gebrauchen."[27]

Mendelssohn points out that the eighteenth century has not succeeded in erasing the barbarism of earlier centuries. Some prejudices remain because it has never occurred to anybody to doubt them; others are confirmed by such authority that not everyone is able to recognize them as falsehoods. Also, some prejudices continue to influence people even after they are no longer believed: "Ueberhaupt ist die Verleumdung von so giftiger Art, daß sie immer einige Wirkung in den Gemüthern zurückläßt, wenn auch ihre Unwahrheit entdeckt, und allgemein anerkannt wird."[28] This latter type of prejudice is an example of what Horkheimer and Adorno call mimesis: a sublimated mimicry of environmental influences that proves resistant to reason.[29] Subliminal mimicry of anti-Semitic attitudes in the society keeps alive centuries-old prejudices even when the stereotype that gives rise to the prejudice is no longer taken seriously.

Often a belief in a false authority works to keep the most implausible of prejudices alive. Mendelssohn gives the example of the Polish town of Posen. Posen accused its Jewish parish of having murdered a Christian child in order to use its blood for a Passover celebration. Two rabbis were convicted and executed for the alleged murder ritual and the parish was compelled to pay a huge fine. Mendelssohn calls this execution, "die schrecklichste, die sich je Barberey erlaubt hat."[30] He recalls speaking to many people in Poland and other lands who firmly believed that Jews commit ritual murders. They back their claim by citing the fairness of the legal process under which the unfortunates were convicted. Mendelssohn argues that a correctly administered legal process does not guarantee justice: the two rabbis of Posen were unjustly convicted after what was probably, in legal terms, a very correctly administered trial. Institutionalized injustice has become a harsh instrument in the persecution of the Jews.

Mendelssohn next takes issue with the argument that the Jews are a social burden. The argument is made that Jews are merely consumers, because they do not produce anything but sell what others have produced. Mendelssohn responds that the merchant plays a valuable role in acting as middleman between producer and purchaser: he prevents defective products from reaching the marketplace, he makes items more easily available, and he frees the manufacturer from having to make sure he always has the correct quantity of a certain item on hand. Mendelssohn also disagrees with an arbitrary division between producers and consumers. Under that kind of logic, all of society, except farmers and manufacturers, would be classified as consumers. "Nicht bloß machen, sondern auch Thun heißt hervorbringen," argues Mendelssohn.[31] He feels that it is unconscionable to call any group of people worthless, for everyone has their function within society. Mendelssohn points to the example of Holland, which has unrestricted freedom for all sellers regardless of religion: "Ihr könnt nirgend so gut und so bequem . . . mit geringerem Verluste alles kaufen als zu Amsterdam."[32] His viewpoint diverges from Dohm's claim that involvement in trade has caused the moral corruption of the Jews. He feels that the Jewish tradesman provides a useful service and should be considered an integral part of bourgeois society.

A leading prejudice against Jews—that they were homeless wayfarers—was grounded in a vestige of reality. Jews were homeless because they were constantly being expelled. In 1749, for instance, Friedrich II expelled 3,000 Jewish families from Prussia because they could not afford to pay for letters of protection.[33] But even obtaining a letter of protection was no guarantee that a Jew could securely reside within his community. Some cities imposed an exorbitant sum of money to be paid annually by the Jews as a poll tax. Dresden imposed such a law as part of its 1772 *Judenordnung* and subsequently exiled half of its Jewish population.[34] In 1777, Dresden's Jewish community was facing further expulsions and turned to Mendelssohn for help. Mendelssohn wrote a letter to Friedrich Wilhelm von Ferber, privy councillor of Saxony, who subsequently arranged to have the expulsion order revoked. Ferber was familiar with Mendelssohn's reputation as a religious scholar and had earlier ordered that Mendelssohn be permitted into Dresden without paying the customs tax usually required of Jewish visitors.[35] In his letter to Ferber, Mendelssohn described the plight of his coreligionists with burning emotion.[36] Mendelssohn's letter contained a veiled warning that the infliction of such grave social injustice upon innocent people could not be without consequence to society: "Und diese härteste der Strafen sollen Menschenkinder leiden ohne Schuld und Vergehung, bloß weil sie andern Grundsätzen zugethan und durch Unglück verarmt sind? Und der Israelit soll ehrlich seyn, an dem Armuth so hart wie Unehrlichkeit bestraft wird?"[37] When Mendelssohn was a child in Dessau, he knew of several otherwise respectable people who, out of sheer despair, joined robber gangs in order to raise the money to buy their right to residency from the government.[38]

Moses Mendelssohn is said to have been the model for Lessing's Nathan, and, indeed, there is a similarity in the outlooks between the philosopher and the fictional character. When Nathan's daughter Recha is rescued from a fire, she views her rescuer as an angel. Nathan disapproves of Recha's attempt to overmystify her experience. As Nathan attempts to enlighten Recha by getting her to view her good fortune through the eyes of reason, so Mendelssohn attempted to enlighten his fellow Jews by encouraging them to view their religion as a temple of reason. Because Jews were segregated in ghettos and prohibited access to education, their religion became isolated from other forms of intellectual endeavor. Therefore, in the words of Sebastian Hensel, "the Jewish religion became stagnant, all life dropped out of its forms, dogmatic subtleties and hairsplittings were more and more spun out."[39] Mendelssohn desired to free Judaism from its intellectual isolationism and unite its traditions with the most valuable elements of modern culture.

Mendelssohn's religiophilosophical outlook had been strongly influenced by the other Enlightenment thinkers, particularly Christian von Wolff (1679–1754). Wolff concerned himself with the practical utility of making men happy: "Do what will make you and your condition and that of your fellow man more perfect." Wolff attempted to secularize precepts of morality. He argued that moral principles must be true whether or not God exists and should be followed for reason's and not for God's sake.[40]

Mendelssohn, while remaining critical of nonreligious modes of thought, such as atheism and agnosticism, promoted a certain secularization of Judaism. Mendelssohn wished to strip Judaism of its layers of overmystification and restore it to what he believed to be its original form. Alan Arkush describes this as an attempted "repristination" of Judaism.[41] Mendelssohn believed that God's role in human life consisted of a single act: divine revelation of the ten commandments to Moses. These ten commandments are primarily a system of religious government. This notion of religion as being based on principles of virtue was known as Natural Religion.[42]

In his 1783 work, *Jerusalem oder über religiöse Macht und Judentum*, Mendelssohn discusses the role and function of religion. He feels that religious teachings can only regulate behavior. Inner thought is to remain free: "Gott bedarf unseres Beystandes nicht . . . keine Aufopferung unsere Rechte zu seinem Besten, keine Verzicht auf unsere Unabhängigkeit zu seinem Vortheil."[43] Mendelssohn feels that Judaism is based on certain principles of reason (i.e., the ten commandments) that all must recognize, but neither church nor state has the right to enforce belief in these rules on anyone. By the laws of reason, there is no worship without persuasion. An act of worship committed under pressure ceases to be one. To be following God's law out of fear is slavery, which cannot possibly be pleasing to God.

Mendelssohn responds to critics who maintain that "bewaffnetes Kirchenrecht" is an integral building block of the Jewish religion. Such people see the church system of Moses as instruction and direction toward responsibility, which is bound with the strongest religious authority. Mendelssohn feels that, "Autorität kann demüthigen, aber nicht belehren; sie kann die Vernunft niederschlagen, aber nicht fesseln."[44] In a situation where there is a conflict between a directive from above and an individual's reason, reason must ultimately reign.

Mendelssohn discusses the issue of religious tolerance. He considers reason to be the highest good in any religion. He believes that a Christian who finds a contradiction between Judaism and reason should not try to provoke a clash with the Jew, but should work together with him in finding the reason for the contradiction. The Christian and Jew together should show either where the contradiction exists or that the supposed contradiction can be rationally explained and is in fact no contradiction.[45] Because Christianity has its foundations in Judaism, it is counterproductive for the Christian to assail Judaism. A similar sentiment is expressed by Lessing in *Nathan der Weise*, when he has the friar say: "Und ist denn nicht das ganze Christentum / Aufs Judentum gebaut? Es hat mich oft / Geärgert, hat mir Tränen genug gekostet, / Wenn Christen gar so sehr vergessen konnten, / Daß unser Herr ja selbst ein Jude war" (4.7).[46]

Mendelssohn maintains that Jews, Moslems, pagans, and followers of Natural Religion are all equally entitled to tolerance. The sincere Christian or Jew should make every attempt to maintain his religion as a temple of reason, and this includes viewing other religions with acceptance and goodwill.

Mendelssohn points out that he has never publicly opposed the Christian religion and would never publicly quarrel with one of that religion's serious adherents. However, there are several points in Christianity that he would disagree with and could easily attack on the basis of what he has learned from Judaism. He feels that Christianity has become overmystified. It is steeped in doctrine, which leads it away from the path of reason. Mendelssohn emphasizes, however, that he is not condemning any particular religion: "Wer Augen hat, der sehe; Wer Vernunft hat, der prüfe, und lebe nach seiner Ueberzeugung."[47]

Mendelssohn discusses the nature of truth. There are two kinds of truth: eternal and historical. Eternal truths are not dependent on a particular time and can be subdivided into necessary and incidental truths. Necessary truths are true in and of themselves. The elements of such necessary truths as mathematics and logic are true because God makes them so. These are unalterable, even by divine power, "weil Gott selbst seinen unendlichen Verstand nicht veränderlich machen kann."[48] The necessary truths are derived from reason and show the possibility or impossibility of combining certain concepts. Whoever wishes to teach them to his fellow man must help the individual see the relations between the concepts himself and not expect him to believe them on authority.

Truths are incidental when they are the best of conceivable possibilities or the only conceivable possibility. Incidental truths such as physics and religion require knowledge as well as reason. If we want to know which rules a creator prescribes for his creation or which general rules alter the environment, we have to accept some things on the belief and observation of others. Our lifespan is not long enough that we can experience and observe everything ourselves. We can accept the observations of others if we feel that the circumstances are still the same and that the observations could be repeated and verified. Other nations, for instance, can take German research into physics for granted.[49] When it is the intention of God to transmit wisdom, he uses the most proficient method of doing so. When it comes to necessary truths, he grants the necessary power of reason. When it comes to laws of nature, he grants the requisite amount of knowledge.

The counterpart of eternal truths are historical truths: things that come true in one time frame and can only be regarded as true within this time frame. In this instance, we are completely dependent on the authority of others. Without the testimony of others, it is impossible to know anything about history. We believe historical truths on the basis of the credibility of the historical source. These truths, according to Mendelssohn, are the only truths that can legitimately be taught by the written word. Eternal truths, on the other hand, are not taught by God through the written word, but by the thing itself and its conditions, which are understandable to all men.[50]

Mendelssohn believes that reason is enough to lead humankind to those eternal truths which are essential for happiness. He feels that it would not have been necessary for God to reveal such truths in a supernatural manner, for he has already given human beings the ability to figure them out for themselves.

Judaism is not a revealed religion: it does not have any exclusive revelations of truths that are necessary for the salvation of humankind. The voice coming out of Sinai to proclaim the ten commandments is an essential teaching, the philosopher maintains, because without it, human beings can neither be virtuous nor happy. However, he views it as being not a miracle, but a historical truth, which he believes on authority. This represents a major contradiction in Mendelssohn's thought. He describes the ten commandments as "revealed legislation," yet he purports not to believe in revelation or miracles. Arkush suggests that Mendelssohn maintained this vestigial belief in revelation in order not to be discredited by his fellow Jews. While maintaining his own belief in Deism, Mendelssohn wished to continue to have influence to combat superstition and ignorance among the Jewish community.[51] Mendelssohn held on to a belief in revelation that contradicted his general philosophy in order to accommodate the rules of exclusion of his Jewish ingroup.

The commandments themselves are grounded in reason, according to Mendelssohn. Every commandment is worded "you shall" or "you shall not" and not "you shall believe." Belief is not commanded, because belief can come about only through persuasion and not through command. Judaism has no symbolic books and no holy relics. Professions and oaths of faith are totally unknown to Judaism. Mendelssohn sees religion in terms of an opposition between faith or belief (i.e., religious teachings) and knowledge (religious commands).

In the beginning, it was forbidden to write about the ten commandments. But in later times, the rabbis reversed that precept and written commentaries on the commandments were permitted. Over the centuries, writings on the commandments proliferated. These writings became teachings and the teachings, Mendelssohn feels, became too prescriptive in telling people what to believe. In time, religious beliefs became too steeped in unnecessary doctrine and overmystification. Mendelssohn gives the example of the Cabbala, a strain of Jewish mysticism that sought ciphers and secret codes in biblical numerals. The purpose of counting numbers is known to everyone. Yet people grow discontented with the obvious and try to make it less mundane by attributing newer, more exotic purposes to it. Therefore, people preach that numbers contain the secrets of nature or that God lies concealed within them.[52] So it is with the ten commandments: people take a straightforward system of religious government and make it more mystifying by applying new teachings to it. The existence of these teachings is later attributed to divine revelation. Like Recha in Lessing's *Nathan der Weise*, people have an inclination toward the divine that makes them want to exaggerate the divinity around them.

Mendelssohn next considers a personal question. He was asked if he would not like to be reassured by a belief in divine revelation that he can be freed from suffering in the afterlife. Mendelssohn's response is no: if his creator inflicts such suffering upon him, it cannot be more than a well-deserved discipline. Mendelssohn does not believe that God would inflict eternal punishment on any of his creations. In God's kingdom, he would let no one suffer except for his own betterment; therefore, the philosopher feels he has no need to fear such suffering. God would surely end the punishment as soon as it was no longer necessary. Mendelssohn sees no need for a belief in divine revelation on this point.[53]

Mendelssohn's view of Judaism as a religion of reason led him to approve of the fact that Judaism could not excommunicate any of its adherents. This brought him into disagreement with the part of Dohm's tract (*Über die bürgerliche Verbesserung der Juden*) urging juridicial autonomy for the Jews. Dohm believed that Jews should have the right to excommunicate recalcitrant coreligionists. Mendelssohn viewed this as being an invitation to interreligious intolerance. In his preface to *Vindiciae Judaeorum*, Mendelssohn argued that a church should discuss religious issues with its dissidents and see what it can learn from them, as well as teach them: "Mit welchem Herzen wollen wir einem Dissidenten, Andersdenkenden, Irrdenkenden, oder Abweichenden den Zutritt verweigern, die Freyheit versagen, an dieser Erbauung Antheil nehmen will, der ist dem Gottseeligen in der Stunde seiner Erbauung höchst wilkommen."[54] A religious community is not entitled to exclude those who do not flow with its tide, unless such persons behave in a harmful and disorderly fashion, in which case they can appropriately be dealt with by the police and the worldly branch of law.

Dohm promotes the right of Judaism to excommunicate recalcitrant members because other churches have that right and he sees that as being a part of granting Judaism equal status with other religions. Mendelssohn argues that abuse of excommunication provisions is inevitable: "Ich sehe keine Möglichkeit den falschen Religionseifer im Zügel zu halten, sobald er diesen Weg vor sich offen findet."[55] An outcast from any religion can still be a worthy and useful citizen. Yet he is ostracized by his own people and is deprived of the right to participate in their religious functions.[56] Mendelssohn feels that the state should not pass a measure that would create such religious problems for respectable citizens. He also feels it would cause unnecessary social problems, because it would unjustly damage people's reputations. What Dohm views as a measure of emancipation is to Mendelssohn another form of oppression. For a Jew, excommunication would have particularly dire circumstances, because, in addition to being shunned by the rest of society, he would be rejected by his own people. The oppressed would turn into oppressors of their own kind. Mendelssohn finds it ironic that what is proposed in the name of emancipation is really another vehicle for intolerance and warns his fellow Jews:

> Ach! meine Brüder! Ihr habt das drückende Joch der Intoleranz bisher allzuhart gefühlt, und vielleicht um eine Art von Genugthuung darinn zu finden geglaubt, wenn euch die Macht eingeräumet würde, euern Untergegebenen ein gleichhartes Joch aufzudrücken. Die Rache sucht ihren Gegenstand, und wenn sie andern nichts anhaben kann; so nagt sie ihr eigenes Fleisch.[57]

Oppression generates a feeling of rage. Instead of directing this rage at the oppressors, the victims vent this rage upon those who are weaker than themselves.[58] Mendelssohn was aware of this tendency and warned his coreligionists to guard themselves against it.

Mendelssohn also pleads for all people to give up the belief that religion needs a strongly enforced orthodoxy.[59] A reliance on the authority of churches to enforce belief is a major cause of both religious and interreligious intolerance. For Mendelssohn, it is through viewing religion as a set of laws (the ten commandments) that it can be set on a tolerant footing. Then religion would be able to exercise its function in an enlightened manner.

Mendelssohn offers a Deistic redefinition of Judaism that has many affinities with Diez's belief that the "Jewish question" could best be resolved by Jewish and Christian adherence to the tenets of Natural Religion. It is clear that Mendelssohn's conception of Judaism was influenced by his contact with Christian heterodox thinkers. His philosophies were very much a result of a combined effort of Jews and unorthodox Christian bourgeois thinkers to gain mutual toleration for each others' beliefs and ideas.

The People and the Ideas of the Haskalah

One of the early progenitors of the Haskalah was the Mannheim physician Elcan Isaac Wolf. He wrote a book of medical advice for his Jewish coreligionists entitled *Von den Krankheiten der Juden* (1777). In this book, he draws a correlation between the adverse medical circumstances faced by the Jews and their adverse social and political situation.

He tries to accommodate rules of exclusion that might hinder him from criticizing the state by historicizing the issue. He maintains that the contemporary situation for the Jews is not as bad as in earlier times, but that current illnesses are the product of past adversities faced by the Jewish people. This is a subtle rhetorical device for criticizing how adverse social circumstances harm the Jews without appearing to be criticizing the government or society: "Noch bluten in ihren Nachkömmlingen die Wunden unserer Vorältern, welche das härteste Schicksal, die grausamste Verfolgung heidnischer Tirannen und zum Theil die äuserste Armut, eine betrübte Folge des nagenden Elendes, in das frische Fleisch der auserwählten Israeliten eingeschnitten haben."[60] One whiplash after the other has been struck on the backs of the Jews. Hunger and thirst, misery, destruction of homes and properties, violence, and illness have victimized the Jews.

Against this background, Wolf expresses gratitude for efforts to emancipate the Jews. He states that the Jews of his century are quite fortunate, because they are governed by humane rulers and live peacefully among decent and virtuous Christians. Prejudices against the Jewish religion are held in abeyance due to humane attitudes.

Wolf presents health tips for Jews at every stage of their lives. Nowhere is he able to separate the medical from the political. He criticizes the forced concentration of Jews in money circulation because he feels it is dangerous to their health. Most people who dedicate themselves to trade and moneylending do not allow themselves enough time to replenish their strength, because it is difficult to make a living through these endeavors. This type of life-style is very exhausting and very deleterious to the health of those who practice it.

The signs of old age appear in Jews at an early point of their chronological age. A fifty-year-old man often has a white beard and is hunched over from the illnesses of his youth and is unable to make a living. Wolf finds himself brought to tears when he views the hard fate of his coreligionists, who are forbidden from practicing most professions. Wolf notes that his coreligionists do not lack the ability to be useful citizens to the state: only difference of religion and Gentile prejudice stand between the state and the Jews' willingness to serve it.

The exclusion from middle-class professions and guilds is a bitter fate for the Jews. It stultifies their creativity and wastes talent, which could be useful to the state. Wolf tells his fellow Jews not to lose courage; they live among virtuous Christians who are upright and humane. In Wolf's tract, we see a pattern that is common in the literature of the Haskalah: expressions of regret over the hard fate of the Jews are juxtaposed with statements of gratitude toward the state and society of which they want to be a part. This is a discursive strategy whereby they can criticize unjust social conditions without offending the Christian majority.

It is interesting that most of the literary production of the Haskalah, like Wolf's book, was nonfiction. One of the few dramas of the Haskalah was *Einige jüdische Familienscenen*, which was written by the

Jewish author Arenhof in 1782. The play, written in the wake of Joseph II's tolerance patent, argued that the emancipatory reforms enabled the Jews to take their places as Germans without abandoning their Jewish identity.

In its opening, the play portrays a Jewish father suffering from despair over the fate of his people. He adjoins his son not to marry because he does not wish to inflict the scourge of Jewishness and the discrimination that accompanies it upon future generations: "Willst Du armen Geschöpfen das Leben geben, die sich krümmen und bücken müssen um nur ein armseliges Leben durchzubringen, die bei jedem Kummer, mit jeder Thräne der Unterdrückung denjenigen vielleicht verwünschen, der ihnen ihr unglückliches Dasein gab."[61] The father's statement is a reflection of the Jewish self-hatred, which was the inevitable consequence of the Jews viewing their Jewishness, their very identity, as a burden and a curse.

The son defends his marriage plans with an argument that Joseph II has brought about a new age of tolerance and that the conditions the father laments no longer exist:

> Sie ist nicht mehr die barbarische Zeit, wo Vorurtheile reagierten, nun herrscht Joseph der Große, der sie alle mit seinen Adlerauge durchschaut, und mit seinem majestätischen Winke verscheucht, der klar sieht, daß jeder Mensch von Gott erschaffen und Mensch ist, daß die Religion, die Lehrerin der gutten Sitten, unmöglich gebieten könne seine Nebenmenschen zu unterdrücken, daß nur Sklaven des Aberglaubens oder des Geldes die besten Menschen durch ihr Prisma von Vorurtheilen zu täuschen und zu blenden trachteten.[62]

Note the dialectical overtones of the statement. On the one hand, it is an assertion of Jewish self-consciousness: the speaker's espousal of the right to be free from the ill effects of bigotry, prejudice, and superstition. Together with this avowal of Jewish identity is an avowal of German identity: an assertion of loyalty and patriotism toward the Austrian state. The son trusts the state to protect his interests and rights as a Jew and as an Austrian. The father chimes in, expressing homage to the Austrian state of Emperor Joseph, "itzt in der goldenen Zeit Josephs Regierung wo sich jedes Würmchen seines Daseins freut, wo die Pest der Menschheit, das Vorurtheil verbannt ist."[63]

For the son, the group identification with his immediate Jewish family is extended into a group/family identification with the Austrian state. The son urges his bride:

Dank unserem besten Vater, er willigt endlich in unsere Verbindung, oder danke es vielmehr dem Vater aller Unglücklichen, unserem gnädigsten Monarchen; Er wurde von unserem unglücklichen Geschichte gerührt, erkennt und behandelt uns als Menschen, zerbricht unsere Fessel, ertheilt unserer Nation die Freyheit, und macht uns dadurch aus elenden Geschöpfen zu glücklichen, und mich zum Glücklichsten.[64]

The play reflects the great hopes and expectations with which Austria's Jewish community greeted the tolerance patent. The tolerance patent was of limited impact: after all, it was to be administered and enforced largely by people who still believed that Judaism was an inferior religion. While the political impact of this tolerance impact can be debated, there can be no doubt that it provided Jews with a tremendous psychological impetus. It gave them the feeling that they, too, belonged to the dominant Austrian society.

Arenhof's criticisms of the excesses and prejudices of Gentile society are enveloped in an expression of gratitude that these excesses have been relegated to the past. The play particularly celebrates the opening up of the differing professions to the Jews. The forced concentration of the Jews in money circulation is described as a terrible situation for the Jews because it draws such hatred upon them:

Welche glückliche Aussicht für unsere Nachkömmlinge, da ihnen verschiedene Wege offenstehen sich als rechtschaffene brave Männer und Bürger ernähren zu können und nicht mehr, wie in den vorigen Zeit des Fanatismus für uns alle Quellen versiegt sind, daß meistens nur die einzige elende Quellen des Geldhandels übrig blieb, um das mit Angst und Schweis Errungene zu zinsen für die hohe Gnade, daß man uns die Luft in einer Welt schenkt, worein uns Gott gesetzt hatte. Und darüber mußten wir die bittersten Vorwürfe des Wuchers wegen dulden.[65]

The statement is a revealing complaint against the hypocrisy of the dominant Christian culture which barred Jewish participation in all professions not dealing with money circulation and, at the same time, made Jews the target of hatred because it viewed the Jews as unduly profiting from that very money circulation which had been forced upon them. As does Dohm, Arenhof points out that most of the Jews who engage in this kind of work can succor only the most marginal subsistence for themselves.[66]

Because he is writing in German and not Hebrew or Yiddish, it seems likely that the intended audience for Arenhof's play is the Christian community. He wishes to communicate his gratitude for the new reforms to the dominant culture and, at the same time, to signal the readiness of the minority to take its place within the dominant culture. Underscoring Arenhof's obvious jubilation is the expectation and hope of inclusion. He signals his desire for inclusion by writing within the paradigm most popular with and accessible to the Christian readership: that of the bourgeois family drama. At the same time, through writing in German, he asserts that Jews, too, are a part of German society.

Arenhof's writing is tentative and amateurish. The way all of the characters chime in with uncritical gratitude toward the emperor is unpersuasive. But in asserting the unrelenting loyalty of the Jewish community toward the emperor, Arenhof gives voice to the desire of his Jewish coreligionists to be regarded as being among the emperor's full-fledged subjects. He demonstrates that the Jews do not wish to be regarded as a state within a state.

Arenhof casts a binary opposition between autonomy of identity and subjugation to the state. On the one hand, a certain Jewish pride underlies the submerged and often indirect assertions of human rights for Jews. On the other hand, the expressions of patriotic feeling toward the Austrian state show a willingness and an eagerness to procure inclusion in the broader society through submission to the authority of the emperor.

The notion of Jews wanting to be included in the larger Austrian community also found expression in a leading manifesto of the Haskalah, *Worte der Wahrheit und des Friedens an die gesammte jüdische Nation*, written by Naphthali Hartwig Herz Wessely in 1782, the same year Arenhof's play was published. The work was originally written in Hebrew and was translated into German by David Friedländer in 1798. Our analysis is based on the Friedländer translation. In this work, Wessely urged Austrian Jews to support the tolerance edict of Joseph II and take advantage of it.[67] His main argument was that Jews should desire integration into the broader society: "Mensch seyn ist eine Stufe höher als Israelite seyn."[68]

He views the Yiddish language as being a significant barrier to inclusion of Jews in the broader society. He describes a typical scenario: without knowledge of grammatical Hebrew, a Polish Jew teaches a German Jewish boy the Holy Scriptures. The boy learns neither the Hebrew language nor the German language correctly. The neglect in teaching him both his own native language and his holy language hinders him in acquiring all sorts of knowledge. There is an inexcusable neglect of the German national language. Jewish coreligionists from

Spain and Portugal have no difficulty with their national languages. In France, Italy, England, and in the Orient, Jews speak their national language. Even Jews in Poland speak at least a pure Polish. Only the German Jews speak a mixed language. Wessely attacks Yiddish as being a jargon that separates Jews from the Christian members of society. Jews should avoid everything that bears the sign of an oppressed person—and, for Wessely, that includes the Yiddish language. He encourages Jews to read Moses Mendelssohn's Bible translation, which used High German with Hebrew characters, as a means of learning German and gaining greater acceptance into society.

Wessely argues that Jews deserve inclusion in the broader society because they are good and loyal subjects of the emperor: "Wir haben jederzeit mit dem aufrichtigsten Herzen an der Glückseligkeit unserer Landesfürsten theilgenommen, und für deren Wohlfahrt zu dem ewigen inbrünstigen Gebete in unsren Tempeln geschickt."[69] Like Arenhof, Wessely portrays Jews as being among the emperor's most patriotic subjects and thereby entitled to full-fledged equality. Wessely defends Jews as being a group of people of high moral character. Even when they are at the lowliest stage of humanity, Jews have the consolation that they are guiltless and that their continuing misery is the effect of outdated prejudices in the hearts of their regents.

Nothing remains for the Jews except to pray to God with folded hands that he turns the hearts of the princes so that Jews find grace and mercy in their eyes. The long duration of their misery had robbed the Jews of all hope. They recognized with gratitude the protection and tolerance that the princes of Europe granted them in later times. But the hopes to be included within the body of the state, to achieve the rights granted other citizens, all hopes for that had been given up until now.

It is interesting how Wessely's assertion of the need to grant human rights to Jews is enveloped within an expression of gratitude toward the German princes. This is an effort to accommodate rules of exclusion—to give due deference to the rulers while underhandedly and politely criticizing them.

Wessely continues by stating that prejudices against Jews were universally enrooted. The examples of many centuries seemed to justify them. It has pleased merciful God to give the world a hero and protector in the person of Joseph II. He has long had the reputation of being among the greatest and most noble of regents: only through him was it possible for society as a whole to develop so much virtue. Joseph is gifted with the highest degree of reason. One is struck by the similarity between the expressions of gratitude for Joseph II expressed by both

Wessely and Arenhof. This expression of fervor for the emperor is a code: by paying homage to Joseph, the Maskilim are hoping to reap the awards of citizenship.

Wessely tells his fellow Jews that they should be incorporated into the body politic. Professions have been opened up to them: arts and sciences are also now accessible to them. They should make themselves worthy of these rights by taking full advantage of them.

While Wessely went to great lengths to accommodate the rules of exclusion of the dominant society, he infringed upon those of his own Jewish ingroup. Orthodox rabbis of Poland, Bohemia, and Austria disapproved of Wessely's work, which they saw as heresy. Rabbi Hirschel Lewin banned Wessely from Berlin. [70] Wessely's encouragement that Joseph's Jewish subjects should embrace the tolerance edict was viewed by orthodox Jews as an attack against the Jewish way of life. Rabbis felt particularly that the Jewish manner of raising and educating children was under attack because Wessely felt education should be reformed to enable better acculturation of Jewish children.[71] Jewish society was anything but a monolith, and the potential was there for reform-minded Jews to come into conflict with their more orthodox coreligionists. In commenting on the situation in Berlin, Steven M. Lowenstein observes, "Berlin Jewry, like modern Jewry as a whole, was characterized by a growing chasm between different types of lifestyles."[72] However, after the death of Mendelssohn, the power and influence of orthodox Jews weakened substantially.[73]

If Jewish society as a whole was not a monolith, neither was the Haskalah. A view of Joseph's reforms diametrically opposed to those of Arenhof and Wessely is expressed by Saul Ascher in his anonymously published *Bemerkungen über die bürgerliche Verbesserung der Juden veranlaßt, bei der Frage: Soll der Jude Soldat werden?* (1788). Walter Grab rightly credits Ascher as being an important and undeservedly forgotten figure in the progressive tradition of German history.[74] He is in any case a unique adherent of the Haskalah; his ideas diverge considerably from those of his fellow Maskilim. However, like other Maskilim, his work can be viewed dialectically in terms of the interplay between the concern for Jewish cultural integrity and the desire for greater acculturation.

Ascher objects to Joseph's plans to induct Jews into the Austrian army, contending that this is premature in advance of their being granted full equal rights. Ascher points to Joseph's war against the Turks as a motivation for making the Jews into soldiers. While Ascher concedes that the emperor can properly demand military service from his other subjects, he does not believe that such service can justly be demanded of Jews. Jews have not reaped the benefits that other subjects have received. Ascher maintains that there is no duty in the world that is so isolated that it does not engender another duty in return. A sovereign has responsibilities toward his subjects, if they have responsibilities toward him. The emperor has not performed all his responsibilities toward the Jews in peacetime and therefore cannot demand such sacrifices from them in wartime.

The social contract that the emperor's government has made with the Jewish nation cannot commit them to military service. When the emperor demands more duties of them, that invalidates the current contract. To demand extra duties without corresponding rights is nothing less than slavery, despotism, and oppression.

Speaking on behalf of the Jewish people, Ascher states that the rights of the emperor's other subjects are fruits they do not enjoy. They therefore owe no duties to the emperor. The emperor promises extra rights for the Jews in exchange for imposing new duties upon them, but the problem is that the Jews have not yet enjoyed anything from the duties that he owes them. Ascher here diverges considerably from Arenhof and Wessely who express their gratitude toward the emperor.

Ascher states that the emperor views the Jews as human beings toward whom he has no duty. This is the first step toward enslavement of the Jewish people. The longer the war lasts, the more the sovereign will demand that the Jews sacrifice their blood for him.

Ascher next explores how military service could harm the Jews, with an eye toward the uniqueness of the Jewish situation. To expect culture from contemporary Jews is a vain hope. They are an infantile people, because they have been discriminated against for so long. No nation is more pursued, despised, and oppressed than that of the Jews. Because a Jew can count on little happiness in this world, he acts in respect to his eternal happiness. Through giving mild alms to the poor, Jews seek to lessen the misery of people in need.

Military service has the opposite character: it will spread disloyalty on the part of the Jews toward the entire system by exerting a negative influence on their moral character. Enlightenment cannot take place without morality. The enthusiasm that the Jews have already begun to show for their sovereign has borne fruit. The proposed reform, however, will alter not their civic status, but their religious status.

Jews do not possess the characteristics that the status of a soldier requires. The emperor should grant the Jews human rights. He would thereby teach them to view the advantage of the state as being not isolated from their own. He would thus awaken in them an inclination toward patriotism and good citizenship and thereby they could be educated toward becoming useful citizens.

While Arenhof and Wessely view Joseph's tolerance edict as an occasion for jubilance and renewed patriotism among the Jewish community toward the Austrian state, Ascher views it as being a Trojan horse which instead of emancipating the Jews could very well bring about their enslavement. In writing seven years after the tolerance edict, Ascher sees the promise of emancipation as being largely unfulfilled.

Ascher explored Judaism with more philosophical depth in his 1792 tract *Leviathan oder ueber Religion in Rücksicht des Judenthums*. Here he asks fundamental questions about the nature and purposes of Judaism. He asserts that Judaism is neither unplanned nor contrary to its established purposes. It was built on a firm foundation, based on healthy principles. Unlike other Maskilim, Ascher deemphasized the role of laws in constituting Judaism and instead emphasized the role of faith or belief. Belief for Ascher is a firm underpinning of any religion. Religion must have adherents who voluntarily submit themselves to belief. In order to submit ourselves to belief in a religion, the religion must agree with the subjective side of our perception.

Reason is the source that leads us to the idea of a Supreme Being, of God. Laws, on the other hand, are necessary to ensure that people fulfill certain responsibilities toward which they feel no internal calling. Nonetheless, Ascher is against placing too much emphasis on laws. Whoever wants to write universally applicable laws is doing so in vain. It is tantamount to trying to create an equal climate for all human beings located everywhere.

Revealed law is not there to be universally applicable, but it is merely a result of rules that have been abstracted from certain phenomena. They are not necessary, we do not need to follow them; in fact, they are arbitrary and the issue is whether reason dictates another rule that goes against these laws. Our understanding gives us laws, but our reason has the ability to destroy them. Therefore we cannot appeal to reason if we find a general law. A general law is nothing more than a general observation that we have to observe and regard as a law. Reason cannot see the necessity of an occurrence and cannot determine a law on its basis: the law is revealed.

Revelation is the exalted constitution of a society: it is the origin of belief. In every religion, the principle of godliness exists not as an idea but as an object of perception. The subjective condition of all revealed religion is belief. The widest possible range of religion is God, teaching, and law. Revelation can fill a gap in a person's subjective perception in an area where he or she feels a need. In order to attain the satisfaction of this need, belief must take place.

Ascher asks, What is the actual purpose of Judaism? Judaism is something divine. It is a source of happiness that God has given to some of his creations. Judaism is a high means that the creator gave to some members of society to ensure their happiness. For the rest of his creations, he provided other sources of happiness under a different form. The founding principle of Judaism is human happiness. Its intent is to sensitize human beings toward the happiness of society.

Faith is the precondition of all revealed religion. Judaism contains the method through which a society of human beings can become accustomed to certain concepts that should bring everybody together. The actual and highest purpose of religion is to make people acquainted with certain truths and make these truths more understandable. God used revelation as a means to assist human beings who could not directly grasp the truth through reason.

Unlike Mendelssohn, Ascher classifies Judaism as a revealed religion. God chose Judaism as a means to teach a group of human beings to think according to a certain formula. No other revealed religion has had the impact of Judaism. The intention of God for the Jews is not to give them laws to regulate their wills. The will is to be left up to the individual. God promised the Jews happiness to the extent that they do not fail to recognize his purpose. Rules for our behavior are intended for the benefit of all the people. They provide protection against transgressions. The laws were given to Moses, who in turn closed a pact with the people after he read them their rights and laws; the people in turn committed themselves to obedience.

When God made a partnership with the Jews, a belief was constituted. Everybody was to submit to a certain bond to be included in a general purpose. The religion was strictly regulative, that is, one was a Jew based on whether one behaved according to constituted norms or according to one's own arbitrary mechanisms. Conditions made it necessary that certain rules become constituted: these became laws. The subjective precondition for Judaism is belief; the objective precondition is revelation. Elements of revealed religion are belief, teachings, and laws. We find in the entire society of Jews not a society of citizens but simply a society that unites out of a religious interest. All their laws are based on natural law. The "rights of human beings" is a different concept from the "rights of citizens."

No member of the Jewish community had a calling to be a citizen of the state. He was simply a human being and a Jew. Thereby the Jewish nation built a character that was uniquely its own. In terms of his relationship to the state, the Jew knew only the duty of defending himself and his people against an outward enemy. Furthermore, he lived according to the religion, which was the only institution that recognized him as a citizen. It seemed to the Jews that their only calling was the religion to which they belonged. Art and science were only cultivated in a way that promoted the Jews' highest calling, their religion; or they were at least promoted in a way that was not to the disadvantage of this religion. Their entire philosophy, their entire manner of thought, was subjugated to religion; their reasoning was grounded in religious ideas.

Jews made no judgments that were not involved with their religion. This led to dissimilarities in Jewish group formation. Misery and oppression brought Jews to new lands and taught them to adapt themselves to the wills and whims of their host cultures in their various lands. The Jewish nation thereby received a dissimilar direction. Some groups sacrificed aspects of their well-being within their host culture to maintain their religion; others surrendered themselves and their religion to fate. This led to great divisions within the Jewish faith.

Ascher critiques three great attempts by Jewish philosophers to systematize Judaism: Maimonides, Baruch de Spinoza, and Moses Mendelssohn. In discussing Maimonides, Ascher points out that his plan was to encompass the entire range of Judaism in principles of reason. Maimonides argues that all transcendental concepts and ideas of reason were distilled from Judaism, and attempts to constitute it as a religion of reason. He does not describe the essence of Judaism but describes it according to principles of reason. He portrays the principles of Judaism in such a way that they resemble Aristotelian principles of reason. This attempt to renew Judaism aroused great attention, but contemporary rabbis saw great harm in it. They feared untoward results and unavoidable revolutions.

Spinoza believed in an absolute division between faith and reason. He rejects everything that is not in harmony with reason, and he only permits those elements of religion which *are* in harmony with reason. Ascher describes Spinoza as an enemy of religion. Spinoza wants to see reason totally separated from religion. He seeks to understand Judaism as being in total contradiction to reason.

Ascher refutes Spinoza's ideas by arguing that reason cannot fathom many truths that can be fathomed by belief. Faith is a support for humanity on a plane on which it is abandoned by reason. To engage in the destruction of belief is to proceed without an awareness of human nature. It is illogical to reproach humankind with a weakness that it has had since the beginning of time. Human beings are no angels and whoever wants to elevate them to this stage loses much of their own humanity. We attempt to elevate human beings as much as possible, but we must never forget that they are human beings.

Next Ascher refutes Mendelssohn. Mendelssohn claims that Judaism has no churchly power. He thereby wishes to prove that the characteristic element of Judaism consists of perception and obedience. Ascher maintains that there is an inconsistency in Mendelssohn's thinking to the extent that Mendelssohn claims that Judaism consists of religious teachings or eternal truths. According to Mendelssohn's system, one must admit that these eternal truths are made known to human beings through laws. Laws are given through revelation. Can reason determine something necessary out of something accidental and arbitrary?

Ascher's intention is to portray Judaism in such a way that every enlightened person can be a believing Jew. The purpose of revelation is to bring a group of people of similar mentality together and create one united body, constituted through the bond of faith. Faith is fortified by revelation. In Judaism, one was unable to constitute general symbols or teachings of faith such as later developed in Christianity. People had not yet been sensitized to the general purpose of Judaism. On the one hand, the teachings could win no recognition. Therefore God determined to give laws to the Jewish nation. These laws were perhaps the only way of maintaining the Jewish faith, but they fell short of their purpose.

Humans became accustomed to mere actions. They thereby believed that they contributed enough to their faith by action alone. Judaism was constituted through laws, and to the extent that they were mostly used as predicates of belief and means to constitute the revelation in Judaism, so they arranged the purposeful into something essential. Judaism is revealed law giving. The result of this is that Judaism has no dogmas or articles of belief that contain its essence. If one views the revealed laws as the essence of Judaism, then one must at the same time claim that the entire purpose of Judaism can be reached through obeying these laws. This reasoning is insufficient.

The original law developed so that it finally reached the stage that the slightest infraction of the laws was viewed as heresy or lack of belief. When the Jewish nation suffered disturbances and laws were thereby broken, people feared a collapse of belief. Teachers began to see that the laws alone were not the essence of the faith. They therefore began to concern themselves more with faith and endeavored to promote greater faith among the people. They sought to make the people attentive toward teachings through certain images, allegories, and fables.

According to Ascher, we see that the greatest people have already come back to the truth that Judaism has dogmas, only they could not or would not explain whether they are essential elements of Judaism.

Ascher, however, claims that the dogmas are an essential component of Judaism, and only they can bring people back to the actual spirit and purpose of Judaism. Through them alone can Judaism be kept pure in times where the laws are neglected.

Who dares to approach faith through the gateway of reason? And who dares to maintain that his faith is actually perception? In all eternity, reason must yield a place for faith. Reason must tolerate faith and attempt to harmonize with it. When reason finds room for doubt, then it can decide for itself, but it cannot extend its rights to the realm of belief. The situation in which reason must decide over religion occurs only when belief disturbs the happiness of people. However, reason may not demand the destruction of all faith. Unlike other Enlighteners—both Jewish and non-Jewish—Ascher believes in reaching some accommodation with the mystical elements of religion. However, as Michael A. Meyer points out, this does not mean that Ascher was not a part of the Enlightenment: "What finally distinguishes Judaism from other religions is that its dogmas, unlike those of Christianity, do not disturb freedom of thought and action."[75]

Ascher differentiates between a thinker and a freethinker. The thinker proceeds upon the path of reason and thereby brings greater harmony to religious endeavor. The freethinker, on the other hand, takes reason as a sine qua non. He is the creator of a new world in which he possesses enough egoism to trust his fellow human beings to abandon the ways of the Almighty under his leadership. If one accompanies the *thinker* on the road of reason, however, reason emerges as a judge who proceeds with the strictest of consciences.

Through the revealed law, Judaism became a constituted religion. Jewish society has built a theocracy or a constitution that takes its rules for behavior and its directives straight from God. Eventually Judaism ceased to be a theocracy. God delegated the management of his religion to true servants. Judaism underwent a transition from a divine government to a human one. The authority of God was handed over to human beings.

The purposes of God and the authority of law were managed according to human perspectives. This was the first constitution of Judaism. Churchly power developed and high priests had the right to prescribe laws for the nation. How can we tear ourselves away from this liturgy that was constituted upon the authority of God? Revealed law does not contain the true purpose of Judaism. The Godhead only granted revealed law to us, until we should learn Judaism's true purpose.

It was Judaism's purpose to bid us to happiness, to help us feel the true value of human beings, and therefore to invite us into society. It is therefore the purpose of God to keep these purposeful laws until the purpose of Judaism is reached. Ascher asks, Why did God not let us recognize this purpose earlier? Why did he let so many centuries go by without awakening us from our slumber? In which of his plans did God make his purpose known to us? Who shall tell us, how far we can go, to what extent we can abandon the purposeful, that is, the laws? To the extent that they are not essential, they can be abandoned. We are committed to let as much stand as will lead us to God's purpose and this will be the eternal bond that will forever unite us.

Ascher asserts that our wise ones in the history of Judaism sought truth prior to the emergence of revelation, and we must seek it as well. They sought with the spirit of Judaism, and we must seek with the light of reason. Faith is a necessary condition of religion and religion is a necessary precondition of an enlightened society.

Every constituted religion should invite its adherents and not coerce them. Some people will change religions. Apostles of faith have never promoted their religion as being more than a matter of choice. It is the actual character of revealed religion to develop gradually and to be constituted in harmony with the society. Accordingly, every religion will need to go through periods of reformation. Reformation in matters of belief occurs when one destroys or modifies the constitution of a religion and builds another. Ascher wishes to give Jewish society a new constitution based on truths made possible by belief. He feels that the Jews should establish a new relation between religion and society the way Martin Luther did for the Christians.

Ascher differentiates between negative reformation and positive reformation. Negative reformation destroys the entire form of belief and builds a new one out of the pieces. Positive reformation is a less radical, but nonetheless substantive, change, such as the one Luther brought about. The age of science makes negative reformation more appealing to many, but Ascher prefers positive reformation. Luther reformed the constitution of religion. It developed itself according to the spirit of enlightenment. But enlightenment for Ascher is not equivalent to rationalism. No matter how much the thinker exercises his powers, human beings are not created for the sake of reason alone—reason is not enough. Objects of belief do not correlate exactly with reason.

Ascher is in favor of a reformation of Judaism. Most adherents favor observation of the law as the essence of Judaism. Judaism is for Ascher more than that. It is superstition to follow laws mechanically. At the time he is writing, Ascher laments that the total Jewish constitution is entirely law. One who breaks the law disobeys the constitution. Ascher bemoans the lack of positive reformation vis-à-vis Judaism. Negative reformation has occurred, but no positive. The question is, What has this negative reformation created for the Jews? Only this, that they think in a more enlightened manner and wish for another profession and recognize the rights the state has over them. This negative reformation benefits the enemies of faith in that faith is neglected.

Transgression of the law is regarded as a forsaking of Judaism. We should alter the current constitution of Judaism and enable people to choose a profession without going against the teachings of Judaism. The current constitution of Judaism consists of simply observing the law. However, civic improvement can come about if Jews undertake a positive reformation of the law. The only possible valid purpose of Judaism is to make its people as happy as possible, to bind them together in a society.

The law is a way of constituting the religion, but does not constitute its entire essence. Through belief, Jews found they were created for one another. However, they did not dispense with rights of individual autonomy. It was never God's intention to rob the Jew of individual autonomy. Jews misunderstood his intention. Because they mistook the constitution of the religion for its essence, they regarded observing laws as the entire form of religion. Outmoded laws became fossilized because they were falsely regarded as the essence of the religion. Christians now claim the Jewish religion is no longer valid for our times; they tell the Jews, "Renounce it and you can become human beings of equal worth."

Do not do that, says Ascher. Remain children of Israel on the path of your parents: our religion is for all times, all people. The Jews must show that their religion can make them human beings deserving of citizenship. Only the constitution of the Jewish religion must be reformed, but the religion itself must never lose its essence. Ascher is a difficult thinker to understand because of the dialectical nature of his thought. On the one hand, his promotion of a positive reformation of Judaism à la Luther points to a desire on his part for greater acculturation of the Jews into the society. On the other hand, his concern for Jewish cultural integrity transcends his desire for acculturation. He is not willing to go to all possible lengths to effect the Jews' assimilation into German society unless the dominant society can come to respect the advantages of their unique cultural attributes.

A similar concern with modernizing Judaism by no longer requiring adherence to outmoded laws was expressed by David Friedländer. Friedländer's work also has much affinity with that of Heinrich Friedrich von Diez. Diez's claim that Jews and Christians should seek common ground on a plane that is neither Jewish nor Christian—for example, through Natural Religion—was echoed by Friedländer, a major figure of the Haskalah. Friedländer took over the intellectual and civic leadership of Berlin's Jewish community after Moses Mendelssohn's death. Friedländer advocated the founding of a Jewish-Christian sect on the basis of religious compromise by the Jews.[76] The state was in turn to reward the Jews' effort by extending civil equality to them.[77] Friedländer was characterized by his desire for an improvement in the Jews' moral condition as well as their political condition.[78]

Friedländer's conception of Judaism differed in many ways from Mendelssohn's. Mendelssohn viewed Judaism as being the most suitable religion for Jews because it was the religion closest to the path of reason, whereas Friedländer viewed Judaism as having strayed from the path of reason and become steeped in mystical principles.

Through utilization of Jewish self-criticism and a push toward moral improvement, Friedländer hoped to increase the status of the Jewish people. He expressed his ideas in the form of an anonymously published open letter to the Protestant minister Wilhelm Abraham Teller entitled *Sendschreiben an Seinen Hochwürden Herrn Oberconsistorialrath und Probst Teller zu Berlin von einigen Hausvätern jüdischer Religion* (1799). Teller rejected the proposals promoted by Friedländer, insisting on the conversion of the Jews into believing Christians as a pretext for any extension of civil rights to them.[79]

Friedländer criticizes many Jewish precepts because he feels that they are not only contrary to reason but in fact keep Jews in an infantile condition:

> Die positiven Gesetze sind peinlich, mit Kosten verknüpft und Zeit raubend; die negativen setzen seiner Thätigkeit im bürgerlichen Leben überall Schranken. Es muß sehr oft in die unbehagliche Lage kommen, sich selbst oder seine Nebenmenschen auf die einfachsten Fragen unbefriedigend zu antworten. Es ist für ein denkendes Wesen nichts Demüthigenderes, als dieser ewige Zustand der Unmündigkeit, ewig, statt vernünftige Gründe über sein Verfahren zu geben, sich auf Autoritäten des Gesetzes berufen zu müssen.[80]

For Friedländer, the irrationalistic and infantile elements within the Jewish religion itself are factors preventing the inclusion of the Jews in the broader society. Friedländer believes that the state should perform a tutelary function in bringing about the moral improvement of the Jews, who are under the influence of anachronistic religious precepts.[81]

Friedländer asserts that the oppression and social disadvantages that Jews face is a valid reason for them to subject their religious precepts to critical scrutiny and initiate reforms that will bring them closer to the Christian mainstream. He favors a reform of Judaism not only because he feels that the laws of Judaism should be subjected to the test of reason, but also because of his concern for the status of his coreligionists throughout Europe. He expresses regret for the heavy burdens they bear, their exclusion from artistic endeavors and social activity, the prohibition on their farming and owning land, and especially the demoralizing hatred to which they are subjected.[82]

Friedländer believes that Jews should transform their religion in order to make it more acceptable to the Christian majority. Contact with Enlightened Christians can lead to a modernization and evolution of Judaism. Like Diez, Friedländer believes that Jews and Christians should meet on the neutral ground of rationalistic philosophy and that such a philosophy could have a modernizing influence on the Jews. Friedländer viewed the "Jewish question" in terms of a quid pro quo: Jews would abandon many of the traditional tenets of their religion in return for full rights of citizenship. Like Ascher, Friedländer has a concern for lessening the influence of outmoded laws on the Jewish religion and on Jewish culture. He does not, however, concern himself with maintaining Jewish cultural integrity to the same extent that Ascher does.

Because this study may benefit from a concrete example of how the Maskilim wanted to reform Jewish ceremonial laws, we will briefly consider the debate between Marcus Herz and Jacob Emden regarding Jewish burial laws. Marcus Herz was a Jewish physician and philosopher, a student and disciple of Immanuel Kant, and a member of the Mendelssohn circle. Jacob Emden was an important orthodox Jewish rabbi of the eighteenth century who was against efforts to emancipate the Jews without the state granting them full legal equality and recognizing Judaism as a religion of equal value to Christianity.[83] He firmly wanted to preserve both the spirit and letter of traditional Judaism.

Laws of ritual cleanliness were the logic behind the practice of early burials, that is, burials on the day of death. Other reasons for same-day burial were the belief that the soul of the deceased was not released until he was buried and the fact that the seven-day mourning period for the family began right after the funeral, and early burials made the process less burdensome.[84] Jews found themselves confronted with demands for change both from the various authorities and from their coreligionists who were part of the Haskalah, because of a fear that the practice could lead to live burials. Emden lent his authority and moral support to various congregations seeking to preserve the traditional burial rites through the writing of letters to public officials. Marcus Herz responded to Emden in a pamphlet entitled *Über die frühe Beerdi-*

gung der Juden (1788). Herz argues that his proposed liberalization of Jewish burial laws is in fact a restoration and repristination of the original intent of the Jewish religion. He argues from a standpoint of original principles: rabbinical laws regarding early burials go against prior established principles of the Jewish religion.

Herz also promotes Enlightenment principles such as the use of reason to rethink the laws that support the Jewish religion: he sees a need to examine their validity and do away with laws that serve no important function. Judaism is a religion that lays great weight on the love of neighbor and the sanctity of human life. Herz therefore feels that it is impossible for the Jewish religion to command that a person be buried as soon as he shows no outer signs of life. Our power of reason shows us that such a person may be able to recover: early burials may be robbing people of life. They bring about a cruel and tortuous death. Suffocation in the grave is a worse death than public execution. According to Herz, the laws commanding early burial have no reason to exist. Herz condemns Emden as a zealot who fails to accept any perspective more wide-reaching than his own orthodox viewpoint.

The Jewish religion during the eighteenth century was going through a period of tremendous change and this change was fraught with controversy. In addition to all this, Judaism was being challenged in the late eighteenth and early nineteenth centuries by a baptismal epidemic or *Taufepidemie*. Before 1770, only about one-tenth of 1 percent of the Berlin Jewish population converted each year amounting to about four conversions a year. Between 1770 and 1800, the rate of conversion increased 74 percent while the Jewish population decreased by 5 percent. Although the number of conversions was still less than 1 percent of the entire Jewish community, about 5 percent of the adult population was involved. Because the Jewish community was not increasing, this meant that in a twenty-year period, an entire generation had left Judaism.[85] Jews felt themselves under siege by this baptismal epidemic and feared the atrophy of Jewish society. To understand better the motivations of these baptisms, we will explore the writings of one of the most famous woman of letters to be affected by this baptismal epidemic—Rahel Levin Varnhagen.

To Escape the Cloud of Otherness: Rahel Varnhagen and Her Writings

Bourgeois writers of the eighteenth century—such as Lessing and others less remembered—promoted a model of Judaism suitable for the emerging capitalistic culture of the bourgeoisie. In portraying "good"

Jews, these authors expressed their expectations as to what constituted a good Jew. The good Jew became synonymous with the successful bourgeois, a factor that had not only literary-historical significance, but also far-reaching sociological implications. Such attitudes on the part of middle-class writers and people in the general public had the tendency to encourage Jews to distance themselves from their own ingroup. Such persons advocated the utopian ideal of "full social absorption of Jews into non-Jewish society." However, Jews remained strangers to the society even when they adapted to the society.[86]

Sander L. Gilman points to the impact which this phenomenon had upon the Jewish psyche: it caused Jews to disdain their own Jewishness. One cannot understand the writings of Rahel Levin Varnhagen without first examining this Jewish self-hatred. Self-hatred results from the minority group accepting the image of themselves that the dominant group generates. Among the dominant group, there exists a liberal fantasy that anyone is welcome to share in the dominion of the group as long as they abide by the rules that define that group.[87] Outsiders can purportedly become one with the dominant group by abandoning their differences.

However, this practice causes what Gilman calls the conservative curse: "The more you are like me, the more I know the true value of my power, which you wish to share, and the more I am aware that you are but a shoddy counterfeit, an outsider."[88] This situation places members of the minority group in a double-bind situation: they are acceptable neither to members of the minority culture from which they come (because of their attempts to assimilate) nor to members of the dominant culture. This creates a self-approbation toward the culture of one's birth.

This tendency gave rise to the heightened desire of Jews to escape their Jewishness altogether and unite with bourgeois society without the cloud of otherness.[89] However, this was easier said than done. Not even the social progress of the Jews due to the Enlightenment could erase their outsiderness. According to Liliane Weissberg, the "Jewish question" was neither a religious question nor a matter of civic rights, but "an anthropological distinction which neither legal equality nor conversion could erase."[90] The French occupation had granted Jews legal equality in Prussia, and Jews were for the most part seen as a separate nation living upon German soil.

The Berlin salons were an important manifestation of the German Jewish culture of this time period. Salons were founded in the early nineteenth century by such Jewish intellectual luminaries as Rahel Varnhagen, Dorothea Mendelssohn Schlegel, and Henriette Herz. These salons represented a breaking down of social barriers: Jews and Gentiles, Germans and Frenchmen, women and men, and noblemen and commoners socialized with one another. These salons brought the Jewish women who founded them to the periphery of social acceptability in the highest intellectual circles of Berlin. But these women were not satisfied with the periphery. The rate of conversion to Christianity among salon women was far higher than the rate of the Jewish population as a whole.[91] The patronesses of the Jewish salons wished to take their place with the dominant society without the burden of otherness.

Rahel Varnhagen gave expression to such desires when she wrote:

> Ich habe solche Phantasie; als wenn ein außerirdisch Wesen, wie ich in diese Welt getrieben wurde, mir beim Eingang diese Worte mit einem Dolch ins Herz gestoßen hätte: "Ja, habe Empfindung, sieh die Welt, wie sie wenige sehen, sei groß und edel, ein ewiges Denken kann ich dir auch nicht nehmen, eins hat man aber vergessen; sei eine Jüdin!" Und nun ist mein ganzes Leben eine Verblutung; mich ruhig zu halten, kann es fristen, jede Bewegung sie zu stillen, neuer Tod; und Unbeweglichkeit mir nur im Tod selbst möglich.[92]

Rahel gives voice to an expression of Judaism being a burden and a curse. Judaism is confirmed upon the infant Rahel not by a loving God but by an extraterrestrial—a supernatural being lacking divine sanction. Jewishness is viewed as being something outside the divine order: confirmed by a being who has supernatural powers, but who lacks the inherent goodness of a God. Jewish history in its entirety was experienced as a bitter product of the ghetto: as the nexus of a personal misfortune from which one should make strides to distance oneself.[93]

In later years, Varnhagen became critical of the dominant Christian society into which she had tried to assimilate and compared its excesses with those for which her own people had been blamed:

> Als Christus für einen Ketzer, Frevler und Rebellen gehalten wurde, waren seine Ankläger und Verfolger die Herrschenden, Betitelten, Uniformierten, mit dem siegenden großen Volk Alliirten. Deren Nachkommen aber, die Juden, sind bis heute, durch ihren bloßen Namen, nach aller Geschmack Ausgesetzte; und die Nachkommen der Anhänger Christi sind die siegenden Verächter geworden. Der Rest gläubiger Juden hält sich aber noch für alte Aristokraten, und verachtet die ganze Christenheit: auf diese Weise gehen die Juden als warnendes Beispiel umher.[94]

The passage is amazingly rich and multivalent in its content: on the one hand, the Jewish self-hatred against which Varnhagen struggled is far from absent. She distances herself from believing Jews who maintain their group identification with pride and still see themselves as the chosen people. She is uncomfortable with any notion of Jewish ingroup identity. But she is also unwilling and unable to uncritically embrace the dominant Christian group. She views Christians as—through their oppression of the Jews—setting an example for their own oppression during a future time when they cease to be the dominant group. The passage reveals a possible awareness of Lessing's Die Erziehung des Menschengeschlechts (1777) with its prophecy that the members of the dominant religion of Europe would someday outgrow Christianity in the same way that their predecessors had left Judaism to embrace Christianity. Rahel Varnhagen was able to feel a sense of belonging neither to the minority group into which she had been born or the dominant society that gave her the impetus for wanting to leave the confines of her birth.[95]

For most of her life, Rahel was torn between two cultures— with neither could she identify or maintain a sense of belonging. She was a remarkably intelligent and well-educated Jewish woman in a society in which both educated Jews and educated women were rare occurrences. While her Jewishness was a barrier to her full acceptance in Gentile society, her contacts with the German intelligentsia of her time and her prodigious learning isolated her from mainstream Jewish society as well. Furthermore, she had converted to Christianity, which meant a full break with the larger Jewish society.[96]

For Rahel Varnhagen, a principal conflict of her life was in determining her relationship to both the Jewish world into which she had been born and the dominant Christian society she wanted to join. Before she died, she did in fact reconcile herself with the situation of being a Jew and at the same time a member of the larger society. As recalled by her husband, Karl August Varnhagen von Ense, her last words were:

> Welche Geschichte! . . . eine aus Ägypten und Palästina Geflüchtete bin ich hier, und finde Hülfe, Liebe und Pflege von euch! Dir lieber August, war ich zugesandt, durch diese Führung Gottes, und du mir! Mit erhabenem Entzücken denke ich an diesen meinen Ursprung und diesen ganzen Zusammenhang des Geschickes, durch welches die ältesten Erinnerungen des Menschengeschlechts mit der neuesten Lage der Dinge, die weitesten Zeit- und Raumfernen verbunden sind. Was so lange Zeit meines Lebens mir die größte Schmach, das herbste Leid und Unglück war, eine Jüdin geboren zu sein, um keinen Preis möcht' ich das jetzt missen.[97]

Rahel Varnhagen's final musings are driven by the awareness of the ways in which multicultural contacts and contexts enrich human experience. This realization brought her to a sense of peace regarding her "otherness." Her statement is permeated with the underlying ideal of multicultural harmony. Although she spent her life trying to escape her Jewishness, her final impressions constitute a celebration of Gentile-Jewish friendship. A lifetime of confronting anti-Semitism motivated her toward a reclamation of her Jewish identity, which she had once tried to renounce.

The more liberal among the Christian writers wished to integrate Jews into the nascent capitalistic society. This situation was complicated by the precapitalistic concentration of the Jews in money circulation. Under the influence of capitalism, money circulation had been extended to all spheres of human activity and Jews appeared to have a certain advantage in reaping the profits of this condition.[98] Jews seemed to profit from capitalism, Enlightenment, and the French Revolution: phenomena through which the masses felt threatened.

The broader masses in the society suffered from the conditions of the revolutionary epoch but were unable to diagnose the multifarious causes of their suffering. They blamed their travails on emancipation which had been accorded the Jews and not themselves. The social pressure to assimilate and to no longer be ghetto Jews became ever more forceful. Assimilation appeared as an escape from anti-Semitic prejudices. The admission of Jews into bourgeois society was realized through submission. Because emancipation in the sense of unconditional liberation proved impracticable, social pressures on Jews to assimilate intensified. Jews encountered social coercion to become Christians and Germans. But this Christian Germanness was laden with anti-Semitism, and if adopted by Jews could only lead to self-hatred.[99]

We have explored various self-manifestations of Jewish identity. We will next explore how Jewish identity was seen by non-Jewish dramatists advocating Jewish emancipation.

4. Emancipatory Drama after Lessing

The Bourgeois Family Drama as a Vehicle for Jewish Emancipation

In our examination of Lessing, we explored the extent to which the emancipatory discourse was a mediated discourse: mediated, and perhaps even somewhat vitiated, through its commitment to the values and social interests of the emerging bourgeoisie of which Lessing was a part. The impact was to send a message to the Jews that if they truly wanted emancipation, it was the bourgeoisie who represented their interests, but the price for this representation was a conformity to bourgeois values. According to Detlev Claussen, assimilated Jews came to epitomize the bourgeoisie. They emulated the bourgeoisie: under the guise of emancipation, they took on bourgeois values.[1]

The concept of Jewish equality, predicated upon the notion that Christianity was not a sine qua non but one of a series of alternative viewpoints, was a suppressed discourse until the Christian bourgeoisie began to question and attack their own religious underpinnings. As the bourgeoisie began to challenge orthodox Christianity as a consensus formation, a discourse emerged through which it was possible to express notions of Jewish equality.

Foucault's notion of sympathy comes into play: sympathy is a making of the "Other" more similar to oneself. It "has the dangerous power of *assimilating*, of rendering things identical to one another."[2] Demands for equality of the Jews were combined with the broader discourse of expression of bourgeois self-interest. The mediation of the one discourse through the other led to oxymoronic and self-contradictory means of expression. As did the anti-Semites, so did philo-Semitic writers recreate the Jews in their own image: the anti-Semites projected their hatred upon the Jews while the philo-Semites projected their sympathy upon them. The liberal Christians therefore tried to modify or compromise the "otherness" of the Jews. This tended to create the expectation that, as a result of emancipation, the cultural differences of the Jews would atrophy. Bourgeois interests and identity became a filter for the more marginalized discourse of Jewish emancipation.

This phenomenon came about because the interests of the bourgeoisie came to be identified with the general interests of humanity.[3] The emerging bourgeois order was viewed as the "natural" order, which would best meet the needs of all of humankind. The belief was promoted that improvement of the Jewish condition could best be met through the dominion of the bourgeoisie.

The representatives of orthodox Christianity had promoted a narrowly defined notion of tolerance as a temporary forbearance of the inferior with the expectation of conversion. In the meantime, the more liberal middle-class writers promulgated a notion of sympathy with the cultural outsiders with the expectation that most of these cultural differences would disappear.

The antiauthoritarian social criticism on behalf of the Jews was grafted onto a literature promoting the authority of the patriarchal family structure.[4] To the extent that Jewish emancipation became a substitute formation for expression of bourgeois values, literary texts at this time had a myriad of internal contradictions. The linking of the "Jewish question" with the not necessarily congruous "bourgeois question" gives rise to a series of paradoxes, which we will explore further.

German bourgeois drama after 1780 shows evidence of a lively and widespread interest in the "Jewish question." The interests of the later playwrights in Lessing's motifs can be found in their own literary reworkings of those motifs.[5] Before we examine specific plays, I would like to view the mechanism through which the emancipatory literature was expressed: namely, the bourgeois drama.

The bourgeois drama of the late eighteenth century is subdivided into several different genres: *comédie larmoyante*, domestic tragedy (*bürgerliches Trauerspiel*), *Rührstück*, *Sittengemälde*, and others. These new dramatic forms that constitute the middle-class drama manifested a criticism of the dramatic status quo of classicistic and heroic tragedy. The programs of these new dramatic genres supported the Enlightenment in two respects: first, in their struggle for the well-being and progress of humankind and, second, in the moral spirit of observations. To put it in other words, the plays promoted realism on the one hand and the moral program of the Enlightenment on the other.[6]

The realism of the bourgeois drama manifested itself in the closing up of the social distance between the portrayed persons and the audience.[7] One paradigm can be found in the substitution of prose for verse in the dialogues, which Szondi characterizes as the "artlessness" of the dialogues.[8] Another change lies in the jettisoning of the traditional *Ständeklausel*. Seventeenth-century reinterpretations of Aristotle taught that the characters in a drama should either be noble or lowly: tragedy is the imitation of human beings who are better than ourselves whereas comedy is an imitation of lowliness or ridiculousness in people. In the previous dramatic tradition, these teachings were bound up with a notion of social class: tragedy portrayed the aristocracy, whereas comedy portrayed the lower classes. This tradition of the *Ständeklausel* was not continued with the reasoning that the nobility should no longer be allowed to monopolize the heroic function: the burgher—and in some cases even the Jewish pariah—were equally entitled to be represented as tragic figures.[9]

The nuclear family was the social and organizational form of the rising bourgeoisie. What the representative pieces of all the genres of bourgeois drama have in common is that they are all primarily family dramas. The portrayal of the family played a central role in the notion of theater being a moral institution. In the portrayals of the family circle, the members handle themselves in a moral and virtuous manner. They represent the positive *Gegenbild* of an undesirable reality.[10] These dramas had as their underlying principle the propagation of bourgeois values.[11] One element of this principle was the portrayal of patriarchal family structures: the family is presented not only as a historical system but also as a value system. The behaviors between the numerous daughters, sons, mothers, and fathers make sense only in the context of this value system.[12] The organizing principle of the family in these dramas is the power of the father. The dramas portray the obedience and deference of nearly everyone else in the house to the authority of the father.[13]

The conventions of the family drama reflect the subordinacy of the bourgeois society toward the political authority of the feudal governments. The place of the authoritative order of the feudal society was substituted with the authoritative order of the bourgeois family.[14] Dramas portrayed paternalistic family structures and the bourgeois behavioral norms that went along with them. The constitution of these bourgeois conditions is understood as the "natural order." These conditions are not themselves the problem but divergences from these conditions are viewed as being painful circumstances.[15] The instinctual structure of the individual and the order of bourgeois society are forced into a convergence: the latter, and not the former, is understood as the natural order.[16]

One element of this natural order was the life of the merchant.[17] The connection to money is a measurement of bourgeois morals.[18] The moral motif of bourgeois emancipatory tendencies in the dramas of trivial authors in the eighteenth century is undifferentiated from economic considerations.[19]

Dramas thematizing the "Jewish question" during this time were written by Gentiles within this bourgeois discourse. By putting bourgeois values into the mouths of Jewish characters, writers unconsciously promoted Jewish assimilation into the middle class.

All of the dramas we will be exploring here can most politely be referred to as the lower literary culture of *Rührstücke*. They are more interesting to us for their historical value than for their literary value. But even the inarticulate have something to communicate. In the same vein, even writers of limited artistry have much to tell us about the reception of the tolerance motif and the push for Jewish emancipation at this time.

The dramas include Karl Lotich's *Wer war wohl mehr Jude?* (1783), Heinrich Reinicke's *Nathan der Deutsche* (1784), the anonymous drama *Vorurtheil und Liebe* (1792), Karl Steinberg's *Menschen und Menschensituationen* (1792), Jakob Bischof's *Dina, das Judenmädchen aus Franken* (1802), and Gottfried Julius Ziegelhauser's *Die Juden* (1807). We will discuss the following themes characterized in these dramas: the Jewish paterfamilias, Jewish philanthropy, exogamy, and tolerance.

The Jewish Paterfamilias

Horst Albert Glaser describes the *Rührstück* and other forms of bourgeois drama prevalent in the eighteenth century as "father dramas."[20] The portrayal of the Jewish paterfamilias was a common device for promoting empathy with the Jewish people. In Lotich's *Wer war wohl mehr Jude?* (1783), the Christian Reichardt is portrayed as a morally inferior father in contrast to the Jewish merchant Wolf. Wolf is supportive of his daughter Marie and his future son-in-law Karl and works to build a stable relationship between them. Reichardt, on the other hand, condemns his son for entering into the relationship with Marie and behaves in a very unfatherly manner. Because Marie is a purported Jewess, Reichardt does not want her in his family notwithstanding her virtuous moral character. In burning bridges with his son and future daughter-in-law, Reichardt violates bourgeois norms of the primacy of the family sphere. Wolf affirms these bourgeois values regarding his role as a father and is a better burgher than Reichardt. By demonstrating that the Jewish character fulfills his patriarchal role, Lotich affirms that Jews can be good citizens. Jews and Christians are both part of a larger extended family.

Reinicke's *Nathan der Deutsche* (1784) also represents the patriarchal social structure of which it is a microcosm. The cornerstone of this structure is the authority of the father. Both Wessels and Jenzsch point to the role of Reinicke's Nathan as "Erzieher." [21] However, he does not show the adroitness of Lessing's Nathan in this area. Lessing's Nathan is effective in understanding the psychological underpinnings of his stepdaughter. In performing his paternal duties, Lessing's character is nonauthoritarian. His emphasis is on his didactic function, and not on exerting any overt means of control. The "Erziehung" of Reinicke's Nathan produces the worst characteristics of patriarchalism. It takes the form of a crude manipulation, a means of using material wealth to exert power over people:

> Heinrich: Ich habe auch schon gebetet.
> Jude: Aus Gewohnheit oder Trieb?
> Heinrich: Das versteh' ich nicht.
> Jude: Sag, warum that Du's.
> Heinrich: Weil Sie es mir befohlen haben.
> Jude: Das wäre etwas.
> Heinrich: Weil ich gar so gut geschlafen habe, und der Schlaf wäre, sagten Sie ja letzthin eine Wohltat des Himmels, dafür wollt ich—
> Jude: Danken, nicht wahr! Schön gedacht! Schön gehandelt! Will dich belohnen.[22]

The patriarchal structure of the family is a manifestation of bourgeois ideology. Obedience toward the authority of the father, even if it means hypocrisy, is a precondition for paternal love.

Reinicke's patriarchalism does not remain within the family circle but extends to the society as a whole. Nathan asserts his own authority in the family circle and he asserts the authority of the ruling powers of the society. Nathan is not presented as a vehicle for criticism of the oppression of a powerless minority, but is in fact a spokesperson for the wealthy. He has assimilated himself into society and does not pursue any emancipatory goals for himself or other Jews. He represents the eighteenth-century bourgeois ideal of a separation between state and society, which manifested itself by creating a barrier between "bourgeois" and "political" society.[23]

A division between the private and public sphere is portrayed. Nathan wants no power in the public sphere, but he reigns supreme within his own private sphere. As the last name "Bieder" implies, Nathan is an obedient citizen, not interested in any kind of political power or autonomy. He is promoted as being an exemplary sort of German Jew through the title *Nathan der Deutsche*. When an invalid laments that his war service is responsible for his unfortunate state, Nathan chides him for being bitter. Nathan is appalled by the cripple's understandably critical stance toward society and refuses to help him. On the other hand, he admires the deserter who serves time in prison, because "Er beklagte sich nie über die zu harte Strafe, wie's Bösewichter gewöhnlich tun."[24]

Reinicke's Nathan is a representative of the dominant values of society—an implausible stance when coming from a member of an oppressed minority. However, the author represents the values of the patriarchal social structure. The cornerstone of this patriarchal social structure is the authority of the father. So long as the father has unlimited control over the private sphere, particularly his family circle, he is willing to accord total legitimacy to the governing structures of society and insists that other people do the same.

In *Vorurtheil und Liebe* (1792), the Jew Kronberg is portrayed as a father par excellence. *Vorurtheil und Liebe* is classified by the author as being a *Sittengemälde*, which is defined by Wolfgang Schaer as a mixing of the serious comedy (*rührend weinerliches Lustspiel*) with the domestic tragedy (*bürgerliches Trauerspiel*). The viewer should not be amused, but rather his own world, his own reality, should be presented before his eyes.[25] Along with this realistic approach, the drama should teach proper behavior. The family circle is the natural setting for dramas of this nature: as such, it is common that the *Sittengemälde* should promote patriarchal family structures. At the same time, writers of this sort of drama are critical of fathers who do not meet the expectations placed upon them in their role as patriarchs.

Through the efforts of the noble Jew Kronberg, the Christian banker Mossau is educated to fulfill his middle-class duties and bring the children he fathered into his home. Duty is a pillar of middle-class morals, and, as such, the piece is typical of the bourgeois drama of this time. What is unusual about this play is that the typically bourgeois emphasis on duty is expressed by a Jew. The Jew as spokesperson for bourgeois values is evidence of the perceived interdependence between Jewish emancipation and bourgeois self-interest. The Jewish figure emulates and upholds bourgeois values and thereby attempts to assimilate into bourgeois society. Accordingly, the anonymous author portrays the everyday reality that Jews were at least as capable as Christians of sustaining bourgeois values.

Bischof, in his drama *Dina, das Judenmädchen aus Franken* (1802), portrays the tragic results of a nonauthoritarian style of fatherhood. *Dina* both conforms to and diverges from eighteenth-century conventions of the bourgeois family drama. Nathan is not the authoritarian, patriarchal father typical of the domestic tragedy and the other forms of bourgeois drama prevalent at this time. This circumstance points to a conceptual fissure in the play: Nathan's nonauthoritarianism is condemned as weakness, yet it is also the source of his tolerance, which the author lauds. If Nathan had acted in an authoritarian manner more typical of other characters in the bourgeois drama, such as Schiller's Musikus Miller or Reinicke's Nathan Bieder, the tragedy would have been averted. Nathan's tolerance of the misalliance between Albert and Dina crosses the bounds of probability when he defends Albert before Dina after Albert's engagement to Bianka is publicly announced. Both Miller and Bieder would have given the wellbeing of their daughters priority over a philosophical objection to the barriers toward a mixed marriage. That Nathan continues to promote the match in the face of such unlikely odds is unpersuasive.

In the logic of the piece, Dina's love for Albert is an act of rebellion against Nathan's nonauthoritarianism. In the character of Albert, she finds the authoritarian male that her father is not. She is therefore slavishly obedient to him to the point of death, causing the tragedy. The play criticizes blind obedience to religion, but Dina replaces it with a blind obedience to her lover, which makes her willing to fulfill the most unreasonable of requests made in his name—hence her credulity when her rival Bianka announces that Albert wants Dina dead. Dina's extreme subservience to Albert is a repudiation of the nonauthoritarianism of her father, which, as said, is the source of Nathan's tolerance. The play thereby works against its own discourse. It attempts to promote independence of thought (at least thought independent of the fetters of religion) but also attempts to promote slavish obedience of a woman to a man.

Two mutually exclusive discourses are thereby promoted. Kant's famous pronouncement was "Aufklärung ist der Ausgang des Menschen aus seiner selbstverschuldeten Unmündigkeit. Unmündigkeit ist das Unvermögen, sich seines Verstandes ohne Leitung eines anderen zu bedienen."[26] Nathan expresses an avowal of independence of thought when he criticizes "blinde[n] Gehorsam gegen den Glauben."[27] Yet Dina's goodness is grounded in her obedience to Albert, in her lack of independent thought. This is an inner contradiction under which the play suffers. An emancipatory discourse is mixed with a repressive one: expressions of bourgeois self-interest regarding gender roles mar the main message of the play, which is sympathy with the pariah. The antiauthoritarian discourse of Jewish emancipation enters into dialogue with the authoritarian bourgeois discourse of patriarchy. Dina is cast as a binary opposition between rebel and obedient slave. Her choosing to pursue her love of a Christian is an act of rebellion, but her blind obedience to him is an act of slavery. Patriarchal dominion is a consensus formation which is so firmly grounded in Christian as well as Jewish tradition that it does not occur to Bischof to put it into question.

Jewish Philanthropy

In *Wer war wohl mehr Jude?* (1783), Lotich contrasts the Jewish merchant Wolf with the Christian merchant Reichardt. Because of his wealth, Wolf is able to give money to people in need. The model merchant who happens to be a Jew amasses great wealth, but he uses that wealth to assist others. The Christian merchant Reichardt, true to his charactonym, believes in an exaggerated version of the the Protestant work ethic: whoever falls into misfortune has not worked hard enough and deserves harsh treatment. He lives according to an interpretation of Christianity that is inimical to humanity. Wolf gains acceptance among the Christian community by amassing great wealth and performing acts of philanthropy. In a footnote, Lotich writes: "Wer vielleicht wider meinen Juden einwenden möchte, er sei ein Ideal, er glaube es auf mein Wort, daß in Berlin viele Judenhäuser christliche verschmähte Armen ernähren."[28]

In Reinicke's *Nathan der Deutsche* (1784), Nathan performs a litany of philanthropic acts, including bringing orphans into his home, reuniting families, and feeding the homeless. He performs as many good deeds as does Lessing's Nathan. What he lacks, however, is the noble sentiment and empathy that make Lessing's character so compelling. Without that lofty spirit, the impact of the character is unconvincing. Since Nathan's good deeds are not psychologically motivated, they are dramatically ineffective.[29] One gathers the impression that Nathan performs his philanthropic acts as a showcase for his wealth. Lessing's message of tolerance is diluted and even effaced by Reinicke's trivialization.

Reinicke's message to Jews is that emancipation is to be brought about through the attainment of raw power and that such power can be achieved through the acquisition of material wealth. For Reinicke, the value of a person has nothing to do with religious affiliation, but is to be determined by a person's economic status. Ironically, those few Jews who were able to follow Reinicke's prescription of emancipating themselves through bettering their material status drew a substantial anti-Semitic backlash upon themselves from impoverished Christians who could not tolerate the economic advancement of a pariah group while they themselves were still in poverty.

The emancipatory intent of the author is clearly vitiated by its mediation through an expression of bourgeois self-interest. One of the few philosophical or ideological messages of the text is the attainment of wealth and material advantage as a road to social advancement.

Jewish philanthropy as a means to emancipation is portrayed more convincingly by Ziegelhauser in his drama, *Die Juden* (1807). The Jews are portrayed as making an indispensable contribution to the welfare of the Christian community. They are portrayed as being a separate, but integral, part of the larger Viennese community. They gain the gratitude of the Christian community by performing a major role as community activists, benefactors, and charity providers. A similarity between the ethical postulates of Christianity and Judaism is underscored through the assertion of Jewish adherence to the principle of neighborly love. The principle is portrayed as a unifying factor forging Christians and Jews into a common community: "Es ist Pflicht, die uns zum heiligsten Gebote ist: Einer muß den anderen helfen; Jud und Christ muß einander die Hand bieten, dem menschlichen Elend zu steuern, es regen sich in beyden ähnliche Gefühle des Mitleids."[30] Herzfeld, the leader of the Jewish community, thereby appeals to the anthropological equality between Christians and Jews to work together for the common good.

The Christian state's appreciation of its Jewish community is represented when the prince officially recognizes the good deeds of the Jews. The prince presents Herzfeld with a portrait of the emperor; Herzfeld accepts it graciously as "ein kostbares Geschenk für mein Weniges."[31] The portrayal of the ceremony constitutes a direct refutation of the accusations made by the philosopher Johann Gottlieb Fichte and by other anti-Semites that the Jews were "a state within a state." As leader of the Jewish community, Herzfeld shows himself to be a loyal and patriotic subject of the emperor.

In keeping with other bourgeois demands for tolerance of the Jews, Ziegelhauser is willing to accord the Jews tolerance at a price: the attainment of education and wealth. Only through their extensive material well-being are the Jews able to make their mark on the larger community. The Jews win the love and respect of their non-Jewish fellow villagers only by proving that they are something exceptional. As such, the play constitutes a dramatization of Joseph II's tolerance edict.

Exogamy

In Alan T. Levenson's study, "Jewish Reactions to Intermarriage in Nineteenth-Century Germany," he noted that intermarriage was seen by many Jews as a path to emancipation. It was viewed as being one of the easiest ways of disappearing into German society.[32] It is therefore not surprising that many Gentile writers portrayed exogamy as a means of expressing their belief in Jewish emancipation. However, the way in which such writers portrayed exogamy was fraught with contradictions, which point to hidden ambivalences on the part of the writers.

In Lotich's *Wer war wohl mehr Jude?*, exogamy is used as a means of combining the tolerance theme with a notion of social taboo. Mixed marriages were forbidden by law at this time and the portrayal of the forbidden was designed to arouse interest. Of course, legal barriers to exogamy were routinely circumvented at this time by conversion. But for the writers under discussion, this possible solution was far too simple.

Lotich symbolizes a Christian-Jewish union through the engagement of Karl and Marie. The relationship is portrayed as being the violation of a social taboo. The author thereby hopes to provoke the audience and arouse its interest. Through portraying a happy union between a Christian man and a Jewish woman, Lotich attempts to minimize the importance of the ingroup-outgroup distinction. Lotich's drama, however, suffers from a serious internal contradiction in that Marie is revealed to have been a Christian adopted by a Jewish stepfather before the wedding takes place. Lotich thereby counteracts his own attempt to use the relationship between Marie and Karl as a model for Christian-Jewish relations. He boldly sets out both to tantalize and to instruct his audience by portraying a mixed marriage, but lacks the courage to follow through with it. The contradiction of the intermarriage theme was presumably an attempt to accommodate social taboos in order to avoid having the play suppressed or encountering other social sanctions. The marriage is Marie's entry into bourgeois society and her retroactive transformation into a Christian is a precondition for this passage. Even portraying Marie as voluntarily converting in order to marry might have been too controversial for contemporary audiences, commonplace as it was in real life. By retroactive transformation of Marie into a Christian, Lotich was able to avoid having his play viewed as a frontal attack on antiexogamy laws, which were sanctioned by both church and state.

A similar situation is thematized in Steinberg's *Menschen und Menschensituationen* (1792). In the play, exogamy is the background for portraying the perennial conflict between individual inclination and social responsibility typical of family dramas. The lovers Paul and Recha have no illusions about the problematic nature of their feelings for one another. As Recha attests: "Ich mache einen Jüngling unglücklich, der mir ewig werth, werther als mein Leben ist. Ich verbreite Traurigkeit in einem Haus, wo man sonst nur Freude kennt. . . . Schöpfer, da du Liebe schufst, war da schon Christ oder Jude? Wir sind alle deine Geschöpfe? Warum sollen wir nicht gegenseitige Empfindungen für einander hegen?"[33] The anthropological equality of all human beings is established in the ability of people from differing religions or ethnicities to feel emotional attachment to one another.

A latent tragedy is introduced, as the legally problematic nature of Paul's love for Recha makes him contemplate suicide. The purpose of this tragedy is to evoke the emotions of the audience in order to bring about its moral improvement. Steinberg thereby hopes to reduce prejudice. The union between Paul and Recha is portrayed as being impossible on a mixed marriage basis and at the same time necessary in order to avert tragedy. Steinberg therefore introduces the aesthetically implausible double quirk of fate whereby Paul and Recha were both adopted and Paul's Christian stepfather is Recha's biological father. In so doing, he, like Lotich, contradicts his own effort to use the exogamy theme to promote tolerance. By making the mixed marriage an important manifestation of his avowal of tolerance and then not following through on it, Steinberg dilutes the message and appeal of his play.

Steinberg and Lotich both attempt to promote tolerance by tying it to a tantalizing element of tabooed sexuality, but then do not have the courage of their convictions in following through on the potentially controversial material. While such a practice may be politically astute as an accommodation of rules of exclusion, it is artistically disastrous. For Recha to marry Paul, she must cease to be a Jew, which is brought about not by conversion, but through a highly contrived retroactive transformation of her identity from birth onward.

Lotich and Steinberg are thus able to manipulate happy endings for their Jewish heroines by retroactively denying their Jewishness. The characters are simultaneously Jews and non-Jews, which greatly compromises their minority identities. Bischof, however, maintains the Jewishness of his heroine in *Dina, das Judenmädchen aus Franken* at the price of portraying her tragic demise. A successful marriage union between Christian and Jew at this time, though not unknown in real life, seems to be a practical impossibility for writers portraying Jews on the stage. At the same time, they cannot resist a certain artistic flirtation with the "forbidden" motif.

The problem of pariah status and love is thematized much more timidly and cautiously by Ziegelhauser in *Die Juden*. Instead of portraying a love relationship between an interfaith couple, he portrays two parallel endogamous relationships: one between a Gentile couple and the other between a Jewish couple. The scenes of domestic happiness in both cases promote a positive view of bourgeois family life. The author portrays the participation of both Christians and Jews in bourgeois society on a "separate but equal" basis. The separate but equal situation portrayed by the two sets of lovers is a microcosm for the play as a whole. By portraying the Jews as conforming to bourgeois family values, Ziegelhauser attempts to posit a "sameness" between Christians and Jews. Possibly he was motivated by the problematic nature of contemporary literature portraying exogamy to portray only endogamous relationships in this drama.

Tolerance

In Lotich's *Wer war wohl mehr Jude?*, notions of tolerance are expressed by the elderly couple Wolf saves from financial ruin and by pastor Grosse. Werner, the husband, describes the Enlightened viewpoint of his pastor: "Wie er uns immer die Welt so schön beschreibt und uns Menschenliebe lehrt. Neulich sagt er mal, Heiden und Juden wären unsere Brüder, Gott liebte sie wie uns. Sie würden so gut selig werden, wenn sie fromm lebten."[34] Lotich advocates that the Enlightenment should infiltrate the Protestant Church because only the church has the ability to influence the masses to embrace Enlightenment teachings. In this respect, Lotich's theological perspective is very close to that of the neologists, who sought to bridge the gulf between Christianity and rationalism.

In the figure of Pastor Grosse, we have Lotich's answer to Pfranger's monk of Lebanon. Grosse adheres to Christianity but eschews any notion of Christian particularism and embraces a genuine notion of religious tolerance. Lotich discovered one strategy with which to assail the consensus formation of orthodox Christianity: by putting the ideologemes of religious relativity and tolerance into the mouth of a likable Christian figure, Lotich attempts to infiltrate Christianity with the ideals of the Enlightenment.

There are some points of comparison between Grosse and Pfranger's monk of Lebanon. Like the monk, Grosse is a Christian figure who espouses tolerance. His tolerance concept is, however, much more flexible and true to form than the monk's. Grosse's tolerance is devoid of the Christian particularism that mars and contradicts Pfranger's text. At the same time, even Lotich's tolerance concept requires a close and critical examination. While it is true that Grosse is willing to accord Wolf's religious beliefs equal status with his own, it is also true that what he most values in Wolf is his ability to financially assist the impoverished Anne and Werner.

Nonetheless, it is also instructive to view how Lotich handles the strictly religious issues. Unlike some of the writers thematizing the "Jewish question," Lotich does not want to assail altogether the status of Christianity as a consensus formation. Rather he wishes to redefine the ideological parameters of Christianity to make it more amenable to the concept of Natural Religion. Lotich attempts to imbue the linguistic sign of Christianity with the ideology of Enlightenment and graft a critical discourse onto the dominant discourse of Christianity. He attempts to circumvent rules of exclusion by working within a modification of the dominant discourse.

In the anonymous play *Vorurtheil und Liebe,* the gentile banker Mossau is a believer in Natural Religion. He expresses the belief that moral principles should be separated from religious dogma, that one should be able to respect all who adhere to precepts of morality, regardless of their faith: "Was in dieser Religion Tugend ist, das ist es in jeder anderen. So, wie überall, so weit umher in Gottes Welt Menschen sind, die richtig denken denken 2 mal 2 = 4 ist, so ist auch überall Tugend—Tugend. Was verschlägt das dem Schöpfer, daß der den Hut abzieht, der andere ihn aufsetzt, wenn er betet? . . . Es giebt nur einen Weg zur Seligkeit, den Weg zur Tugend."[35] Mossau's friendship with the Jew Kronberg enables him to entrust his son to Kronberg's care, without any concern that his son is being raised according to the Jewish faith. Mossau is only interested in religion that teaches virtue, and does not care about by which mythological conventions it defines itself. There is however a conceptual fissure in the text: Mossau is unconvincing as a spokesman for noble principles precisely because of his status as an absentee father. While the son Kronberg raises is well-off, the other son lives in poverty. Mossau lacks the moral authority to be an effective spokesperson for tolerance.

Steinberg in *Menschen und Menschensituationen* also thematizes the issue of tolerance. The Jewish merchant Mendel describes himself as a *Weltbürger.* He feels that all human beings are part of the same family. By having Mendel assert an avowal of world citizenship, Steinberg demonstrates a continuity with Lessing. Like Lessing's Nathan, Mendel distances himself from any notion of ingroup identification with other Jews: "Alle Menschen sind meine Brüder, ich tue jedem Gutes, so viel ich kann, verachte den schlechtdenkenden Juden und ehre den rechtschaffenden Christen."[36] There is an implicit avowal made by the Gentile author that for Jews to distance themselves from their ingroup is a route to emancipation. Notions of ingroup identification are replaced by an appeal to the anthropological equality of all human beings.

Nathan, the father in Bischof's *Dina, das Judenmädchen aus Franken,* also advocates the notion of anthropological equality as a basis for human relations, and he laments the fact that it is not consistently put into practice. Because of the existence of prejudice, he has serious misgivings about the love match between Albert and Dina. Nonetheless, he feels that this relationship is justifiable under the laws of anthropological equality:

> Eure Liebe ist unschuldig. Natur und Vernunft verdammen sie nicht, aber die Menschen werden sie verdammen. Noch nicht allgemein erwärmt die Herzen diese Wahrheit: das Mensch Mensch ist, wir alle Kinder eines Vaters sind, der uns alle mit gleicher Liebe liebt, wir mögen ihn so oder so verehren, wenn sie nur gut und reines Herzens sind—Unter den Christen gleichen die wenigsten unserem Linau, und wie ich mit meinen Glaubensgenossen stehe, das weißt Du selbst. Längst schon bin ich ihnen ein Dorn im Auge, weil sie mich für einen heimlichen Anhänger des Gekreuzigten halten.[37]

While Nathan fears that his daughter and her lover will face the untoward consequences of prejudice, he acknowledges that their love is perfectly legitimate under the rules of reason. Nathan's speech is an ideologeme representing the relativity of religious belief. The fact that he is regarded by his fellow Jews with some suspicion is the result of his not being a traditional Jew. The tolerance of the Jew for members of other religious groups leads to his distancing and isolation from the Jewish ingroup.

The fact that other Jews regard Nathan as a closet Christian dilutes Nathan's sense of common identity with them. His tolerance toward Christians is equated with his "outsiderness" among Jews. Emancipation is cast in terms of a quid pro quo requiring the members of the minority group to alienate themselves from their own ingroup in order to be accepted into the larger society.

We have seen that Christian bourgeois dramatists concerned themselves quite extensively with the issue of Jewish emancipation, portraying "good" Jewish characters in the medium most popular with middle-class audiences at that time, that of the family drama. The bourgeois writers, however, often walk a fine line between promoting unconditional emancipation of Jews and demanding Jewish assimilation. In portraying Jews in a manner with which they can sympathize, the playwrights often recreate them in their own images. In a very real sense, the bourgeois portrayal of the Jews constituted a restructuring, domination, and exertion of authority over them.[38] The good Jew is consistently portrayed as being wealthy enough to materially contribute to the less well-off in his or her community, when in fact Jews were often among the least well-off. Portrayals of the Jews by Christian writers often have more to do with the Gentile world than they do with the Jewish world. The literary representations constitute little more than cardboard, artificial enactments of Gentile conceptions of emancipated Jews. Because Gentiles had the more powerful culture, they had the ability to give shape to the popular image of the Jew. Although these authors deserve credit for trying to upgrade the Jews' popular image, these efforts must be viewed through a dialectizing optic.

By portraying Jews as improbably noble and incredibly rich and generous, authors promoted unreasonable expectations of the Jewry and underestimated the difficulties they would have in adjusting to the dominant culture after emancipation. But even those Jews who could live up to bourgeois expectations did not have it made. They drew the wrath of the antibourgeois elements, such as the peasants and aristocracy, upon themselves.

Bourgeois writers promoted a model of Judaism suitable for the emerging capitalistic culture of the bourgeoisie. In portraying "good" Jews, these authors expressed their expectations as to what constituted a good Jew. The good Jew became synonymous with the successful bourgeois, a factor that had not only literary-historical significance, but also far-reaching sociological implications. Such attitudes on the part of middle-class writers and people in the general public had the tendency to encourage Jews to distance themselves from their own ingroup. Such persons advocated the utopian ideal of "full social absorption of Jews into non-Jewish society."[39] However, Jews remained strangers to the society even when they adapted to the society.[40] In the meantime, anti-Semitic writers had a chance to regroup and make their views more widely known in German society.

5. Myths of Ethnic Homogeneity: Anti-Semitic Literature after 1800

Anti-Semitic Political Pamphleteers

Although the Enlightenment—to a certain extent—successfully modified the status of Christianity as a consensus formation, it was unable to prevent more pernicious forms of group formation and ingroup identification from arising.

The struggle against Napoleon's domination led to the emergence of a quasi-religious nationalism. The effort to throw off the yoke of the French occupation led to an "urgent search for German authenticity . . . [and] redemption" which led to the "messianic notion of the Germans as a new chosen race."[1] This gave rise to the notion of an unchanging ethnically homogeneous identity which manifested itself in a lauding of everything German and a denigration of everything non-German, including the Jews.[2] German "insecurity and resentment" were inflamed by the situation of Jews having "escaped from the ghetto, becoming 'German' in appearance but still remaining Jews either in a religious, or, more insidiously, in a social or psychological sense."[3]

The primacy of the Christian ingroup no longer revolved as much upon religious as upon national identity. Nationalism provided a secular outlet for the need to feel group kinship. On the other hand, it also supplied sustenance to racist ideologies. The notion of "national character" was a precursor for racist thinking and was a major component in the development of modern anti-Semitism.[4]

According to Elenore Sterling, nationalistic-Germanic anti-Semitism was the ideology of an authoritarian state. On account of the revolutionary changes in France and the resulting social transformations in Germany, the governing powers had become unsure of their absolutist status and had to clothe their ideology in a more irrationalistic manner. Anti-Semitism was at the same time, paradoxically, an ideology of political expression for an oppressed people. They had been made aware of their social and economic needs through the Wars of Liberation, but did not yet understand the advantages of a liberal-parliamentary government.[5]

Anti-Semitism was an expression of the political powerlessness of the broad masses. It was a misguided protest against the social problems of the time. It can therefore be seen as a means of diverting the people against their own interests and using them for reactionary purposes.[6] The Germans were disappointed by the French Revolution and did not want to repeat its mistakes. Instead of viewing the French Revolution in a differentiated manner, to take cognizance of its progressive moments and to attempt to improve on these, they tried to revive a prerevolutionary social ideology: the cult of *Germanentum*.[7]

German nationalism was rapidly becoming a major consensus formation at the beginning of the nineteenth century. As we have already discussed, group formation is largely linguistic in character. Propaganda is one widely used medium for cementing a group together. Although various studies of literature and propaganda have appeared, the most useful work in this area is still Jacques Ellul's sociological study, *Propaganda: The Formation of Men's Attitudes* (1968), which will here be quoted at length.

By its very nature, propaganda addresses the masses: "The individual is of no interest to the propagandist, as an isolated unit he presents too much resistance to external action."[8] Propaganda's goal is monologue: propaganda ceases where dialogue begins. The individual is never considered as an individual, "but always in terms of what he has in common with others. . . . He is reduced to an average."[9]

Propaganda appeals to what Horkheimer and Adorno call the mimetic impulse.[10] Ellul calls the presuppositions upon which propaganda is based "a collection of feelings, beliefs, and images by which one unconsciously judges events and things without questioning them or even noticing them."[11]

To be effective, propaganda not only has to try to engender new consensus formations but must utilize and exploit existing ones. Often they are consensus formations of mythic proportions, which exert unconscious influences on their subjects: "The myth expresses the deep inclinations of a society. . . . It is a vigorous impulse, strongly colored, irrational, and charged with all of men's power to believe."[12]

Propaganda by its very nature depends upon the dynamics of group identity and formation: "Propaganda is effective not when based on an individual interest, but when based on a *collective* center of interest, shared by the crowds."[13] A tightly organized group formation tends to foster the active and effective use of propaganda. On the other hand, the absence of such a group formation is inimical to the success of propaganda.[14]

The attempts of Lessing and other authors of the Enlightenment to distance the Christian majority from a rigid sense of ingroup identification by criticism, dialogue, and tolerance were contrary to the spirit of propaganda: whoever succeeds in keeping aloof from an intense ingroup identification is usually outside the influence of propaganda, whereas "the individual who is part of an intense collective life is prone to submit to the influence of propaganda."[15]

Propaganda exploits latent drives that are vague, unclear, and generally unfocused and makes them powerful, direct, and precise, transforming them into prejudices.[16] It encourages individuals to think that they are right in harboring such prejudices and reinforces antagonisms and hatreds toward people outside their own group context.[17] Propaganda utilizes and directs an individual's hatreds.[18] It supplies people who before had only some unspecified notions with prefabricated judgments.[19]

Stereotypes are homogenized with a resulting codification of political, social, and moral standards.[20] Propaganda is a major element in the construction of consensus formations. Whereas Lessing and other emancipatory authors sought to enter into dialogue with the Christian hegemony and extend the range of permissible discourse, the propagandistic literature that followed these authors promoted monologue. Propaganda seeks to build monolithic individuals: "It eliminates inner conflicts, tensions, self-criticism, doubt" and creates "a system of opinions which may not be subjected to criticism."[21]

This phenomenon results in the formation of rules of exclusion, which limit the field of thought and make rapprochement with unlike or nonidentical persons less likely. Propaganda is one means through which the agents of the dominant group define and limit the discourses and parameters of group identity. This will at times evoke minority responses, which reinforce the hostility of the dominant group.[22]

One sign of the growing trend toward anti-Semitism was the growing popularity of Carl Wilhelm Friedrich Grattenauer, an author of anti-Semitic pamphlets. His earliest pamphlet, *"Über die physische und moralische Verfassung der heutigen Juden"* (1791) was read by almost nobody. But the later *Wider die Juden* (1802) had a wide readership and went through numerous printings.[23]

Grattenauer, a Prussian jurist and public official in the Justice Ministry, combined religious, nationalistic, and economic elements in his anti-Semitism. *Wider die Juden* is subtitled *Ein Wort der Warnung an unsere christlichen Mitbürger*. It shows a familiarity with the anti-Semitic literature that preceded it and contains several unattributed quotations from such sources as the notorious early eighteenth-century anti-Semite Johann Andreas Eisenmenger and the idealistic philosopher Johann Gottlieb Fichte, also known for his strident anti-Semitism.

In Grattenauer's text, both the paranoic quality of anti-Semitism and the neurotic nature of propaganda in general become clear: Grattenauer claims that Jews will dominate over and enslave the Gentile population if they are given full equal rights.[24] Grattenauer plays on the economic fears of his readership. He attempts to give these fears body and definition by uniting them with his interpretation of the "Jewish question." He recreates the Jews in his own image: a member of the powerful dominant group represents an oppressed minority as being powerful.[25] He thereby inverts Dohm's arguments that empowerment of the Jews will make them more useful citizens.

The Jews are viewed as being the primary beneficiaries of the labors of Christians. He seeks to exploit Jew-hatred and give definition to it and thereby make it part of the prevailing ideology. Grattenauer proceeds with a historical account alleging Jewish misdeeds since ancient times. Timeworn prejudices against Jews are repeated, such as blaming them for the poisoning of wells in the Middle Ages. The prejudices recounted here are such as those already refuted by Menassah ben Israel in his *Vindiciae Judaeorum* and by Mendelssohn in his preface to the German version of that work.

Grattenauer's discourse is irrational and self-contradictory:

> Auch in Wien, wo die Juden seit einiger Zeit so mächtig geworden sind, wurden sie . . . wegen vorübter Mordthaten, Diebereien, und ruchlosen Laster am 4. Febr. 1670 sämmtlich vertrieben. Nach den neuesten Nachrichten haben sie jetzt von neuem die ehrlichen christlichen Kaufleute so bedrückt, daß alle, die nicht 20,000 Floren Vermögen nachweisen können, die Stadt räumen sollen.[26]

The claim that Jews are powerful is a false projection of power onto them. Fear is a powerful mobilizer of hatred. Grattenauer's argumentation is specious on its face. The Jews are said to "oppress" Christian merchants, when they are in fact the oppressed: poorer Jews are driven out of the city.

Grattenauer makes the claim that Jews are murderous, which is a false projection of his own violent, aggressive hatred toward Jews. Jews committed fewer murders than Christians. Yet Grattenauer denies that Jews have any vestige of humanity. Grattenauer is astonished that the Jews show sympathy for the sufferings of other Jews and attributes it to physical factors, because he maintains they do not have the same sympathy for Gentiles. This is a dehumanizing false differentiation of the Jews from the Gentiles. He finds Jewish sympathy inexplicable because he views Jews as being a murderous and cowardly race. The renowned psychologist Otto Fenichel explains the prejudice that Jews are murderous with the fact that they are uncanny: they dress differently and speak differently and live in ghettos. The murderous fantasies and impulses are forbidden; therefore, the subject must dispel of them somehow. He dispels of them by projecting them onto an uncanny people, that is, the Jews.[27]

Horkheimer and Adorno describe the anti-Semites as paranoids following the laws of their own sicknesses. They do so by attempting to make their environment more similar to themselves.[28] They therefore project their forbidden impulses onto the outside world, for example, onto a weaker people. Grattenauer projects his own violent impulses onto the Jews. In order to do this, he must dehumanize them by making their humane characteristics into objects of wonder.

Grattenauer argues that Jews are incapable of being integrated into bourgeois society: "Vergeblich ist jede Hoffnung, daß sich der verderbliche der bürgerlichen Gesellschaft höchst gefährliche, allen Völkern feindselige Geist des Judenthums je ändern, und in einem freundlichen wohltätigen Genius der Menschheit verwandeln wird."[29] He maintains that Jews are unsuitable for integration because Jewish religious precepts only apply in relation to other Jews. He believes that Jews are therefore permitted to cheat Gentiles. He argues that the provision for the forgiveness of sin in the Jewish religion allows Jews to cheat, or even assault, Gentiles and be forgiven for it.[30]

This is quite ironic in view of the fact that Christianity contains a similar provision for forgiveness of sin. His claim that Jews are permitted to commit violent acts against Gentiles is another sign of his paranoia. This argument did not originate with Grattenauer, but was lifted from Johannes Andreas Eisenmenger's *Entdecktes Judentum* (1711). Because he views Jewish religious precepts as only applying in relationships with other Jews, Grattenauer believes that a total apartheid system should exist between Jews and Gentiles: "so lange Juden- und Christenthum existirt, muß jedes in sich geschloßen, und eine große Kluft dazwischen gefestigt bleiben."[31]

He views Judaism as being an inherently inferior religion to Christianity: the Christian religion demands a belief in the incomprehensible and eternal elements, whereas Judaism attempts to explain the contradictions of this life. Grattenauer lauds Christianity as a mystical religion and condemns Judaism as an earthbound, rationalistic religion. His conception of Judaism as a rationalistic religion reveals a familiarity with Moses Mendelssohn. The theological duality he sets between mystical/good and rationalistic/bad is similar to that established by Tralles and Pfranger (see Chapter 2).

118 Myths of Ethnic Homogeneity

Grattenauer is, on the other hand, much more hateful in his attitude toward Jews. Pfranger seeks patiently and forbearingly to convert the Jews, Grattenauer is against conversion. He maintains:

> Soll man einen Juden von Geburt, der länger als bis in sein zehntes Jahr im Judenthume erzogen ist, zum Christenthume aufnehmen; und wenn es nicht gehindert werden darf, welche Vorsichtigkeits-Maaßregeln sind bei seiner Aufnahme erforderlich, und welche Beweise seiner Bekehrung kann man von ihm fordern? ["]Wäre es nicht weit leichter und zweckmäßiger, statt die Juden die Köpfe zu waschen, sie ihnen unmaßgeblich gleich abzuschneiden, und andere anzusetzen, in denen sich nicht eine einzige jüdische Idee befindet? ["][32]

The last sentence of this passage is an unattributed quotation from the anti-Semitic philosopher Fichte. Grattenauer rejects Mendelssohn's arguments for tolerance that were based on the mutual interdependence between Judaism and Christianity because Judaism is the parent religion. Grattenauer maintains that the derivation of Christianity from Judaism cannot be proved. He refers to "die diametrale Antithese der christlichen Religion gegen alle Religionen der Welt."[33] His is a chauvinistic, particularistic conception of Christianity. To acknowledge Christianity's relationship to other religions such as Judaism would be to acknowledge the legitimacy of other religions. Grattenauer is an advocate of the reactionary ideology of monologism: he wishes to wipe alternative discourses off the face of the earth.

Grattenauer's anti-Semitism is different from the religiously motivated anti-Judaism of Pfranger. Pfranger would have been satisfied with the conversion of the Jews, but Grattenauer shows a hatred toward the Jews regardless of whether they convert or not. Grattenauer is an early advocate of a "racial" approach to the "Jewish question."

He believes that Jews are absolutely unfit for inclusion in broader society: Jews cannot be citizens because they do not live among Christians but from them. Their culture and their religious maxims do not promote the ethical values that will make them good citizens, maintains Grattenauer. Grattenauer postulates a strict dichotomy between Germanness and Jewishness: uniquely Jewish traits such as religion, differences in values, and instruction and raising of the young are seen as being incompatible with belonging to the German ingroup. Grattenauer demonstrates a total inability to accept any kind of outgroup differentiation from rigidly defined norms.

The lawyer Grattenauer expresses many prejudices that had already been refuted by Dohm. He believes that Jewish religious values

Myths of Ethnic Homogeneity 119

and ethical teachings would interfere with Jews taking an active role as citizens, and that therefore, citizenship should not be granted them. Grattenauer shows many economically motivated prejudices toward Jews, resulting from their involvement in money circulation: "Sind sie [die Juden] nicht in der Regel so wenig Produzenten als Künstler, und plündern sie dennoch nicht beide durch ihren Handel und Wucher? Ruinieren Sie nicht die Fabrikanten, und ergeben nicht die Akten der Finanzbehörden, daß zwei Drittheile aller Manifakturisten Bettler sind, die das Unglück haben, israelitische Entrepreneurs in die Hände zu fallen?"[34] Again Grattenauer exploits the economic fears of the general populace to give the appearance of substance to his propaganda.

Grattenauer's criticism of the Jewish specialization in money circulation is hypocritical because it fails to acknowledge that Christian society excluded Jews from practicing most other professions. He makes the exaggerated claim that Jews create a need to borrow money by controlling most of the money in circulation: "Hätten die Juden aber nicht hier und da mehr als die Hälfte des koursierenden Landesgeldes in Händen, so würde man selten in die Verlegenheit kommen, etwas borgen zu müssen."[35] Grattenauer is trying to enlist the support of the debt-ridden peasants and handworkers, as well as the equally indebted lower nobility, for his expression of anti-Semitic ideology.

Grattenauer's anti-Semitism also shows signs of having been influenced by the new nationalistic fervor and anti-French feeling. He views Jewish emancipation as an undesirable and outdated byproduct of the French Revolution. Grattenauer supports German nationalism as a new consensus formation, whose rules of exclusion include a prohibition of "sansculottisms." By defining Jewish emancipation as a sansculottism and as a Jacobin blasphemy, Grattenauer attempts to make it seem non-German and specifically to unite it with the hated discourse of the French Revolution. Grattenauer tries to work against Jewish emancipation through an appeal to German national fervor, which has the rejection of the nonidentical as one of its central components.

Grattenauer's *Wider die Juden* is—like much of the anti-Semitic literature of this era—a transitional work between a traditional religiously based anti-Semitism and an anti-Semitism that defined Jews in terms of their economic functions. Grattenauer's anti-Semitism contains both traditional religious and modern economic terms. Grattenauer tries to suppress critical discourses promoting ethnoreligious tolerance and to promote the monologic hegemony of a mystical Christian-based nationalism.

Grattenauer's tract helped popularize his brand of anti-Semitism and won him many imitators and emulators.[36] One of these emulators was Friedrich Buchholz, an impoverished scrivener and would-be civil servant who expressed his own anti-Semitic leanings in the pamphlet *Moses und Jesus oder über das intellektuelle und moralische Verhältniß der Juden und Christen* (1803). Although he purported to be a Deist, Buchholz's discourse is laden with Christian particularism. He never abandoned his need for a fervent ingroup identification with Christianity. Buchholz tries to disengage dialogue between the Christian and Jewish communities through his defamatory rhetoric against Moses Mendelssohn. To many Christians, Mendelssohn represented a convincing proof that Christians and Jews could harmoniously coexist. Buchholz seeks to remove this barrier to a monolithic Christian consensus formation by inflaming hatred against Mendelssohn: "Moses Mendelssohn in seinem *Jerusalem* behauptet: Jesus sey mit vollem Rechte gekreuzigt worden. Dies Urtheil rührt blos daher, daß Moses Mendelssohn nie das Mindeste von der Tendenz des Christenthums und dessen ganzen Wesen begriffen hat."[37] By falsely accusing Mendelssohn of advocating Christ's execution, Buchholz attempts to inflame old prejudices that the Jews were guilty of deicide and thereby impose a Christian monologism upon German society.

He openly accuses all Jews of being deicidal and maintains that Mendelssohn only confirmed them on their path of error. Buchholz tells the Jews that their ancestors crucified a saint only because he wanted to convert them from Judaism, and they praise those who confirm their path of foolishness. He condemns Mendelssohn for having strengthened the Jewish faith, and thereby prevented conversions to the one "true" belief. Buchholz disparages Judaism by maintaining that all present and future generations of Jews share a collective guilt for the death of Christ. He views Judaism as somehow posing a threat to his own culture and is unwilling to accord it any degree of tolerance. His writings are further evidence of the paranoic nature of anti-Semitism. Judaism is portrayed as something that must be stamped out.

He rejects Mendelssohn's argument that Christianity is partially dependent on Jewish traditions by asserting:

> Das Christenthum verhält sich zu dem Judenthum, wie die Newtonsche Philosophie zu der Astrologie des 13. und 14. Jahrhunderts. So wie diese Philosophie eine höhere Entwickelung der ihr vorangegangener Astrologie ist, eben so ist das Christenthum eine höhere Entwickelung des Judenthums, und so wenig jene ihre

Beweise aus den Werken der Astrologen schöpft; eben so wenig schöpft dieses seine Wahrheit aus den Nazionalbüchern der Juden.[38]

Buchholz's argumentation is similar to that of Johann Georg Pfranger, who felt that Judaism is a primitive and inferior religion. Both men eschew any notion of giving Judaism equal status with Christianity, but Buchholz goes even farther than Pfranger. Buchholz maintains that the major purpose of Christianity from its very founding was to extirpate Judaism from the world. He thereby maintains that anti-Semitism is an integral part of Christianity, wished upon it by Christ himself. Through his anti-Jewish rhetoric, Buchholz attempts to argue that Christ himself was anti-Semitic and that, therefore, no one can maintain a group identification with Christianity without adopting an anti-Semitic stance. He argues that tolerance and adherence to Christianity are two mutually exclusive propositions. Only with the decimation of Judaism, maintains Buchholz, can morality in life and society be promoted.

By portraying Jews as being inimical to morality, Buchholz attempts to unify his Christian ingroup under the banner of Jew-hatred. Like Grattenauer, Buchholz seeks to prey upon the fears of his audience regarding their own economic well-being. He maintains that Jews have a perverted, fetishistic relationship to money: "Der Jude liebt das Leben um des Geldes willen, indeß der Christ (und jeder Nicht-Jude) das Geld nur um des Lebens Willen liebt."[39] Buchholz argues that Jews have an inherent predisposition toward money and that this obsession with money prevents them from participating in the broader German culture. Their single-minded consideration of money limits their value to society as a whole. Buchholz fails to comment on the arguments advanced by Dohm, Mendelssohn, and other emancipatory writers that the Jewish concentration in the money industry was a direct result of the dominant Christian society prohibiting them from other pursuits. Buchholz instead attributes this money concentration of the Jews to their inherent moral failings: Jews despise everything that does not have to do with money and, because they already think they know everything, they cannot be instructed to do other things with their lives.

He does not even attempt to adapt his rhetoric to arguments about the extent to which the Jewish concentration on money circulation was imposed on them by the restrictions of the dominant Christian group. He views any restrictions placed upon Jews as being per se legitimate.

He argues not only that usury is inherent in Jews, but also argues, quite unconscionably, that it is unique to them: "Der Wucher liegt in dem staatsbürgerlichen Verhältnis des Juden zum Christen, aber er liegt nicht in dem Verhältnis des Christen zum Christen, außer etwa, in sofern der Jude ihn auch hier erzwingt."[40] He attempts to exploit the economic fears of the working class and mobilize it into a united front of anti-Semitism. Buchholz warns economically troubled Christians that the working class is beginning to hate its fatherland, because of the "monetary despotism" of the Jews. Buchholz makes Jews a scapegoat for the economic woes of the entire populace and thereby seeks to unite a Christian hegemony against them. He argues that the presence of Jews prevents German Gentiles from loving their land. The oppression of the Jews is suddenly elevated into a "patriotic" stance.[41]

The elevation of anti-Semitism into such a stance of patriotism reaches its most extreme in the work of the national Romantic poet and pamphleteer Ernst Moritz Arndt. The political Romantics espoused the ideals of German nationalism and conservatism, which had the effect of raising the state to the highest ideal. The state took on many of the functions previously reserved for religion, such as providing an outlet for feelings of social kinship and enthusiasm.[42] Arndt sought to exploit religion by subordinating it to the interests of the state: his ideal was Christianity in the service of Germanness.[43] He viewed a national religion as being a necessity in order to effect the codification of national customs.[44]

The emergence of a *Volksgeist* depended upon the sustenance of a "national" religion.[45] Arndt unceasingly tried to draw parallels between Christianity and Germanness to raise nationalism to a consensus formation of the level of which religion had been.[46] In Arndt's eyes, the struggle for the fatherland in the form of the anti-Napoleonic Wars of Liberation was a struggle for God: Germans were to be bound together through a great communal hatred toward the French, which was to reach religious proportions.[47] The entire struggle for the fatherland against the tyrant contained the character of a religious devotion: the goal of God's tribunal was the support and encouragement of the German *Volk*.[48]

According to Arndt, the Germans were the children of God, because they were not "corrupted" through intermarriage with foreign peoples, but were a "pure" and "original" people.[49] Léon Poliakov described Arndt as "a fierce gallophobe [who] advocated a system of watertight bulkheads between the peoples of Europe."[50] Arndt subscribed to the philosophy of the cult of the Germanic race. Poliakov continues, "The Germanic obsession with purity of blood led to a condemnation of the Jews even in the absence of a specific hatred. It produced the German prototype of the patriot who was not subjectively an anti-Semite but who was hostile to Jews because he professed the myth of race."[51]

Arndt was principally known as the poet who "called his people to arms, urging them to drive out the foreign tyrant."[52] But "the idea of 'impure blood,' blood which was required to water the furrows on both sides of the Rhine, in Germany, quickly became that of inferior blood."[53] Arndt expressed his views on the "Jewish question" in his pamphlet *Blick aus der Zeit auf die Zeit* (1814), particularly in the chapter "Noch etwas über die Juden." Arndt is a sophisticated propagandist in that he knows how to work the written word in a devious and manipulative manner. He starts his chapter with soft words of sympathy for the Jews but gradually becomes more and more anti-Semitic. Arndt thereby gives his monologic, authoritarian voice the false appearance of dialogism. This is an effective propaganda technique in that it gives a veneer of fairness and objectivity to the work and therefore confirms people in their prejudices by making them feel justified in their anti-Semitism.

Arndt begins with a disclaimer against those who would castigate him for his inhumane views. He denies that he is anti-Semitic and deigns to have sympathy for the Jews: "Der menschliche Mensch muß die Juden als Opfer ansehen, und sie wenigstens bedauern, wenn er sie nicht ehren kann."[54] However, he does not hesitate to condemn Judaism as an outdated religion: he describes Jews as being "Verstockt und versteint gegen die Stimme der warnenden und rufenden Geister der Zeit."[55] Jews are to him inherently unequal to German Gentiles: "Man kann sie [die Juden] bedauern und man muß sie bedauern, aber lieben kann man sie nicht, denn Liebe wird nur gebohren aus dem Gleichartigen und Geselligen, welches diesem Volke fehlt, das in seiner abgeschloßenen Art und Weise und mit seinem wunderbaren Gesetze unter den europäischen Völkern dieser Zeit wie ein Fremdling ist."[56] Arndt's discourse is permeated with the hatred of otherness: whoever has "foreign" customs cannot possibly be regarded as an equal and can justifiably be further oppressed. According to Arndt, the only concession the good German has to grant members of the oppressed minority is to pity them their status as nonidenticals. But he is totally against any measures that would lead to a respect for ethnic and religious otherness. On the contrary, he views Jews as a threat against which German Gentiles must be protected: Jews do not fit into the German state. They are a completely foreign people and should not be allowed to increase their population. Germans should be discouraged from miscegenation with foreign peoples, and therefore the society needs to be protected against Jews.[57]

Arndt advocates the continuation of oppressive policies that were designed to control the population of the Jews, such as the imposition of special taxes and financial penalties upon them. Arndt's view of the "Jewish question" goes beyond either religious or economic anti-Semitism and can best be described as racial anti-Semitism.

Arndt believes that modern society can only be constructed under the principles of religioethnic homogeneity: "Fast allen unseren Einrichtungen, Ordnungen, und Gesetzen fremd, sind sie [die Juden] durchaus unfähig, in einem christlichen Staate volle Bürger zu seyn: denn wie mag alle Bürgerrechte haben, wer nicht alle Bürgerpflichten erfüllen kann?"[58] Arndt despised the theological views of eighteenth-century rationalists who advocated religious tolerance and cosmopolitanism: he believed that rationalistic theology took religion away and drove humankind toward atheism.[59]

But more than religious homogeneity, Arndt desires racial purity and decries any developments that will lead to mixtures between differing ethnic peoples: "Das Geschlecht der Mischlinge auf dem Gränzscheiden der Völker [ist] gewöhnlich ein leichtfertiges, zuchtloses, und treuloses Geschlecht."[60] Arndt views the Jews as being an ethnically mixed, and hence inferior, race whereas he views the Germans as being a bastion of ethnic purity. He feels that the entrance of other ethnic groups into Germany poses a substantial threat: "Weil es [Deutschland] der Mittelpunkt des Welttheils ist, so dringt man von allen Seiten das Fremde darauf ein, und auch von den Juden bekömmt es jährlich einen zu reichlichen Zufluß."[61] He maintains that "Teuschland hat aber das traurige Schicksal, daß es . . . von einer Judensündfluth bedroht wird" and tries to unify a German ingroup opposed to Judaism.[62] Arndt tries to build ingroup identification not only around concepts of religion, but to an even greater extent around notions of blood and soil. His ideology goes beyond orthodox Christianity and may have been influenced by superstitious uses of Nordic mythology, which Arndt considered to be more "genuine" and "unmediated" than orthodox Lutheranism.[63] Poliakov sees Arndt as one of the architects of the "Aryan myth" and points out that the Nazis saw him as one of their ideological precursors.[64]

In addition to the largely economically motivated anti-Semitism of Grattenauer and Buchholz and the clearly racially motivated anti-Semitism of Ernst Moritz Arndt, the more "traditional" religiously motivated anti-Semitism proved to have considerable staying power well into this era. This situation is best demonstrated through an examination of the Berlin historian Friedrich Rühs's pamphlet *Ueber die Ansprüche der Juden an das deutsche Bürgerrecht* (1815). Rühs is opposed

Myths of Ethnic Homogeneity 125

to the notion of separation of church and state: he views German society as being a Christian society and therefore postulates that Christian belief should be a prerequisite for full participation in that society. He posits an indivisibility between Christianity and Germanness:

> Das wahrhaft sittlich Leben, dessen Beförderung der letzte Zweck aller Staaten sein soll, kann unter den christlichen Völkern nur ein christlicher seyn, mithin sind auch die Staaten, worin sie zerfallen, christliche. Der größte Theil unsrer bürgerlichen Rechte und Verpflichtungen fällt unmittelbar mit unserem Glauben zusammen und es ist von der wahren Aufklärung zu erwarten, daß sie immer genauer wieder mit demselben in Verbindung gesetzt werden.[65]

Like so many other people during this era, Rühs wishes to impose a Christian monologism upon German society. He therefore cannot accept the presence of Judaism, because Judaism by its very existence signifies that there is an alternative to Christian belief and inflicts fissures upon the bullwark of the Christian consensus formation: especially if Judaism were to be granted equal civic status with Christianity, then the conclusion would be inescapable that there are at least two legitimate religious points of view. The society would therefore be dialogized and democratized. Rühs wishes to avoid this and therefore maintains that equal rights should be granted to Jews only if they convert to Christianity:

> So lange die Juden Juden bleiben wollen, erklären sie sich für eine besondere und abgesonderte Nation; sie erklären, daß sie nicht mit dem Volk, unter welchem sie leben, zu einem Ganzen verschmelzen wollen. . . . [Ein] Gegensatz findet zwischen Juden und Deutschen statt; die Erhaltung ihrer Volkseigenthümlichkeit ist an ihre Religion gebunden, die zugleich eine trennende politische Tendenz hat.[66]

Rühs's position is basically a recapitulation of Fichte's infamous formulation of the Jews being "a state within a state." Nonetheless Rühs's pamphlet also shows the impact of traditional Lutheran teaching on the "Jewish question" in that he seeks to convert Jews to the "superior" religion of Christianity. In a stance reminiscent of Tralles and Pfranger, Rühs advocates a temporary forbearance of the Jews in order to convert them to Christianity: a sort of "pretextual tolerance." In the meantime, Rühs promotes the continued imposition of career restrictions on the Jews and the extraction of special taxes upon them in the form of letters of protection. Rühs demands that Jews be further relegated to a status as second-class citizens and that, at the same time, they should acknowledge their right to live within German society under conditions of oppression as a privilege granted them by the Germans. He rejects the contentions of the Enlighteners that granting Jews equal rights will make them better citizens: "Der Charakter eines Volks wird durch mannichfaltige Einwirkungen bestimmt. Außer der ursprünglichen Anlage sind am wichtigsten Religion und Staatsverfassung: aus diesen beiden Elementen muß man das Eigenthümliche des jüdischen Charakters erklären; der in Spanien wie in Polen derselbe war."[67] Rühs maintains that the moral failings he believes exist in the Jews are caused not by their oppression but by their religion. He therefore wrote his pamphlet urging the Congress of Vienna not to support the Napoleonic-imposed emancipation of the Jews. His ideas are motivated by the all-too-prevalent hatred of the nonidentical.

Although the forms of anti-Semitism expressed by Grattenauer, Buchholz, Arndt, and Rühs were all differing aspects of the dominant discourse of this time, such views did not go altogether unrefuted. Some marginalized voices from the periphery of society rose to challenge these pernicious elements of a new nationalistic anti-Semitism. Most notable among these minority voices was that of Saul Ascher, the German Jewish Enlightener and popular philosopher, in his pamphlet *Die Germanomanie* (1815).

Ascher's polemic does not take the form of a direct argumentation, but an alternatively shocked and bemused repetition of his opponents' positions which adequately voices his disapproval of them. He ridicules Rühs's arguments regarding restricting the population of and the eventual conversion of the Jews: "Man soll ferner der Juden Vermehrung in Deutschland durch Einwanderung verhindern! Als wenn dies nicht schon längst geschehen wäre. Und soll endlich der Juden Uebergang zum Christenthum befördern, damit sie zu Deutschen umgebildet werden! Als wenn das Christenthum die unumgängliche Bedingung der Deutschheit wäre."[68] Ascher is obviously not writing to win new converts to his point of view, but is addressing those who already share his viewpoint. He does not go so far as to debate or refute formally the anti-Semites, but regards an accurate rehashing of their ideas as refutation enough. Ironic understatement is an important element to his mode of argumentation.

He shows a highly developed sense of irony when he examines the attempts of the German nationalists to combat the "tyranny" of foreign elements by making the society more repressive, monolithic, and monologic: he ridicules notions that Germany can only overcome foreign tyranny through unity of religion and ideas.[69]

Ascher makes further use of his sense of irony to point out the ludicrousness that a Germany which has throughout its history profited from foreign influences should now close itself off from such influences:

> Der Deutsche, den die Natur gleichsam ausersehen zu haben schien, in sich vielseitige Kultur aller Zeitalter und Nationen aufzunehmen, sowohl in Hinsicht der Religiosität, als der Staatsverfassung und Geisteskultur, sollte nach den Ansichten dieser deutschen Adepten oder Germanomanen, sich plötzlich von allem auswärtigen Einfluß absorbieren. Fremde Sitte und Sprache sollte er von sich weisen und die entferntesten Verhältnisse, die ihm etwas ausländisches aneignen könnten, aufgeben.[70]

Through his sarcastic mode of expression, Ascher goes to great lengths to distinguish foreign influence from foreign tyranny: "Ist denn Deutschland einer andern Macht unterthan worden, weil es fremde Sprachen übte, fremden Sitten huldigte, und dem Auslande in Kultur in Industrie nachzustreben sich beeiferte?"[71] Ascher attempts to counter the "Christian-Germanic, romantic-nationalist" atmosphere which greatly weakened "the position of Jews in the field of politics, religion, and culture."[72]

In 1817, in a book burning at the Wartburg Festival held by the *Burschenschaften*, Ascher's antinationalistic tract was thrown onto the fire.[73] Saul Ascher commented on the book burning: "They probably burned my *Germanomanie*, because I said that all men are made the same way as Germans, and that Christianity is not a German religion."[74] It is one of the profound ironies of German history that the Maskilim embraced the Enlightenment in order to help bring about the acculturation of Jews into German society, yet, after the Congress of Vienna, members of the Jewish intelligentsia such as Ascher and David Friedländer were almost the only adherents of the Enlightenment in the German-speaking countries.

The Rise of Defamatory Humor: Anti-Semitic Dramas

If the hateful form of invective in the political pamphlets was one popular form of anti-Semitic propaganda, then the equally hateful defamatory humor of bigoted dramatists was another.[75] The anti-Semitic dramatists made use of a vicious humor to differentiate themselves from the Jewish outgroup and strengthen their own group identity. Humor in all of its forms is a vehicle for group formation. As Sigmund

Freud pointed out, one cannot enjoy a joke by oneself. A joke produces a need for someone else's laughter.[76] Humor creates its own group dynamic: "Every joke calls for a public of its own and laughing at the same jokes is evidence of far-reaching psychical conformity."[77]

The subscribers to a certain sort of humor compose an ingroup of sorts and therefore it should come as no surprise that some groups will attempt to foment humor by deriding the members of outgroups. Such humor is a manifestation of the aggressivity of the outgroup toward all those who deviate from its norms.[78] This sort of derisory humor deserves closer examination.

There is a certain satisfaction in the use of derisory humor: it offers members of the ingroup the pleasure of viewing themselves as superior to others.[79] Favorable personal comparisons showing ingroup members to be better than their "enemies" may contribute to amusement.[80] Derision provides a certain happiness increment by providing feelings of superiority or heightened self-esteem: it thereby manifests itself as a pleasurable release of resentment toward enemies.[81] Deriding someone else causes members of the subject group to reappraise themselves more favorably.[82]

Humor of this nature had been attacked by the dramatists and literary theorists of the Enlightenment. The comic theory of such authors as Lessing and Diderot was anathema to the notion that comedy manifested itself in the production of laughter at the expense of "lower" people.[83] They were more interested in teaching people how to laugh at themselves in order to promote recognition of the comical incongruities of society. Lessing believed that comedy should ridicule social habits or moral failings that are subject to being remedied: "Comedy wants to improve through laughter but not through derision."[84]

The Enlightened concept of comedy was a didactic one: "criticizing the conditions that breed ignorance, intolerance, and prejudice; by means of laughter it intended to make society more reasonable, self-critical, and tolerant."[85] However the decimation of the philosophy of the Enlightenment through the increasing nationalism also led in large measure to a jettisoning of the literary conventions of the Enlightenment and the return to derisory humor as a common element in the theater.

The early nineteenth century was a time of reinforcement of group identification with Germanness and Christianity. Derisory humor regained popularity because of the largely subliminal nature of laughter, which made it an ideal means of appealing to the suggestibility of the individual. A coldness toward the victim is promoted by humor of this sort.[86] Therefore the laughter promoted by this sort of humor is an effective expression of the opposition between the larger collective and the noncomforming individuals the collective wishes to humiliate.[87]

The relation of these concepts of derisory humor to our topic of anti-Semitic propaganda becomes clearer through analysis of a concrete example. We will therefore make an examination of the anti-Semitic farce of 1804, *Der wuchernde Jude am Pranger*. According to Detlev Claussen, a key concept of modern anti-Semitism is viewing the Jew as a synecdoche for money circulation.[88] The Jews became a scapegoat for the economic woes of the entire populace. The author of *Der wuchernde Jude am Pranger* tries to elicit laughter out of his audience by deriding the Jews for what was perceived to be their economic role. The piece is introduced with the words: "Heute wird von den Juden ein Stück aufgeführt, / Wie sie durch Wucher die Erde regiert. / Doch heute wird ihnen der Fell abgezogen, / Gezeigt wie sie uns Christen erbärmlich betrogen."[89] Bjørn Ekmann argues that certain kinds of laughter emerge as a defense mechanism against a threat or fear: the fear is deflected into a relaxing mechanism.[90] The peasant or burgher who is in fear for his economic well-being may find the opportunity to laugh at a designated culprit a welcome diversion from his troubles. At the same time, it helps mobilize him against the maligned outgroup by appealing to his suggestibility. The piece demonstrates how interethnic hostility is created by feelings of deprivation and anxiety about the future on the part of the ethnocentric individual.[91] A substantial amount of power is projected on the Jews with the implication that they should somehow bear responsibility for the economic troubles of this era. The Jews are portrayed as the willing and cheerful beneficiaries of contemporary economic conditions. A Jewish character proclaims: "Doch wär es mein Seel! ein närrischer Streich, / Wenn man uns verböte das Leihen auf Pfändern, / Das Schachern, das Wuchern, das Handeln mit Bändern; Denn würde es schlecht mit den Juden aussehn— / Doch, Gott sey gelobt! das wird nie geschehen."[92] By portraying Jews as wanton and usurious villains, the author endeavors to build a Christian ingroup identification based on a common persecutor: the majority group is appealed to as being oppressed by a "powerful" minority.

In order to help members of his own Christian ingroup appraise themselves favorably, the author draws a dichotomy between the bad Jewish banker Ruben Herz and the good Christian lawyer Müller. Ruben is, true to stereotype, unscrupulous: "Gewissenhaft handeln bringt leider nichts ein . . ."[93] and obsessed with money: "Wer Gelder besitzet, dem lachet die Welt. . . ."[94] He is devoid of sympathy for his fellow human beings and is a harsh taskmaster toward his debtors: "Ei sieht doch, da sollt ich gewissenhaft seyn / Nein, nein, gebt Geld oder zeigt mir den Schein—Darum lach' ich wenn Jemand von Eid und Pflicht / Und von Gewissen viel pralet; / Ich gebe gewiß keinem Schuldner verzicht / und quäle ihn, bis er mir zahlet."[95] Appeals to fear are a powerful motivator for the effectiveness of any propaganda and by convincing economically troubled Christians that Jewish creditors will subject them to unconscionable debt harassment, the author shrewdly plays on their fears.

The author attempts to deepen an "us-identification" with the majority group and deepen prejudices against the minority by portraying Ruben in his mistreatment of an impoverished widow: "Ey denkt sie durch Klagen mich h'rum zu bekommen? / Nein, Ruben Herz läßt sich nicht Näßchen andrehen / Kurz, einmal für immer. / Geld muß ich bekommen, / Woher sie dieß auftreibt, da mag sie zusehen."[96] The speech is calculated to deepen paranoia against the social pariah by attributing heinous attitudes to him. Humor of this sort can best succeed by disparaging an object of repulsion while enhancing an object of affection.[97] In order to disparage his object of repulsion, the author introduces his object of affection as a contrast figure: the heroic lawyer Müller. Müller proclaims his own goodness by declaring what an evil man Ruben is and how he intends to put a stop to it: "Und zeigen will ich der ganzen Welt, / Welch Unheil verursacht der Wucher mit Geld, / Zwar hat mancher nicht Ruh noch Rast / Bis er sein Geld und Gut hat verpraßt, / Doch mancher auch ohne Schuld leidet Noth / Und fleht vergebens ums tägliche Brodt / Er ward vom Wucher ins Elend gestürzet / Und so ihm die Freuden des Lebens verkürzet."[98] The author encourages his audience to think that they are right in harboring prejudices against the Jews by reinforcing antagonisms against the outsiders. The Jews are portrayed as posing a danger to the welfare of Christian citizens. The only way the author can make this work amusing to a Christian audience is by having the Christian hero triumph over the Jew. Laughter thereby becomes a gesture of blind superiority.

Müller does triumph over Ruben when he entraps the Jewish banker into perjuring himself in front of witnesses. The result is that Ruben is forced to pay a fine and stand in the pillory and thus, in the logic of the play, good triumphs over evil. Such technical details as the unethical nature of Müller's entrapment of Ruben apparently did not bother the author of this farce. His concern is with the laughter of triumph and despisal.

The laughter of the anti-Semitic audience is elicited as Ruben stands in the pillory declaring: "Ich möchte vergehen, denn ich muß sehn, / Mein Geld in fremden Händen; / Gern ertrug ich Schimpf und Spott /

Könnt ich dieß abwenden."[99] The fact that Ruben is more worried about the loss of some money than the loss of his dignity makes the audience feel justified in laughing about the loss of dignity and, at the same time, reinforces stereotypes that Jews are fixated on money.

The play concludes with the choir proclaiming and reinforcing a litany of defamatory stereotypes against the Jews: "Wer sich der Waysen gut anmaßt, / Und arme Witwen drücket, / Dem Redlichen nur dient zur Last, / Und andere gern berücket, / Der Reichtum hält für seinen Gott, / Der werde endlich auch zum Spott / Er möge am Galgen sterben."[100] *Der wuchernde Jude am Pranger* is formally in the tradition of German farce, which is a sort of comedy. Comedy, according to Lessing, is the genre in which human folly is laughed at and the possibility for self-improvement is diagnosed. However, by portraying a member of a socially disadvantaged group as the mainstay of folly and the object of laughter, the author of *Der wuchernde Jude* reinforces stereotypes and promotes a demeaning image of the Jews. As such, he attempts to appeal to people's more negative instincts. In contrast to Lessing's comedy *Die Juden*, where prejudice is portrayed as the object of laughter and exposed as folly, *Der wuchernde Jude* promotes prejudice by portraying Jews as hardhearted, powerful, and greedy.

As Georgina Baum points out, an important question for comedy is, "Who laughs at whom?" The artistic representation of the comical requires the author to take a stance toward the represented object. The figure at whom laughter is directed is portrayed from a specific standpoint. That standpoint is either an affirmation or negation of the portrayed person.[101] In the case of *Der wuchernde Jude*, Ruben is negated through the author's portrayal. As Baum points out, critical laughter is only justified when the person portrayed represents socially inhibiting factors. Falsely stereotyping a character on the basis of his religioethnic identity does not constitute such a justification.

If the author of a comedy attempts to side with backward or reactionary forces, and make fun of progressive ideals, he can then only count on a short-lived impact within a circle of people who think the same way he does.[102] In *Der wuchernde Jude am Pranger*, the anti-Semite laughs at the Jews and thereby sides with the reactionary forces that reversed the progress of the Enlightenment in regard to Jewish emancipation. As such, the comedy can only have a humorous impact on people who agree with the author's attitude toward the Jews.

The author rejects both the teachings and the literary conventions of the Enlightenment. The comedy of the Enlightenment is an unsuitable vehicle for his intolerant message so he becomes a dramaturgical antiquarian and revives the *Fastnachtspiel* of the sixteenth century. He employs a kind of *Knittelvers* reminiscent of the sixteenth-century author Hans Sachs. Sachs's literary production was meant for the lower strata of society and thereby lacks a certain sophistication and was a suitable model for the author of *Der wuchernde Jude*. Furthermore, Hans Sachs was a fervent Lutheran who shared Martin Luther's Judeophobic views.[103] The influence of Sachs on the author of *Der wuchernde Jude* can best be demonstrated by examining a portion of Sachs's Judeophobic *Fastnachtspiel, Der Teufel nahm ein altes Weib* (1545): "Drin in der Stadt ist ein steinern Haus, / Da wohnen zwei alte Juden drinnen, / Die großes Gut mit Wucher gewinnen, / Die mit Finanz und vielen Lügen / Die Leut bescheißen und betrügen."[104] The similarity of these lines to some of the anti-Semitic statements in *Der wuchernde Jude am Pranger* in terms of both content and form amply show why the anonymous 1804 author imitated Hans Sachs instead of some more contemporary author.

Der wuchernde Jude am Pranger represents in many respects a modern kind of anti-Semitism because, unlike the Lutheran Judeophobia of the sixteenth century, it is not primarily religiously motivated. It is an example of the emergence of a new authoritarian consensus formation. Even secularized Christians often maintained their hatred against the Jews, because of the Jews' involvement in money circulation. Whereas Grattenauer's anti-Semitism contains both traditional religious and modern economic elements, *Der wuchernde Jude* is a seminal work of a secularized anti-Semitism that defined Jews only in national and economic terms. In the prosaic epilogue of the piece, the author condemns the economic activity of the Jews:

> Was uns aber wider die Juden, und, wie mich dünkt, mit dem vollsten Rechte aufbringt, ist nicht ihre Religion, sondern ihr schändlicher Hang zum Wucher, der ihnen angeboren zu seyn scheint. Wider diesen zu eifern, dessen Schandthaten zu enthüllen, das sey jeder Biedermanns rechtlicher Wunsch. Aber nicht dabei stehen bleiben, sondern ihn bey seinen Grundpfeiler anzugreiffen und zu schüttern, das ist ächter Patriotismus.[105]

Because this author bases his anti-Semitism solely on the Jews' economic activities, he casts aside the pleas for tolerance based on the Jews' religion, which had been promoted by such authors as Lessing, Mendelssohn, Diez, and Bischof. He argues that religion is not the key issue: "Wohl unserem Zeitalter, wenn dieser Streit, der sich anfangs auf die Religion und Nation der Juden einschränkte, auf ihren stinkenden Geiz sich ausdehnte."[106] This statement is a clear rejection of the Enlightenment; the author argues in favor of an anti-Semitic stance despite the arguments for Jewish equality based on the Jews' religion.

The Enlightenment did, in fact, try to come to terms with the issue of the Jews' economic activity. Dohm, for instance, advocated the opening up of all professions to the Jews in order to decrease their dependence on moneylending. Mendelssohn also pointed out that the economic activities of the Jews were mainly due to Christian-imposed restrictions. The author of *Der wuchernde Jude* ignores these authors because, like a true propagandist, he wishes to impose his own monologue upon his audience and not extend an invitation to dialogue.

Those who sought to introduce a monologic anti-Semitism into German society had powerful opposition in the form of that Magna Charta of the German Jewry, Lessing's *Nathan der Weise*. Anti-Semitic authors did everything they could to marginalize Lessing's critical discourse, including the writing of hateful and mean-spirited travesties based on Lessing's drama. Wolfgang Karrer points out that the knowledge and capabilities of writers of travesties have generally been minimal, and the anti-Lessing travesties are no exception.[107] Travesty is characterized by a negative attitude toward the original author and an opposition to the positive reception of the original.[108]

The goal of the author of the travesty is to "overcome" the message of the original by influencing the overall reception.[109] It is the intention of the travestier to make his recipients laugh at the original and therefore make the original author despised.[110] The criticism indicates a negative social judgment.

The travesty has such goals as humor, criticism, and ridicule but the effects can often be disgust, boredom, and aggression.[111] Particularly when the original is an admired work, rejection of the travesty is often a result. Again, it is a question of who is laughing at whom, and where the sympathies of the recipient lie.

The anonymous travesty *Nathan der Weise travestirt und modernisirt* (1804) combines elements of a traditional religious anti-Semitism with the emerging nationalistic anti-Semitism. The author attacks tolerance for the Jews along with Natural Religion, the French Revolution, and the Napoleonic conquests. The play attempts to reaffirm the status of Christianity as a consensus formation as well as promote nationalistic and anti-Semitic beliefs. In the prologue spoken by the templar, Lessing is attacked as being non-Christian and non-German: "Und Lessing wird Nase und Ohren geschlitzt, / Weil er weder Türke, Jude, noch Christ, / sondern ein wilder Araber ist."[112] Lessing's sympathy for Natural Religion is attacked as nonbelief.

Lessing appears as a character in the play, taking the role of the dervish. He addresses Nathan with the following words: "Ruhe und Frieden dem jüdischen Weisen / Seit dem Durchgang im rothen Meer, /

Bis nach Wolfenbüttel kreuz und quer. / Nicht wahr ihr seid zwar tüchtig beschmutzt, / Aber ich habe euch trefflich benutzt, / Und euch von Mosen und alle Propheten / Nichts weiter gelassen as Singen und Beten / Ihr kennt meine göttlichen Fragmente schon?"[113] By imparting his own terms to what he believes is Lessing's standpoint, the author attempts to impose a mystical Christian monologism upon society. He attacks Lessing for his portrayal of Nathan as a nonbeliever, claiming that Lessing has thereby corrupted the Jews. He disapproves of what he views as the secularization of Moses and the prophets, seeing it as reducing them from figures of spiritual importance into empty songs and prayers. The travestier opposes the calling of divine revelation into question. Also a target of criticism is Lessing's release of the *Wolfenbüttler Fragmente*. The travestier considered Lessing to be a scurrilous disbeliever, because he viewed Lessing as the author of the fragments.[114]

The author is offended by the invitation to dialogue extended to the Jewish and the heterodox Christian communities by Lessing. He is unwilling to accommodate the reality of multiple consciousness that Lessing wishes to legitimize. He wishes to impose a single consciousness upon society: his own. But this is quite impossible. As Mikhail M. Bakhtin commented: "No Nirvana is possible for a *single* consciousness. A single consciousness is *contradictio in adjecto*. . . . Those worldviews that recognize the right of a higher consciousness to make decisions for lower ones . . . transform them into voiceless things."[115]

The author makes his resistance to the critical discourses unleashed by Lessing and Reimarus clear. He attacks the Enlightenment in favor of a conservative religious orthodoxy when he has his character Lessing utter the words:

> Herr Nathan der Weise! / Ich habe meine Ehre bei ihm versetzt, / Darum bin ich von ihm sehr hochgeschätzt, / Ich habe die Eurige [i.e., die Christen] angegriffen, / Drum bin ich von allen Priestern gepfiffen. / Ich habe die Bibel hübsch persifliert/ Den Deismus überall eingeführt. / Aber kaum haut ich der vielköpfigen Hyder / Flink und rüstig ein Köpgen hernieder, / So singen und beten die Anderen schon wieder. / Heute setzt man Vernunft auf die Thron, / Und morgen kauft jeder Absolution / Heute gibt jeder den Priestern die Knute / Und morgen küßt jeder die kirchliche Ruthe.[116]

The travestier rejects Lessing's critical discourse that calls the absolutism of Christianity into question and asserts the strength and resilience of the dominant discourse of orthodox Christianity. Natural

Religion is dismissed as a trend, destined to whither away. Orthodox Christianity is asserted as having more staying power than Deism and other heterodox beliefs comprising the critical discourse of this time. This author, like so many others, promotes a reactionary utopia of monologism. Christian doctrine is posited as being an unassailable consensus formation.

The author's resistance to the notion of tolerance toward the Jews is expressed in terms of his recasting Nathan in terms of a hurtful stereotype: greedy, materialistic, and unscrupulous. An anti-Semitic utterance is placed in Nathan's mouth: "Ihr wißt, / Das der Jude Vater und Mutter vergißt, / Ist vom Gelde nur die Rede."[117] Instead of directing the laughter at human folly in the best German comical tradition, the author directs laughter at a member of a disadvantaged minority with the intent of further marginalizing the status of that minority. He also, much like other anti-Semitic propagandists, feeds the fears and paranoias of economically troubled Christians and provides them with the Jew as scapegoat.

Nathan is portrayed as being unscrupulous and gifted in managing money when he proposes that Saladin name him finance minister: "Macht mich nur hurtig zum Finanzminister, / Glaubt ich beschneide Juden und Philister, / Aus allen Nestern hol' ich goldne Eier."[118] The travestier makes it clear that he feels that the reason Jews are better at managing money is because of their lack of morals: "Ein Jude, nur ein Jud' taugt zum Finanzminister / Den kümmert weder Pfaffe her, noch Küster . . ."[119] Nathan is also presented as willing to give Recha to the templar, if the price is right. When Daja begs Nathan to give Recha to the templar, he responds, "O ja, hätt er nur Geld; auch zur Maitresse gern."[120] This is designed to inculcate hatred against the Jews because Recha is described as being "so jungfräulich keusch wie Mutter Maria," yet Nathan is virtually willing to sell her to be the templar's mistress.[121]

Through the figure of the monk, the travestier expresses his opposition to the French Revolution: "Die Jakobins sind todt; der Streich ward gut vollführt."[122] Wessels points to the anti-Napoleonic polemic in the piece; Saladin is an embodiment of Napoleon.[123] In recreating Saladin as Napoleon, the author tries to present Napoleon as an infidel and therefore attempts to build a Christian ingroup opposition to Napoleon. The anti-French sentiment of the piece, like the anti-Semitism, is influenced by feelings of German nationalism which overcame the influence of the Enlightenment in the early nineteenth century.

The goal of the travesty was to try to influence the reception of the original by heaping ridicule upon it, to try to bring about a scornful attitude toward Lessing's critical discourse and thereby defend conservative values. The piece exemplifies the reemergence of the consensus formation of orthodox Christianity, accompanied by the newer consensus formation of German nationalism, asserting themselves against the critical discourse demanding tolerance for the nonidentical. Accordingly, the play constitutes a regressive attempt to silence the minority voices which tried to enter into dialogue with the dominant society.

Along with rejecting Lessing's worldview, the anonymous travestier rejects the literary innovations favored by Lessing, particularly the use of blank verse. Like the author of *Der wuchernde Jude am Pranger*, the travestier revives the *Knittelvers* of Hans Sachs's works. The characters used by Lessing are tilted on their heads and used to promote and intensify a reactionary viewpoint which had been espoused by Sachs more than two centuries earlier. Therefore both anonymous authors view the obsolete form of the *Fastnachtspiel* as a suitable vehicle for the message they wish to convey.

As did the anonymous travestier, so did Julius von Voss attempt to influence the reception of *Nathan der Weise* through a scornful rewriting of it in *Der travestirte Nathan der Weise* (1804). Voss's travesty was also an attempt to counter the critical discourse mounted by Lessing with a conservative discourse. The Jews are portrayed as being alien to German culture and inevitably unsuitable to inclusion in the society. In this manner, Voss asserts the rules of exclusion accompanying the new nationalism against Lessing's avowal of tolerance.

He attempts to direct laughter at the original play and make it seem ridiculous through employment of a burlesque incongruity with the original. The fateful fire that nearly claims Recha's life is in Voss's version set by Daja as part of an insurance fraud scheme. Nathan, portrayed by Lessing as the concerned father has a callous attitude toward the near death of Recha in Voss's version. He only thinks of repairing his house and replacing his wares. This is in marked opposition to Nathan's anxiety toward Recha in the original version. In Voss's travesty, Nathan shows no sign of gratitude for the templar's selfless rescue of Recha, but is instead concerned with whether the templar harmed her. Voss therefore tries to convey the impression that Jews are inherently mistrustful of Christians and that the two cultures do not mix.

There is an enormous difference in the characters of the two Nathans. The original Nathan is a noble Jew, a man of high principles, tolerant toward members of all religious groups. Voss's Nathan, on the other hand, is intolerant toward non-Jews. He believes that it is ethical to deceive and cheat Gentiles and that this right is grounded in the fact that the ancient Hebrews were permitted to lie to the Egyptians in order to escape slavery. He feels that Jewish religious and moral precepts only apply in interactions with other Jews. This portrayal is similar to accusations made against the Jews by Eisenmenger and Grattenauer. In repeating these accusations, Voss expresses a principle that Jews are only suited toward interaction with other Jews and that problems arise when Jews interact with Gentiles.

This principle is further developed by Voss in his portrayal of Recha as an assimilated Jew. Through the character of Recha, Voss tries to parody salon Jews such as Rahel Varnhagen and Dorothea Schlegel. She tries—unsuccessfully—to conceal her Jewish identity by assuming the language of educated Germans: "Hört, ich spreche keinen Dialekt mehr, weiß die Rede / Der höheren Bildung wie mein Aschre [i.e., ABC] . . . Man merkt mir nimmer noch die Jüdin an—."[124] Voss equates Jewish assimilation with religious nonbelief when he has Recha utter, "Ich bin zwar über alle positive / Religion indifferent, die echte Schellingianische Philosophie / Umarmend."[125]

In travestying both the traditional Jew and the assimilated Jew, Voss places Jews in a no-win situation.[126] Voss thereby shows his per se disdain for Jewishness: whether that Jewishness is represented by a stereotyped itinerant peddler and moneylender such as Voss's Nathan or by someone with the undisputed intellectual vitality of a Rahel Varnhagen. According to Jeffrey Grossman, Voss uses Recha to satirize the German-Jewish ideal of attaining acculturation through *Bildung*.[127] Voss believes that there is an inherent Jewish nature and that no amount of acculturation can change this.[128]

Another example of Voss's utilization of racist humor is his manner of directing laughter toward the exogamy laws that prohibited marriage or sexual relations between Jews and Christians. In Lessing's *Die Juden* (1749), the exogamy laws are the target of a progressive humor: through the "naive" question of the baron's daughter as to why she could not marry the Jewish traveler, the laws are condemned as folly and a righteous laughter is directed against them. In Voss's travesty, he tries to present Nathan's fear of prosecution under the exogamy laws as a reason for laughter: he portrays Recha as the child of an illicit union between Nathan and Frau von Stauffen. In finding humor in the fears faced by a Jew for transgressing these laws, Voss voices his approval of them and confirms his principle of separation between the races. He directs the laughter of the audience not toward the exogamy laws themselves but toward those who oppose and fail to abide by them.

Numerous scholars including Stümcke (1904), Wessels (1979), and Albertsen (1984) attempt to defend Voss against charges of anti-Semitism. Stümcke points out that the non-Jewish characters are also travestied, that the Christian templar is hardly portrayed any more positively than Nathan.[129] However, what is criticized on the part of the templar is his willingness to convert to Judaism in opposition to Voss's principle of the separation of cultures. The templar is criticized for not adhering more faithfully to Christianity and Nathan is travestied for adhering too closely to his supposedly "Jewish" characteristics. Wessels remarks that Voss wanted to criticize the one-sidedly idealistic portrayals of Jews by Lessing and others, but denies that Voss intended to attack the underlying principles of Jewish emancipation.[130] He points to Nathan's defense of Judaism. This defense, however, does not constitute a major element to the clearly anti-Semitic elements of the play. In his defense of Jews, Nathan says:

> Jetzt ist er doch / Zerstreut in aller Welt, er bleibt ein Jud—Kein Mensch zwingt ihn zu seiner Religion / Kein Papst, kein Imam, unter fremden Henkern / Wirft man ihn oft drob auf die Folterbank; / Er bleibt ein Jud / Er hat kein Vaterland / Und ist der größte Patriot, viel hundert Nationen hat der Zwang vernichtet. Der Jud, ich sag's, wird alles überleben. . . . Und sind die Eltern so geehrt / Von ihren Kindern wo, als bei den Juden? Und er ist gesund / Und wird auch alt und zieht die Kinder auf / Nach des Levitischen Gesetzes Weisung, / Und pflanzt so tief ins junge Herz das niemand es mehr ausjäten kann.[131]

People who cite this passage as proof that Voss was basically tolerant fail to understand the racist nature of Voss's separatist stance. By maintaining that there are elements of Jewish culture that he has respect for, Voss attains a veneer of tolerance, but at the same time he maintains that problems arise from Jews living in the midst of German culture. Nathan's defense of Judaism is motivated by Voss's belief that it is right and proper for Jews to resist contact with Christians because they do not fit in well with the surrounding culture.

Even Voss's explicit denial of anti-Semitism is permeated with a bizarre contradictoriness:

> Ich bitte es mir aber von einer löblichen Judenschaft aus: mich nicht, weil ich einen anderen als den Lessingschen Nathan darstellte, in die Rubrik ihrer Feinde zu verzeichnen. Das Loschen-Kaudesch und gewisse Hausgebräuche können keinem Israeliten anstößig werden, da sie der Nachlaß der Väter sind. Der Handel in den Händen des Geizes sieht unter allen Völkern sich gleich, und durch das Gespräch mit dem Tempelherrn glaube ich mir selbst um die Juden erworben zu haben, indem ich die Consequenz ihres Theosophen, die bürgerliche Festigkeit, die ihre Gesetze hervor-

bringen und ihre Entfernung von manchen Verderbniß anderer Völker beleuchtete. Ich bin gewiß in Hinsicht ihrer die Neutralität selbst, denn meine an sie verlorenen Proxenetica, Abzüge, Prolongationsgebühren und Zinsen erhalte ich nicht wieder.[132]

Voss's denial of anti-Semitism must be regarded with skepticism. He maintains that his use of mock Yiddish and German Jewish dialect should not be offensive to Jews because it is purportedly a part of their heritage: yet he uses a pseudo-Yiddish for its comic effect in order to direct derisory laughter toward the Jewish community.[133] Therefore his denial of anti-Semitism on this score cannot be taken too seriously.

Furthermore, by juxtaposing his denial of anti-Semitism with a lament over the money he has lost to Jewish moneylenders, Voss contradicts his avowal of neutrality toward Jews. In avowing respect for some aspects of Jewish culture, Voss stops short of maintaining the feasibility of Jewish-Christian coexistence.

Leif Ludwig Albertsen dismisses the charge of anti-Semitism out of hand, but fails to present a convincing counterargument: "Das ist Unterhaltung aus der Froschperspektive der Zeit, wenn Teile des Gehirns vor dem Schlaf ausgeschaltet sind; das ist nicht Antisemitismus."[134] The "Froschperspektive" of this time was also largely anti-Semitic, and it should not be surprising that a play directed toward this sort of audience should also be anti-Semitic.

Voss displays both an animosity toward assimilated Jews and repeated efforts to demonstrate the incompatibility between German and Jewish culture. Though he does not discuss any of Voss's works in detail, Jenzsch views Voss as having, along with Grattenauer and Sessa, attempted to stop the development of Jewish equality through promoting a national racist kind of anti-Semitism.[135]

Whereas Lessing signaled his nonconformity with the dominant elements of his Christian ingroup through identification of the pariah whom he portrays as being noble of character and capable of inducing sympathy, both Voss and the anonymous travestier signal their belonging to the dominant ingroup through their portrayal of the pariah as being ignomious and ridiculous. Lessing wishes for people to be touched by the good Jew and less inclined toward harboring prejudices, but the travestiers wish to relegate the Jew to a position of permanent inferiority and thereby advance derisory and contemptuous attitudes toward him. An unhealthy laughter that gives rise to a false feeling of superiority based on ingroup idenitification is encouraged.

The followers of the Romantic School were contemporaries of Julius von Voss. Under the influence of the Napoleonic incursions and the resulting nationalism, most of the followers of the Romantic School became anti-Semitic. Achim von Arnim and Clemens Brentano, among the most significant writers of German Romanticism, were founding members of the Christian-German Dinner Society (*Christliche-Deutsche Tischgesellschaft*), which excluded Jews, Frenchmen, "Philistines," and women from its membership. Since the emergence of the Mendelssohn circle and the Jewish salons, Jewish society was an important part of the intellectual life in Berlin. Scholars, artists, and authors met in mixed Jewish-Christian circles. Reactionary writers wanted an alternative.[136]

The Christian-German Dinner Society attacked the Enlightenment and the Jewish salons. According to Deborah Hertz, the reason that the dinner society was "such an attack on the Jewish salons was not simply that the club's founders set themselves to rebuild the Christian state, but that they envisioned a conservative and a Christian version of that state."[137] In a speech before the dinner society, published in 1811 under the title "Der Philister vor, in und nach der Geschichte," Brentano attacked Enlighteners and Jews alike. The Enlighteners were disparaged as being "Philistines" who tended to make life mechanistic with their rationalistic concepts. Alfred D. Low has summarized Brentano's speech: "Philistines and Jews, while displaying different traits of character and even showing hostility to each other, were both representatives of a cold, barren rationality which could only harm humanity."[138] It is interesting that the term "Philistine" to denote a banal and valueless individual was borrowed from the name of a Semitic people.

In his opening remarks, Brentano applauds the demise of Jews and Philistines, whom he regards as endangering the Romanticist from differing directions:

> Gleich den Flüssen nun hat diese edle Tischgesellschaft gesammelt, aus reinen ursprünglichen und fröhlichen Herzen, und hat ausgewiesen auf ewig von sich, nicht aus eigenem Dünkel, sondern aus frommer Achtung gegen die Geschichte, die Juden und die Philister, über welche die Fluche der Schrift längst wahr geworden, welche nur als Wahrzeichen ihres Untergangs, als unauslösliche Blutflecken einer bösen Schuld, als Gespenster ihres nicht seeligen historischen Todes, als eine alte Essigmutter der Sünde auf Erden verweilen, und sind sie über die ganze Erde verbreitet, heißt das doch nur so viel, als ihre Asche in den Wind gestreut.[139]

Brentano's speech marks a resurgence of a religious anti-Semitism: the reference to "Blutflecken der Schuld" is an avowal of the belief that the entire Jewish people share an eternal collective guilt for the death of Christ. Judaism is further condemned as being a moribund religion.

Nationalistic sentiment appears in the statement that Jews are homeless wayfarers whose "ashes are scattered in the wind."

Brentano attempts to promote an ingroup identification based on exclusion. The privilege of belonging to the group is made conditional on not belonging to certain other groups, namely, the Jewish community. This exclusiveness tends to promote a certain monologism and a reinforcement of exclusive, reactionary ideals.

Similar conceptions of Judaism were expressed by Achim von Arnim in a play with anti-Semitic overtones entitled *Halle: Ein Studentenspiel* (1809–11). The two Jewish characters who appear in the play are Ahasverus and Nathan. Nathan is an all-too-stereotypical merchant and moneylender and is negatively portrayed. He is prejudiced against Christians, whom he regards as frivolously lavish in their lifestyles: "Ein Christ, ein Verschwender, einer mehr, der andere weniger—Wenn eines meiner Kinder sich wieder taufen läßt, so will ich's enterben."[140] The miserly Jew is portrayed as being bitter and jealous toward well-off Christians and therefore desiring to extract money from them. The wealthy aristocrat Arnim thereby promotes the privileges of rich Christians and at the same time displays their paranoia toward the Jewish people.

Arnim shows signs of a modern economic anti-Semitism when he maintains that dealings in money are something inborn to Jews. One example of this is in the scene in which Nathan's grandchildren simulate lending money and play the role of stern creditors. Nathan is thankful for this sign of "Jewish" nature: "Du, gnädiger Gott unsrer Vater, dein Segen ruht auf den Samen deines Volkes, abwaschen kann ihn nicht die Taufe."[141] Arnim views money circulation as something culturally inculcated into and indivisible from the Jews from childhood onward.

The alternative to participation of the Jew in the Jewish community, assimilation, was also something which Arnim condemned. Nathan makes a statement against baptized Jews: "Ich habe nichts gegen das Taufen, laß ich doch meine Kinder waschen alle Tage, aber das Taufen löscht den Kredit aus, da wollen sie Staat machen, wie die Christen, sprechen von das [sic] Literatur, sind nervenkrank, was ich spar' bei der Lampe, verbrennt beim Wachslicht, Tee und Schokolade alle Tage und Zucker."[142] Nathan's statement is particularly directed against the salon Jews, who frequently let themselves be baptized and discussed art and literature with Gentile society. Arnim was against this sort of assimilation because it promoted contact between Jews and Christians on a secularized basis. He demands the conversion of all Jews into believing Christians.

Ahasverus, the eternal "wandering Jew," represents Arnim's answer to the "Jewish question." Ahasverus is the Romanticist's model for the renunciation of Judaism.[143] He seeks the Christianization of all Jews:

> Bis ihr Juden all getaufet, kann ich keine Ruhe finden, muß durch alle Länder ziehen, seh' euch martern, quälen, schinden, wie ihr dabei lächerlich. . . . Euren Glauben ihr verlasset, hasset doch den Christenglauben, rauben laßt ihr willig alles, alles, alles, nur kein Geld, stellet euch an fließend Wasser, lasset eure volle Kasten tief hinein, klein ist nur, was ihr verlieret, zieret euch der Glaube, leicht beflügelt ist der Glaube, hebt so schwere Last nicht auf, werdet arm, ihr werdet selig.[144]

Arnim argues that by failing to become believing Christians, Jews are accepting needless suffering. He rejects any notion that Jews adhere to Judaism out of a feeling of kinship and ingroup identification with other Jews. Nathan shows no signs of pity for or solidarity with his suffering coreligionists:

> Es soll sein ein Abgeordneter von den Juden in Jerusalem, daß wir ihnen geben Geld, damit sie kaufen los ihre Juden, die da schmachten in die Gefangenschaft von den Türken, es soll sein, er hat seine Briefe, aber was geht's mich an, schickt mir einer aus Jerusalem ein Geld, wenn ich meine Wechsel nicht bezahlen kann und komm' in die Gefangenschaft von den Christen, er soll's sein, wenn er nun mit dem Gelde geht in die weite Welt?[145]

The Jew is stereotyped as being selfish, obsessed with money, and totally without a sense of community or group identification with other people. Jewishness is portrayed as a social evil, which isolates human beings and deprives them from a sense of belonging to others.

Arnim's play combines traditional religious with modern economic anti-Semitism. According to Paul Lawrence Rose: "Confessing the fervent hope of medieval Jew-hatred that the Jews would be redeemed by conversion to Christianity, Arnim portrayed Ahasverus as a convert whose full redemption must await the general conversion of the Jewish people."[146]

The Romantic anti-Semitism of Brentano and Arnim influenced a Breslau physician named Karl Borromäus Alexander Sessa (d. 1813) to write one of the most successful and notorious of the plays against Jewish emancipation. Sessa, in his farce *Unser Verkehr* (originally entitled *Die Judenschule*, written in 1812, but published in 1815) also reveals Voss's influence. As with Voss, there is an exploitation of pseudo-Yiddish dialogue for its comic effect. With both authors, this is a means of differentiating the Christian ingroup from the Jewish minority and thereby strengthening German Gentile group identity.[147] This differentiation provides both author and audience with an opportunity to view their ingroup as superior to others and thereby allow themselves some amusement at the outgroup's expense.

The play begins with a defamatory attack representing the author's view of Jewish family values. The viewer is introduced to the family circle of Abraham and Rachel. They are poor Jewish peddlers who sell old clothing. They are portrayed as being obsessed with material things and very stingy as they kick their son Jakob out of the house. Abraham's values are revealed in his charge to Jakob as Jakob leaves home: "Loß dich treten von de Leit, Loß dich werfen aus de Stuben, Loß dich verklagen bei de Gerichte, loß dich setzen ins Hündeloch, loß dich binden mit Stricke und Ketten, loß dich paitschen, loß dich martern halb taudt, aber (*drohend*) du mußt doch werden raich."[148] In this speech, Sessa promotes the stereotype that Jews are masochistic. Jews are portrayed as being more willing to suffer tribulations than to take an active role against them. The viewpoint is promulgated that Jews are a people lacking dignity and pride, and hence deserving of the inferior status to which they are relegated by the Christian majority. The entire Jewish community is made out to be ridiculous and therefore deserving of the scorn that Gentiles heap upon them. Thus the effort is made to bolster the self-esteem of the Christian audience through a feeling of belonging to the "superior" ingroup.

The stereotype that Jews are single-handedly motivated by the pursuit of money is also present. Sessa tries to reconfirm the parameters of the group he is trying to cement together by making the point to his audiences that the outsiders are justifiably the objects of hatred.

Jakob's first goal as he is on his own is to seek assimilation into non-Jewish society: "Ich will werfen den Jüden bei Seit, ich bin doch aufgeklärt—ich hob doch gar nischt Jüdisches an mer!"[149] Sessa posits an incongruity between German and Jewish society by having Jakob disavow his Jewish identity in a purportedly Yiddish-tinged dialect. Sessa tries to portray the Jews as being inherently non-German and thereby heap aversion and contempt on them in the nationalistic climate of Napoleon's defeat.

Sessa symbolizes Jakob's yearnings for assimilation into non-Jewish society as he attempts to enter a Christian church. He seeks to gain entrance by accompanying Lydie, the daughter of the assimilated Jew Polckwitzer. Out of a combination of snobbery and Jewish self-hatred, she tells him that the church has no room for him. He tries to gain admission to the church from the sexton with the argument, "Es kümen

144   Myths of Ethnic Homogeneity

doch mehr von unsere Leit rein."[150] The sexton responds, "Schande genug, aber's sind reiche Leute, können blechen, man muß ein Auge zudrücken. (*giftig*) Aber du kannst nicht hinein, Schacherjude."[151] Entrance into the world of the dominant culture is to be accorded only to wealthy Jews, who are in turn resented because of their wealth.

Jakob himself soon comes to the realization, "Ach ja! das Glück sucht nur heim de Reichen! Mit en Gelde kümmt der Verstand, mit en Geld de Gewalt und de Tugend und's Recht."[152] Sessa portrays Jews as lacking any underlying moral system, but only being interested in material gain. There is a degree of hypocrisy in this portrayal, because Christian society placed restrictions and taxes upon Jewish subjects that could only be surmounted through attainment of appreciable wealth. Wealth is made into the only path of empowerment and those who seek it are then condemned.

Money is portrayed as being the backbone of the Jews' value system. That is evidenced by Abraham when he learns of Jakob's supposed reversal of fortune through the lottery: "Du bist geworden raich—Du hast mer gemacht äne grauße Freude—sell dich segnen Jehova dervor."[153] The father, who had no qualms about ducking his parental responsibilities when he threw Jakob out of his house, now makes his parental rights into a matter of principle: "Voter und Sohn sind von anem Fleisch: was der Sohn hot, hot der Voter."[154]

The alleged winning of the lottery has other benefits: Lydie, who had earlier pretended not to remember Jakob, greets him as a childhood friend. Polckwitzer, also wishing to share in Jakob's newfound wealth, reverses his earlier opposition to granting his daughter's hand in marriage.

Jakob's temporary reversal of fortune is overturned when it turns out that the lottery was not won by him: he was proclaimed winner through an error. His parents abandon him to his fate and Polckwitzer takes back the offer of his daughter's hand in marriage. Jakob gives up his earlier aesthetic leanings and hopes of assimilation through being cultured and dedicates himself to trade: "Mit der Demuth fangt mer an! Mit der list kümmt mir weiter, mit der Dreistigkeit setzt man's durch, mit dem Stolz un de Sucht zu glänzen, kann mer enden."[155]

Sessa's entire play is an exercise in triviality and banality, not to mention mean-spiritedness. But even his overt anti-Semitic message is undercut by its own conceptual fissures: he seeks to condemn the Jewish striving for wealth by maintaining that Jews are only interested in money and are not interested in higher things. At the same time, he parodies a common Jewish characteristic that directly contravened this supposed obsession with money, namely, the Jewish intellectual vitality and striving for *Bildung*. In the figure of Isidorus Morgenländer, Sessa parodies the Jewish itinerant scholar of the Haskalah which was best exemplified in the person of Salomon Maimon, a philosopher of the Mendelssohn circle. Maimon was a man who was the very antithesis of materialism and greed for effortless financial gain and who was known for the absolute primacy of his philosophical and other intellectual pursuits. The character of Jakob is also not without his interest in intellectual and aesthetic pursuits, which indicates that Sessa was aware that this element of intellectual vitality existed in the Jewish community. Instead of praising it, he makes it into an object of ridicule. This would indicate that the lack of appreciation for the finer (non-material) things in life for which Sessa was willing to condemn the Jews was in fact present in Sessa himself. This constitutes a false projection of Sessa's own shallowness and unsatisfactory value system onto the Jews.[156]

Another element that Sessa makes into an object of derision is the fact that Jews treat other Jews with money differently from the way they do people without money. But the play itself inadvertently makes it clear that this element is not restricted to Jews. The sexton also treats rich people differently: he bars Jakob from admission to the church, but permits Polckwitzer and Lydie to enter unimpeded. Wealth is just as much a measure of status in Christian bourgeois society as it is in Jewish society, if not more so.

Sessa tries to heap hatred upon the Jews through expressing the belief that the only thing that matters to Jews is money, whether they be believing or converted Jews. Sessa is prejudiced not only toward practitioners of Jewish religious belief but also toward Jews who have taken up the Christian faith.

The reaction to Lessing's critical discourse demanding tolerance for the Jews has completely changed. Conversion is no longer a prerequisite for the Jews' acceptance into society; they are not to be accepted whether they convert or not. There is no longer a conflict between two religious points of view (although that continued to exist) but a conflict between the discourse demanding emancipation and a nationalistic anti-Semitism, which views Jews as a racial group. The dominant discourse demanding the linguistic hegemony of orthodox Christianity was replaced by a dominant discourse demanding the linguistic hegemony of Germanness. One authoritarian discourse was replaced by another, more pernicious one.

Sessa's authoritarian discourse had wide resonance. *Unser Verkehr* had an impact vastly out of proportion to what one would expect, given its tastelessness and lack of artistic merit. According to Low,

"Sessa was to attain a greater applause from a wider audience than Lessing had ever enjoyed."[157] *Unser Verkehr* fictionalized anti-Semitic *ressentiment* in the wake of the Prussian emancipation edict of 1812 and comparative laws in other German states.[158]

Stage performances of *Unser Verkehr* dominated the public cultural life of Berlin in 1815. The original production had appeared in the Breslau theater under the original title, *Die Judenschule* in 1813. After two performances, the controversial play was banned by the censor.[159]

For the Berlin production the title was changed to *Unser Verkehr* in an effort to attract less attention from the public officials whose approval was needed in order to stage the play. The performance was forbidden by Karl August von Hardenberg, the chancellor of Prussia, because he feared the piece could incite violence against the Jews and because he felt it offended Jewish religious sentiments:

> [Ich halte] es für sehr unanständig . . . ,
> wenn religiöse Begriffe, welche der Staat duldet, und [die] sich mithin seines Schutzes zu erfreuen haben, auf der Bühne lächerlich gemacht und verächtlich dargestellt werden.[160]

Ironically the act of censorship served to make more possible the elements that led to the performance's success. The suppression gave rise to a clamoring of people wishing to see the play.[161] One journal proclaimed its opposition to the censorship with anti-Semitic overtones: "Die Juden sollen es nicht durchsetzen."[162]

Because of threats against the theater, the theater management lobbied for a lifting of the ban. The Berlin chief of police also feared violence from the banning of the play and pressed Hardenberg to rescind the censorship.[163] A bowdlerized version of the play was approved by Hardenberg and had its premiere on September 2, 1815, in the Berlin Opera House. Censorship, controversy, and a scandal over one of the actors all ignited interest in the play: the leading actor Albert Wurm was put on trial for homosexuality and acquitted.[164]

The success of the play was overwhelming: it attracted considerable attention not only among the middle classes but also among the lower classes, who were less likely to frequent the theater.[165] The play was also performed in Halle, Braunschweig, Kassel, Bremen, Königsberg, Hamburg, Breslau, and Cologne.[166] That such an artistically inferior exponent of the anti-Semitic message as Sessa could attain such success points to the popularity of the message.

Unser Verkehr inspired considerable commentary on the part of contemporary journalists and critics, some of which will be examined here. In writing about the Berlin premiere in 1815, Friedrich Julius Schütz (*Zeitung für die elegante Welt*) took an anti-Semitic, essentially pro-Sessa stance. He argued in favor of performing the piece. He felt that it should not be banned for the sake of the Jewish community, because Sessa had a right to criticize sects that did not fit in well with German society: "In den Juden wird hier überdem auch nicht ein *Volk* lächerlich gemacht, weil sie keinen Staat mehr haben, nicht mehr sind, sondern blos Unterthanen andrer Staaten, die wie die auch schon auf die Bühne gebrachten Quäker, nur eine in ihren Gebräuchen zu unseren Staatseinrichtungen einmal nicht passende Sekten bilden."[167] Schütz defends Sessa's farce, because he agrees with Sessa's underlying premise that Jews should be excluded from participation in the broader German society. He views Jews as having customs that do not fit in well with German social institutions and compares them with the Quakers in this regard. He therefore applauds the politics of racism and exclusion promoted in *Unser Verkehr*.

Even Schütz, however, could not overlook the obvious aesthetic weaknesses of the play. He suggested that a more talented author should rework the play in order to bring out better the anti-Semitic message:

> Es wäre darum zu wünschen, da der unglückliche Verfasser nicht mehr, wie er wollte, sein Stück noch einmal überarbeiten konnte, ein andrer geistreicher und gewandter Lustspieldichter es übernähme, diesen Versuch als eine bloße Anlage zu einer höheren Ausführung, in der das ganze Eingreifen der Juden in unsere moralische und politische Weltordnung, durch Handlung dargestellt würde, benutzen, oder das Stück wenigstens nur durch Einlegung wirksamerer Szenen, wie zum Beispiel die ganz treffliche des Nathan in Arnims *Jena* [sic] *und Jerusalem*.[168]

Although he may have had some relatively minor disagreements with Sessa over aesthetics, he fully approved of the notion of using literature as a tool for anti-Semitic agitation. Therefore he had fervent regard for both Sessa and the more talented but equally reactionary Achim von Arnim for their racist stances.

Not all Christians agreed with Schütz's view of the play. In 1824, a liberal Christian journalist writing in *Agrippina* took a stance against the injustice and reaction promoted by Sessa. His commentary on the "Jewish question" was reminiscent of the opinions voiced by Dohm some forty years earlier:

> Wir Christen, die einen großen Schuld-Antheil haben an dem den Juden eingefleischtes Unwesen durch Unduldsamkeit und Unterdrückung, wir ziehen verfolgend gegen sie los und stellen sie verächtlich auf der merkenden Kinderseele, daß sich ewig fort-

pflanze das Vorurtheil und die Ungerechtigkeit, und daß diese sich einpflanzen, noch ehe die Zeit der eigenen reifen Ueberlegung den eigenen Geist eines Bessern belehrt.[169]

According to this author, the problems in German-Jewish relations arose because of the exclusionary attitudes and the oppression perpetrated by the Christian majority. He is therefore offended by the hateful image of the Jew advanced by Sessa's play: "Es ist unverantwortlich, einem solchen Schauspiel mit Lust und Trieb beizuwohnen."[170] The farce fails to be humorous to him, because he does not support the derision and disparagement of the Jewish minority, which the farce champions. He is not susceptible to joining the "community of laughter" to which the play is an invitation, and therefore does not fall under the influence of racist elements that were seeking to revoke the progress accorded to Jews in the area of equal rights.

More journalistic resistance to Sessa's authoritarian discourse came from other quarters. One of the viewers of the 1815 Berlin premiere was a young German Jewish political journalist who was later to become one of the major writers of the "Young Germany" movement. Ludwig Börne (1786–1837), a staunch defender of Jewish civil rights, denounced the nationalistic rejection of the notion of equal rights for religioethnic minorities.[171]

In his review of Sessa's farce, the twenty-nine-year old Börne displays a keen awareness of the ambivalences inherent within the written form. On the one hand, he wishes to unmistakably condemn the play. On the other hand, he does not wish to fuel the flames of controversy surrounding the play and thereby add to its success. He does condemn the nationalistic and anti-Semitic sentiment expounded by the play, but shows a somewhat contrived degree of restraint in so doing:

> Die Aufführung dieser Posse zu Berlin fiel in jene Zeit, wo einige Hauptstädter, die sich für das deutsche Volk hielten, alles von sich abstießen, was nicht deutsch war, oder sie gleich den Juden für undeutsch erklären wollten. Wie es entnervten Menschen eigen ist, daß sie in den Gebärdungen des Zorns und des Hasses sich gefallen, weil sie solche äußerungen als Zeichen des Kraftgefühls und eines selbstständigen Daseins geltend machen möchten, so haben auch jene Schwächlinge, um Volkstümlichkeit und Vaterlandsliebe zu offenbaren einen Haß gegen Juden, der oft ihrem eignen Herz fremd war, den Bessern aufzudringen gesucht.[172]

Börne viewed the play as being basically a work of low-level propaganda designed to serve as a unifying factor for proponents of a na-

Myths of Ethnic Homogeneity   149

tionalistic race-hatred. But he is skeptical of the persuasive efficacy of the play. Jew-hatred is viewed by him as being a misguided expression of patriotism, which fails to convince even the perpetrator on any kind of serious level: anti-Semitism of the sort promoted by Sessa was for Börne an expression of weakness but not of evil. He did not consider even the monoculturalistic and anti-Semitic proponents represented by Sessa to be immune from a certain internal dialogism which would prevent them from seriously hating the Jews. In this statement, Börne seems to underestimate the potential efficacy of the play as a fomenter of hatred. But Börne's statement may have been motivated by a desire not to blow the play out of proportion and thereby make Sessa's work more controversial than it deserved to be, because such action would ultimately guarantee its success.

If Börne did not regard the play as dangerous, he certainly did consider it to be offensive. He distinguishes between what he considers to be rightful satire and the more pernicious practice of defamatory humor. First he describes rightful satire,[173] in which characteristics of individuals within certain groups are criticized and these individual characteristics might be condemned, but no attempt is made to incite hatred against the group as a whole. Defamatory humor, on the other hand, is characterized by the wholesale condemnation of an entire group of people:

> Wenn aber Judenmanieren auf der Bühne gebracht werden, und diese wie in "Unser Verkehr" das ganze Spiel ausfüllen, so müssen solche Darstellungen den jüdischen Glaubensgenossen mit Recht verwünschenswert sein.... [Die] Zuschauer ... werden ... die bei solchen Anlässen empfangenen Eindrücke mit sich aus dem Schauspielhause tragen und die auf die Bühne mit Treue oder Überladung vorgespielten Gebrechen der Juden überlicherweise allen diesen Glaubensbekennern anrechnen.[174]

Börne denounces the false stereotyping inherent within defamatory humor, because it is based on condemnations of entire groups, rather than individual characteristics of particular members of certain groups. A humor which is targeted toward alterable individual characteristics constitutes legitimate social criticism because it does not foster hatred toward an entire group of people. On the other hand, such humor as that championed by Sessa wrongly foments prejudice.

The pamphleteers and playwrights who wrote on behalf of a nationalistic Christian Germanness sought to promote and reinforce a monologic identity. But the uniformity they sought could only be implemented through rigidly differentiating themselves from the outsiders.

A rigid conformity was advanced and implemented through unifying German Christians against common enemies, including but not limited to the Jews. This was done in part by playing on the fears of the populace, particularly the economic fears, and encouraging the preconception that the Jews constituted a threat to the financial well-being and economic survival of the Christian majority. Often this was done through hateful invective, which offered the struggling masses a cathartic outlet for their anger and thereby manipulated them into taking an anti-Semitic stance. Other times this was done even more insidiously through subjecting targeted audiences to a barrage of derisory humor and thereby appealing to the desire of the downtrodden masses to feel good about themselves. In this humor, Gentiles were portrayed as being morally and existentially superior to the Jewish outgroup and these authors made the self-image of their constituencies dependent upon the hatred of and disdain for the "other."

The Enlightenment had attempted to appeal to humankind's most noble characteristics: tolerance, humanism, and rationalism and a type of humor that induced self-criticism and that was directed at social improvement. It was supplanted by a nationalism and religious chauvinism that appealed to the worst characteristics that humankind had to offer by promulgating the notion that religioethnic minorities were responsible for all social ills. Therefore, the implication was that there was no need for the members of the majority group to improve themselves, since they were already superior to the members of the minority. Since people believed that the minorities were the cause of social evils, improvement in the human condition was to be attained not through bettering the society as a whole, but through oppressing the members of minority groups.

6. Concluding Remarks: Beyond the Tolerance Debate

Have you thought there could be but a single Supreme?
There can be any number of Supremes—One does not countervail another, any more than one eyesight countervails another or one life countervails another.
—Walt Whitman, "By Blue Ontario's Shore"

The question remains, what does the tolerance debate have to teach the current generation?[1] While progressive forces have tried to redefine tolerance as an "indulgence of diversity" and a "freedom of conviction," it still carries much of the baggage of the earlier and narrower Christian definition of "concession," of a temporary sufferance or forbearance of evil as a pretext for conversion to the superior religion and culture.[2] Such a restricted definition of tolerance must of necessity impinge on the ability of the tolerance concept to bring about equality between differing religioethnic groups.

Much of the paradoxical nature of tolerance is wrapped up in Max Horkheimer and Theodor W. Adorno's statement in their famous tract, *Dialektik der Aufklärung* (1947):

> Der Antisemitismus heute gilt den einen als Schicksalsfrage der Menschheit, den anderen als bloßer Vorwand. Für die Faschisten sind die Juden nicht eine Minorität, sondern die Gegenrasse, das negative Prinzip als solches; von ihrer Ausrottung soll das Glück der Welt abhängen. Extrem entgegengesetzt ist die These, die Juden, frei von nationalen oder Rassenmerkmalen, bildeten eine Gruppe durch religiöse Meinung und Tradition, durch nichts sonst. . . . Indem die liberale These die Einheit der Menschen als prinzipiell bereits verwirklicht ansetzt, hilft sie zur Apologie des Bestehenden.[3]

Horkheimer and Adorno's ironically expressed but basically true statement that racists have a more consistent position than do tolerant liberals merits further thought and reflection. We have examined writings thematizing the "Jewish question" from both tolerant and anti-Semitic perspectives. The writings of the proponents of multiculturalism are, for the most part, beset by conceptual fissures. This comes about, for the most part, because multiculturalists seek to enter into a dialogue with "Otherness." But in order to do so, multiculturalists must first enter into an internal dialogue with themselves. Conceptual fissures arise because elements of this internal dialogue often remain unresolved. Attempts to resolve the dialogue often manifest themselves in a superficial assimilation of the "Otherness": an attempt to make the other more similar to oneself rather than to appreciate the otherness for what it is and resolve it in a spirit of mutual respect.

Many will contend that there is a utopian aspect to tolerance and hence that it is unrealistic. Consider Hannah Arendt's critique of the internal contradictions inherent in the position of the eighteenth-century advocates of tolerance: "The particularly tolerant, educated, and cultured non-Jews could be bothered socially only with exceptionally educated Jews. . . . Jews were exhorted to be educated enough not to behave like ordinary Jews, but they were, on the other hand, accepted only because they were Jews, because of their foreign exotic appeal."[4] Gershom Scholem, the famous Jewish theologian, writing in 1965, goes even further than Arendt does. He states that the willingness of the Germans to enter into dialogue with the Jews was done "under the presupposition that Jews were willing to give themselves up as *Jewish* to an ever more progressive extent."[5] Rapprochement with the outsiders was made dependent on their willingness to distance themselves from their own ingroup: all sense of Jewish collectivity was to be abolished and the Jews were to be reconstructed as "universal" human beings possessing no group, but only individual, characteristics.[6] This worldview was dependent upon a largely ahistorical view of humankind as being a series of individuals always the same in all times and at all places.

But is the monoculturalist position demanding ethnic and religious homogeneity any less utopian? Its ultimate goal is to impose a unitary consciousness upon its own ingroup through fossilization of consensus formations. Through a process of dissimilation and false projection, the monoculturalist also recreates the minority in his own image: hatred cannot be sustained through healthy social conditions but only through mass neuroses and psychoses.

Through rigidly defined rules of exclusion, monoculturalism seeks to impede uncomfortable modes of thought. In so doing, it must of necessity exclude the outsiders who will be inevitably forced to mount challenges to social a prioris and will seek to enter into dialogue with the dominant society. The dominant society will be increasingly compelled to resist communication by attempting to compel its opponents to restrict themselves to "officially" sanctioned discursive formations.

And it will rest content in the belief that their way of seeing things is the only conceivable way of viewing them. But the price will be rampant injustice and a stymieing of social progress, with potentially devastating results. Jean-Paul Sartre pointed to the utopian pretensions of the ethnocentric reaction in his 1948 study, *Anti-Semite and Jew*.[7]

Through fighting the pariah, monoculturalists convince themselves of the righteousness and sanctity of their own a prioris, making racism an indispensable unifying element. The monoculturalists hate the pariahs, but they cannot live without them: "If the Jew did not exist, the anti-Semite would invent him."[8] One aspect of bigotry is the interchangeability of the victim: assimilation of the Jews must inevitably lead to the "construction" of new pariahs: blacks, Asians, Arabs, Turks, and Gypsies, or whoever else falls outside the parameter of the consensus formations. Ethnocentrists and monoculturalists must oppose all those who contradict their "single Supreme," their principle of unitary consciousness.

As has been previously mentioned, both the anti-Semitic and the philo-Semitic writers recreated the Jews in their own image. Anti-Semitism and liberal pretextual tolerance are vastly differing political visions of reality, yet they both construct an unbridgeable gulf between familiarity and otherness.[9] As Edward W. Said points out, all cultures "impose corrections upon raw reality." Cultures are "inclined to impose complete transformations on other cultures; receiving those cultures not as they are, but as, for the benefit of the receiver, they ought to be."[10]

Whereas the anti-Semite wishes to exaggerate ethnic differences and make them into reasons for the rejection of otherness, the liberal wishes to deny the importance and existence of these ethnic differences altogether in order to, in Sartre's terms, "isolate the Jew from his religion, from his family, from his ethnic community, in order to plunge him into the democratic crucible whence he will emerge naked and alone, an individual and solitary particle like all the other particles."[11]

The desire to "tolerantly" bring about the assimilation of the minority leads to an intolerant backlash when members of the minority group refuse to comply. As Julia Kristeva points out in her recent book, *Strangers to Ourselves*: "the absorption of otherness proposed by our societies turns out to be inacceptable to the contemporary individual, jealous of his difference—one that is not only national and ethical but essentially subjective, unsurmountable."[12] Neither the principles of the anti-Semites nor those of the advocates of the tolerance ideology were acceptable to the Jewish community as a whole. The anti-Semite wishes to deny the Jew status as a human being and "leave nothing in him but the Jew, the pariah, the untouchable," whereas tolerant liberals wish to deny the Jews status as Jews and leave nothing in them but the human being, "the abstract and universal subject of the rights of man and the rights of the citizen."[13]

A pretextual tolerance that is based on the principle of assimilation and demands that the minority give up its differences leads to ethnic self-hatred: members of the minority who do assimilate live in fear that their behaviors will correspond to the negative stereotypes the dominant culture has of their group.[14] As in the case of Rahel Varnhagen, many Jews wanted to lose themselves in the Christian world, yet they remained fixed in the Jewish milieu.[15]

This dilemma can only be escaped if tolerance as a pretext for assimilation can be superseded as an ideology for race relations. It should be replaced by a recognition of cultural difference and nonconformity not as an anomaly but as a legitimate and inevitable factor in human relations. Pretextual tolerance with the hope of absorption should give way to a genuine multicultural understanding. It falls upon our educational institutions to continue the direction of trying to impart greater degrees of multicultural literacy to its students and to the broader public. The time is past when the dominant culture could expect the unquestioned dominion of its cultural *a prioris*. As Kristeva points out, "A new homogeneity is not very likely, perhaps hardly desirable. . . . A paradoxical community is emerging, made up of foreigners who are reconciled with themselves to the extent that they recognize themselves as foreigners."[16] Ethnic and religious minorities of various sorts in today's society are increasingly reconciling themselves to their roles as pariahs and preferring that situation to the path of the parvenu.

In applying this condition to the "Jewish question," Arendt points out that emancipation should have been "an admission of Jews *as Jews* to the ranks of humanity, rather than a permit to ape the Gentiles or an opportunity to play the *parvenu*."[17] In the absence of such full acceptance of otherness, pariahdom is preferable to conformity to an unjust society. It accords a stance from which to criticize that society. The parvenu is not "born to the system, but chose it of his own free will, and . . . is called upon to pay the cost meticulously and exactly, whereas others can take things in their stride."[18]

For Arendt, the question of being a parvenu or a pariah is nothing less than a choice between social ambition and political consciousness. Only a pariah can develop a true political consciousness because only pariahs can affirm their ethnic identity and push politically for minority rights.[19] Pariahs tend to be resisters, whereas parvenus tend to be politically malleable.[20] It is for this reason that the Jewish pariah became the symbol for Lessing's attacks on the orthodox Christian hegemony of the feudal order in *Nathan der Weise*. There was no ready-made element in the majority culture to which Lessing could turn in order to launch his social criticism. He was therefore forced to express his disapproval of the majority culture through celebrating the pariah.

A society devoid of pariahs will be bereft of a major source of social progress in the form of the oppositional currents that conscious pariahs provide. Such a society will be built upon ossified consensus formations, which will either impose permanent limitations on that society or be surmounted with the greatest of difficulties. A society that defends the right to be different and extends that right to its pariahs will be assured of critical currents, which may lead to real social alternatives being extended to the majority. Only through diversity of outlook can the possibility of social progress be safeguarded.

The existence of minority groups who fall outside the parameters of consensus formations and the other vagaries of group identity guarantees that a conceptual alternative to those consensus formations will exist, should such consensus formations prove to be unduly repressive or inimical to the interests of a large number of individuals within the society. Much of the secularization of modern society, which benefited Christian heterodox thinkers as well as Jews, would not have been possible had it not been for the Jewish community because of the role it played in the "disappearance of that state which had its foundations in theological principles."[21]

Lessing's family circle in the concluding scene of *Nathan der Weise* is an invitation to a multicultural utopia. There is no question as to whether we will be utopianists in the long run. The real issue is whether we will be utopianists for the ideal of tolerance and multiculturalism or utopianists for the far-from-ideal situation of monoculturalism, reaction, and bigotry. History is our guide: the ultimate choice is our own.

Notes

Chapter 1

1. Reichmann, *Hostages of Civilisation*, 172.
2. Arendt, *Antisemitism*, viii.
3. Indeed, some of the most valuable research into the nature of anti-Semitism was done in the 1940s and 1950s.
4. Turn-of-the-century investigations of the portrayal of Jews in German literature, such as those carried out by Herbert Carrington in his dissertation, "Die Figur des Juden in der dramatischen Litteratur des 18. Jahrhunderts" (Heidelberg, 1897), and Heinrich Stümcke in his 1904 study, *Die Fortsetzungen, Nachahmungen und Travestien von Lessings "Nathan der Weise,"* are high on plot summaries but low on analysis. They are useful primarily for their bibliographical references and, in the case of Stümcke's book, for the reprints of rare early nineteenth-century plays. The notorious Nazi dissertations of Elisabeth Frenzel ("Judengestalten auf der deutschen Bühne," 1940) and Hans Karl Krüger ("Berliner Romantik und Berliner Judentum," 1939) are certainly devoid of scholarly merit and only the bibliographical references have any value.

Helmut Jenzsch's 1974 dissertation from the University of Hamburg, "Jüdische Figuren in deutschen Bühnentexten des 18. Jahrhunderts," concerns itself with formalistic issues and restricts itself to the positive and "neutral" portrayals of Jews during the eighteenth century and does not examine the transition from the enlightened literature of the eighteenth century to the largely anti-Semitic literature of the early nineteenth century. In many of the plays discussed by Jenzsch, Jews play only minor roles and political issues are not thematized.

The political and ideological issues surrounding Jewish emancipation come more to the forefront in Hans Friedrich Wessels's 1979 monograph, *Lessings "Nathan der Weise": Seine Wirkungsgeschichte bis zur Ende der Goethezeit*. Wessels offers a comprehensive overview of the journalistic reception of *Nathan* and he also provides an insightful sociological analysis of the plays written in reaction to *Nathan*. He restricts himself to those dramas which were earlier discussed by Stümcke. Wessels blurs the transition from the emancipatory literature of the late eighteenth century to the anti-Semitic literature of the early nineteenth century. The historical transition from emancipation to nationalistic anti-Semitism becomes clearer through examination of a broader base of literature from this era.

Rose Schipper Wightman's dissertation, "The Changing Image of the Jew as Reflected in German Drama in the Time of Lessing and Heine" (Wayne State University, 1967) focuses primarily on major authors such as Lessing and Heine. Her analysis of minor works dealing with Jews is frequently based on secondhand knowledge and is rife with inaccuracies. Charlene A. Lea provides a useful analysis of the portrayal of Jews in nineteenth-century dramas in her monograph *Emancipation, Assimilation and Stereotype: The Image of the Jew in German and Austrian Drama, 1800–1850* (1978). Most of the plays she discusses are from after 1815, so the circumstances surrounding the literary reflection of the first manifestations of Jewish emancipation and counter-emancipation are not examined in detail.

5. Rürup, *Emanzipation und Antisemitismus*, 11.
6. Katz, *From Prejudice to Destruction*, 1.
7. Ibid.
8. Ibid., 2.
9. Ibid.
10. Low, *Jews in the Eyes of the Germans*, 18–19.
11. Ibid., 19.
12. Spiel, *Fanny von Arnstein*, 73.
13. Low, *Jews in the Eyes of the Germans*, 20.
14. Ibid., 20.
15. Ibid., 21.
16. Ibid., 22.
17. Barton, "Der lange Weg zur Toleranz," 11.
18. Ibid., 33.
19. Ibid., 13.
20. Spiel, *Fanny von Arnstein*, 80.
21. Stern, *Der preußische Staat und die Juden*, 3:7–8.
22. Low, *Jews in the Eyes of the Germans*, 23.
23. Ibid., 24–26.
24. Ibid., 27.
25. Ibid., 28–29.
26. Ibid., 103.
27. Ibid., 105.
28. Rürup, *Emanzipation und Antisemitismus*, 17.
29. Ibid., 78.
30. Poliakov, *The History of Anti-Semitism*, 3:461.
31. Sterling, *Judenhaß*, 26.
32. Ibid., 31, and Claussen, *Grenzen der Aufklärung*, 19.
33. Sterling, *Judenhaß*, 29.
34. Ibid., 30.
35. Ibid., 31.
36. Ibid.
37. *Encyclopedia Judaica*, 1:87.
38. The continuing validity of Sumner's research is evidenced not only by its inclusion in *The Authoritarian Personality* (1950), the classic study by Theodor W. Adorno, Else Frenkel-Brunswik, Daniel J. Levinson, and R. Nevitt Sanford, but also by its inclusion in Werner Bergmann's 1988 study, *Error without Trial: Psychological Research on Antisemitism*, and in numerous other

sociological and psychological studies. See Bergmann, "Group Theory and Ethnic Relations," 139. See also Sumner, *Folkways*, 27.

39. Bergmann, "Group Theory and Ethnic Relations," 139. and Sumner, *Folkways*, 27.
40. Bergmann, "Group Theory and Ethnic Relations," 140–41.
41. Ibid., 141.
42. Ibid.
43. Ibid.
44. Sartre, *Anti-Semite and Jew*, 27.
45. Fein, "Explanations of the Origin and Evolution of Antisemitism," 9.
46. Rubin, *Anti-Semitism: A Disease of the Mind*, 103.
47. Adorno, Frenkel-Brunswik, Levinson, and Sanford, *The Authoritarian Personality*, 43.
48. Ibid., 48–49.
49. Ibid., 147.
50. Ibid.: "The ethnocentric individual feels threatened by most of the groups to which he does not have a sense of belonging; if he cannot identify, he must oppose; if a group is not 'acceptable,' it is 'alien.' The ingroup-outgroup distinction thus becomes the basis for most of his thinking, and people are categorized according to the groups to which they belong."
51. Ibid., 149.
52. Reichmann, *Hostages of Civilisation*, 22.
53. Ibid., 23.
54. Ibid., 24.
55. Ibid.
56. Ibid.
57. Ibid., 25.
58. Ibid., 27.
59. Rubin, *Anti-Semitism: A Disease of the Mind*, 93.
60. Sartre, *Anti-Semite and Jew*, 67.
61. Reichmann, *Hostages of Civilisation*, 29.
62. Ibid., 31–33.
63. Fein, "Explanations of the Origin and Evolution of Antisemitism," 9.
64. Adorno, Frenkel-Brunswik, Levinson, and Sanford, *The Authoritarian Personality*, 149.
65. Horkheimer and Adorno, *Dialektik der Aufklärung*, 153.
66. Fenichel, "Elements of a Psychoanalytic Theory of Anti-Semitism," 13–14.
67. Sartre, *Anti-Semite and Jew*, 43–44.
68. Simmel, "Anti-Semitism and Mass Psychopathology," 37.
69. Adorno, Frenkel-Brunswik, Levinson, and Sanford, *The Authoritarian Personality*, 485.
70. Ibid.
71. Glock and Stark, *Christian Beliefs and Anti-Semitism*, 208.
72. Ibid., 21.
73. Ibid., 35.

74. Ibid., 208.
75. Ibid., 210–11.
76. Adorno, Frenkel-Brunswik, Levinson, and Sanford, *The Authoritarian Personality*, 310.
77. Ibid., 310.
78. Ibid., 730.
79. Ibid., 759.
80. Ibid., 95.
81. See ibid., 730.
82. Ibid., 233.
83. Bettelheim and Janowitz, *Social Change and Prejudice*, 107.
84. Ibid.
85. Adorno, Frenkel-Brunswik, Levinson, and Sanford, *The Authoritarian Personality*, 233–34.
86. Bettelheim and Janowitz, *Social Change and Prejudice*, 200.
87. See Adorno, Frenkel-Brunswik, Levinson, and Sanford, *The Authoritarian Personality*, 239. The opposite tendency can be observed among anti-authoritarian personalities. Their tendency to reject the overriding values of their ingroup manifests itself as an identification with the pariah group. The outgroup is thereby idealized and becomes a symbol of a rejection of the dominant powers. See the analysis of Lessing in Chapter 2.
88. Horkheimer and Adorno, *Dialektik der Aufklärung*, 168.
89. Bettelheim and Janowitz, *Social Change and Prejudice*, 137.
90. Horkheimer and Adorno, *Dialektik der Aufklärung*, 172.
91. Orr, "Anti-Semitism and the Psychopathology of Everyday Life," 89.
92. Fenichel, "Elements of a Psychoanalytic Theory of Anti-Semitism," 20–21.
93. Ibid.
94. Ibid.
95. Ibid.
96. Ibid., 17.
97. Simmel, "Anti-Semitism and Mass Psychopathology," 35.
98. Sartre, *Anti-Semite and Jew*, 30.
99. Simmel, "Anti-Semitism and Mass Psychopathology," 36.
100. Berding, *Moderner Antisemitismus in Deutschland*, 17.
101. Morais, *A Short History of Anti-Semitism*, 109.
102. Berding, *Moderner Antisemitismus in Deutschland*, 17–18.
103. Reichmann, *Hostages of Civilisation*, 45.
104. Léon, *The Jewish Question: A Marxist Interpretation*, 171.
105. Berding, *Moderner Antisemitismus in Deutschland*, 19.
106. Reichmann, *Hostages of Civilisation*, 43.
107. Ibid., 44.
108. Horkheimer and Adorno, *Dialektik der Aufklärung*, 155–58.
109. Ibid.
110. Ibid.
111. Poliakov, *The History of Anti-Semitism*, 3:6–7.
112. Sombart, *The Jews and Modern Capitalism*, 6.

113. Poliakov, *The History of Anti-Semitism*, 3:13.
114. Sombart, *The Jews and Modern Capitalism*, 119.
115. Ibid., 132.
116. Poliakov, *The History of Anti-Semitism*, 3:49.
117. Morais, *A Short History of Anti-Semitism*, 110.
118. Poliakov, *The History of Anti-Semitism*, 3:7.
119. Sombart, *The Jews and Modern Capitalism*, 135.
120. Ibid., 150, and Poliakov, *The History of Anti-Semitism*, 3:11.
121. Sombart, *The Jews and Modern Capitalism*, 151, and Poliakov, *The History of Anti-Semitism*, 3:7.
122. Poliakov, *The History of Anti-Semitism*, 3:8.
123. Ibid., 11.
124. Baron, et al., *Economic History of the Jews*, 71.
125. Ibid.
126. Ibid.
127. Ibid.
128. Ibid.
129. Ibid.
130. Sterling, *Judenhaß*, 29.
131. Sartre, *Anti-Semite and Jew*, 68.
132. Arendt, *Antisemitism*, 25.
133. Scholem, "Jews and Germans," 74.
134. See Frank, *What Is Neostructuralism?*, 106.
135. Foucault, "The Discourse on Languages," in *The Archaeology of Knowledge*, 216: "In a society such as our own, we all know the rules of *exclusion*. The most obvious and familiar of these concerns what is *prohibited*. We know perfectly well that we are not free to say just anything, that we simply cannot speak of anything, when we like or where we like; not just anyone finally, may speak of just anything. We have three types of prohibition, covering objects, ritual with its surrounding circumstances, the privileged or exclusive right to speak of a particular subject; these prohibitions interrelate, reinforce and complement each other, forming a complex web, continually subject to modification."
136. Voloshinov, *Marxism and the Philosophy of Language*, 23.
137. Brugger, *Philosophical Dictionary*, 421.
138. *Lexikon für Theologie und Kirche*, edited by Josef Höfer and Karl Rahner, 239–46.
139. Voloshinov, *Marxism and the Philosophy of Language*, 9, 10, 11.
140. Ibid., 21.
141. Ibid., 23.
142. Frank, *What Is Neostructuralism?*, 184.
143. Foucault, *The Archaeology of Knowledge*, 27.
144. Freud, "Repression," 424.
145. Ibid., 427.
146. Foucault, *The Order of Things*, xx.
147. Ibid.

148. Ibid. xxi.
149. Foucault, "Discourse on Languages," in *The Archaeology of Knowledge*, 228.
150. Ibid., 226.
151. Foucault, *The Order of Things*, 23–24: "Sympathy is an instance of the *same* so strong and so insistent that it will not rest content to be merely one of the forms of likeness, it has the dangerous power of *assimilating*, of rendering things identical to one another, of mingling them, of causing their individuality to disappear—and thus rendering them foreign to what they were before."
152. Bauer, *Kirchengeschichte der neueren Zeit*, 586–91.
153. Katz, *From Prejudice to Destruction*, 8.
154. Ibid., 23.
155. Ibid.
156. Stephan and Laube, *Handbuch der Kirchengeschichte*, 4:104.
157. Ibid., 105.
158. See François-Marie Arouet de Voltaire, "Jews" (1756), in Mendes-Flohr and Reinharz, *The Jew in the Modern World*, 252.
159. Katz, *From Prejudice to Destruction*, 25.
160. Berding, *Moderner Antisemitismus in Deutschland*, 53.
161. Low, *Jews in the Eyes of the Germans*, 37: "The Enlightenment had a considerable influence on the relationship between Germans and Jews. The flourishing of individualism and cosmopolitanism, the simultaneous recession of national and religious exclusiveness, and the popularity of Deism, the religious fashion of the age, all tended to establish closer links between Germans and Jews."
162. Katz, *Zur Assimilation und Emanzipation der Juden*, 84–85: "Daß die Emanzipation der Juden mit der Säkularisierung der europäischen Staaten und der Gesellschaft zusammenhängt, ist unbestreitbar. Innerhalb des von der christlichen Kirche gelenkten Staates wäre die Aufnahme der Juden als gleichberechtigte Bürger undenkbar gewesen. So könnte man die Anfänge der Judenemanzipation mit den Anfängen des Säkulisierungsprozeßes gleichsetzen."
163. Pinson, *Pietism As a Factor in the Rise of German Nationalism*, 105.
164. See Pütz, *Die deutsche Aufklärung*, 19. See also Stephan and Laube, *Handbuch der Kirchengeschichte*, 4:107.
165. Prignitz, *Vaterlandsliebe und Freiheit: Deutscher Patriotismus von 1750 bis 1850*, 43.
166. Ibid., 59–60.
167. Berding, *Moderner Antisemitismus in Deutschland*, 58.
168. Ibid., 58–59.
169. Ruether, "The Theological Roots of Anti-Semitism," 42.
170. Ibid.
171. Reichmann, *Hostages of Civilisation*, 53.
172. Katz, *From Prejudice to Destruction*, 76.
173. Ibid., 87.
174. Reichmann, *Hostages of Civilisation*, 61.
175. Ibid., 122.

Notes to Pages 29–36 163

176. Ibid.
177. Ibid., 123.
178. Ibid., 133.
179. Ibid., 135.
180. Ibid., 136.
181. Ibid., 137–38.
182. Ibid., 140.
183. Ruether, "The Theological Roots of Anti-Semitism," 43.
184. Pinson, *Pietism as a Factor in the Rise of German Nationalism*, 27.
185. Ibid., 34.
186. Ibid., 33.

Chapter 2

1. The works mentioned in the notes to this chapter by no means cover the full range of Lessing scholarship. I have instead tried to concentrate on that secondary literature that was most relevant to the narrow confines of this study. For a history of scholarship on Lessing's *Nathan*, see Jo-Jacqueline Eckardt's recent book, *Lessing's "Nathan the Wise" and the Critics*.
2. Johann Melchior Goeze, "Ein Predigt gegen fremde Religions-Verwandte" (1771), quoted in Meyer, *The Origins of the Modern Jew*, 191.
3. Gilman, *Jewish Self-hatred*, 56.
4. Lessing, *Werke*, 7:129.
5. *Encyclopedia Judaica*, 10:1208–09.
6. Johnson, *A History of the Jews*, 208.
7. Wilson, *Humanität und Kreuzzugsideologie um 1780*, 60.
8. Ibid., 73.
9. Lessing, *Werke*, 2:299.
10. Mayer, "Der weise Nathan und der Rauber Spiegelberg," 364–65.
11. Jenzsch, "Jüdische Figuren in deutschen Bühnentexten des 18. Jahrhunderts," 299.
12. The English Christian religious reformer Leonard Busher had demanded the extension of religious liberties to Jews as early as 1614 in his tract, "Religious Peace, or a Plea for Liberty of Conscience."
13. Mosse, *German Jews beyond Judaism*, 15–16.
14. Fischer-Gardner, "Der obskure Traum der Toleranz," 5.
15. Bennett, *Modern Drama and German Classicism*, 91.
16. Ibid., 8.
17. Suesse-Fiedler, *Lessings "Nathan der Weise" und sein Leser*, 291–92.
18. Mayer, "Der weise Nathan und der Rauber Spiegelberg," 364.
19. Bennett, *Modern Drama and German Classicism*, 84.
20. Lessing, *Werke*, 2:253.
21. Politzer, "Lessings Parabel von den drei Ringen," 357.
22. König, *Natürlichkeit und Wirklichkeit*, 45.
23. Barner, Grimm, Kiesel, and Kramer, *Lessing: Epoche, Werk, Wirkung*, 303.

24. See Berghahn, "Der Jude als der Andere: Das Zeitalter der Toleranz und die Judenfrage," 22.
25. Mayer, *Outsiders: A Study in Life and Letters*, 303.
26. Pütz, *Die Leistung der Form: Lessings Dramen*, 269–70.
27. Hernadi, "Nathan der Bürger: Lessings Mythos vom aufgeklärten Kaufmann," 342–43.
28. Cases, "Lessings 'Nathan der Weise,'" 334.
29. Bizet, "Die Weisheit Nathans," 303–4.
30. Ibid., 306.
31. Suesse-Fiedler, *Lessings "Nathan der Weise" und sein Leser*, 170–71.
32. Claussen, *Grenzen der Aufklärung: Zur gesellschaftlichen Geschichte des modernen Antisemitismus*, 55.
33. Barner, Grimm, Kiesel, and Kramer, *Lessing: Epoche, Werk, Wirkung*, 307.
34. Ibid.
35. Politzer, "Lessings Parabel von den drei Ringen," 358.
36. Atkins, "Die Ringparabel," 165.
37. Zymner, "Kunstapotheose in der Ringparabel," 89.
38. Ibid., 92.
39. Leventhal, "The Parable as Performance," 509.
40. Ibid., 509, 511.
41. Ibid., 512, 512–13.
42. Ibid., 515, 516.
43. Ibid., 520–21.
44. Bennett, *Modern Drama and German Classicism*, 84.
45. Wessels, *Lessings "Nathan der Weise*," 19.
46. Quoted in ibid., 31.
47. Quoted in ibid., 32.
48. Schmidt, *Lessing*, 380–81.
49. Wessels, *Lessings "Nathan der Weise*," 69.
50. *Reichs-Post-Reuters*, February 17, 1780, quoted in Wessels, *Lessings "Nathan der Weise*," 39.
51. *Vossiche Zeitung*, 1780, quoted in Wessels, *Lessings "Nathan der Weise*, 41.
52. Holquist, *Dialogism*, 34.
53. Ibid., 52.
54. G. E. Lessing, quoted in Schmidt, *Lessing*, 343.
55. Tralles, *Zufällige . . . Betrachtungen*, 44, 30, 32.
56. Ibid., 56.
57. See Foucault, "Polemics, Politics, and Problematizations," 382.
58. Borgius, *Lessings "Nathan" und "Der Mönch vom Libanon": Zum hundertjährigen Gedächtnis beider Dichtungen*, 4. See also Wessels, *Lessings "Nathan der Weise*," 282.
59. Johann Georg Pfranger, quoted in Borgius, *Lessings "Nathan" und "Der Mönch von Libanon*," 4. In a letter to his wife, Pfranger commented on the impact which Reimarus's and Lessing's writings had on him: "Ich muß Dir gestehen, daß diese Tage die unglücklichsten meines Lebens waren. Zweifel der Religion marterten mich, das ist der unglücklichste Zustand, den ich mir

denken kann. Aber Gott sei Dank sie ist überwunden und desto stärker ist mein Glaube."

60. J. E. Berger, 1794, quoted in Wessels, *Lessings "Nathan der Weise,"* 282.
61. Pfranger, *Der Mönch vom Libanon*, 40.
62. Ibid., 41.
63. Ibid., 51.
64. Ibid., 43–44.
65. The term "ideologeme" was coined by members of the Bakhtin Circle to denote discourse that is infused with ideology.
66. Ibid., 108.
67. Ibid., 100.
68. Ibid., 172.
69. Ibid., 130.
70. Ibid., 135.
71. Ibid., 69.
72. Ibid., 79.
73. Ibid., 213.
74. Ibid., 263.
75. Wessels, *Lessings "Nathan der Weise,"* 292.
76. Arendt, *Antisemitism*, 29.
77. Pfranger, *Der Mönch vom Libanon*, 265–66.
78. Ibid., 149.
79. Said, *Orientalism*, 27–28.
80. Lessing, *Werke*, 2:253.
81. Pfranger, *Der Mönch vom Libanon*, 262.
82. Wessels, *Lessings "Nathan der Weise,"* 293.
83. Schmidt, *Lessing*, 379.
84. Borgius, *Lessings "Nathan" und "Der Mönch vom Libanon,"* 6.
85. Ibid., 10.
86. Wessels, *Lessings "Nathan der Weise,"* 290.
87. Heinze, *Das deutsche Märtyrerdrama der Moderne*, 12.
88. See Szarota, *Künstler, Grübler und Rebellen: Studien zum europäischen Märtyrerdrama des 17. Jahrhunderts*, 5.
89. Klüger, "Kreuzzug und Kinderträume in Lessings *Nathan der Weise*," 201.
90. See Demetz, "Lessings 'Nathan der Weise': Wirklichkeiten und Wirklichkeit," 169.
91. See Berghahn, "Comedy without Laughter: Jewish Characters in Comedies from Shylock to Nathan," 22.
92. Kettner, *Lessings Dramen im Lichte ihrer und unserer Zeit*, 346.
93. Lessing, *Werke*, 2:317.
94. Wolfram Mauser observed in one of my seminars at the University of Freiburg that Nathan's recounting of the pogrom in which his wife and seven children were murdered was the most moving moment in Ernst Deutsch's famous on-stage portrayal of Nathan.
95. Kettner, *Lessings Dramen im Lichte ihrer und unserer Zeit*, 343.

96. Ibid., 296.
97. Ibid.
98. Ibid., 54–55.
99. Katz, *Zur Assimilation und Emanzipation der Juden*, 88.
100. Reuss, *Christian Wilhelm Dohms Schrift "Über die bürgerliche Verbesserung der Juden" und deren Einwirkung auf die gebildeten Stände Deutschlands*, 21.
101. Sorkin, *The Transformation of German Jewry*, 23.
102. Liberles, "Dohm's Treatise on the Jews," 34.
103. Sorkin, *The Transformation of German Jewry*, 27.
104. Berding, *Moderner Antisemitismus in Deutschland*, 24.
105. Dambacher, *Christian Wilhelm von Dohm: Ein Beitrag zur Geschichte des preußischen aufgeklärten Beamtentums und seiner Reformbestrebungen am Ausgang des 18. Jahrhunderts*, 175–76.
106. Ibid., 183.
107. Reuss, *Christian Wilhelm Dohms Schrift "Über die bürgerliche Verbesserung der Juden" und deren Einwirkung auf die gebildeten Stände Deutschlands*, 30.
108. Ibid., 37.

Chapter 3

1. Breuer, "Das Bild der Aufklärung," 135.
2. Sterling, *Judenhaß*, 36.
3. Ibid., 36–37.
4. Breuer, "Das Bild der Aufklärung," 135.
5. Lowenstein, "Two Silent Minorities: Orthodox Jews and Poor Jews in Berlin," 5.
6. Ibid., 6.
7. Ibid., 9.
8. Ibid.
9. Ibid., 16.
10. The Hebrew-language writings of such orthodox Jews as Jacob (Ja'akov) Emden are unfortunately outside of the scope of this study.
11. Katz, *Aus dem Ghetto*, 59–62.
12. Altmann, *Moses Mendelssohn*, 194.
13. Arendt, *Antisemitism*, 59.
14. Schallück, "Moses Mendelssohn und die deutsche Aufklärung," 18.
15. Arendt, *Antisemitism*, 56.
16. Schoeps, *Moses Mendelssohn*, 12.
17. Hensel, *The Mendelssohn Family*, 6.
18. Moses Mendelssohn, quoted in Schoeps, *Moses Mendelssohn*, 70.
19. Schoeps, *Moses Mendelssohn*, 76.
20. Altmann, *Moses Mendelssohn*, 116.
21. Moses Mendelssohn, quoted in Dubnow, *Geschichte des jüdischen Volkes*, 8:375.
22. Katz, *Aus dem Ghetto*, 63.

23. Although Mendelssohn's original appointment was to be unpaid, it was with the understanding that he would be moved to a paid position later in his tenure.
24. Horkheimer and Adorno, *Dialektik der Aufklärung*, 207.
25. Altmann, *Moses Mendelssohn*, 464.
26. Mendelssohn, *Gesammelte Schriften*, 8:6.
27. Ibid.
28. Ibid., 7.
29. Horkheimer and Adorno, *Dialektik der Aufklärung*, 215.
30. Mendelssohn, *Gesammelte Schriften*, 8:9.
31. Ibid., 13.
32. Ibid., 16.
33. Dubnow, *Geschichte des jüdischen Volkes*, 8:306.
34. Altmann, *Moses Mendelssohn*, 426.
35. Ibid., 430.
36. Mendelssohn, *Gesammelte Schriften*, 12–2:102. The text of his letter reads: "Gütiger, allwohltätiger Vater! wo sollen diese Elenden mit ihren schuldlosen Weibern und Kindern hin . . . wenn das Land, in welchem sie um ihr Vermögen gekommen sind, sie ausschleudert? Das Vertreiben ist für einen Juden die härteste Strafe: mehr als bloße Landesverweisung, gleichsam Vertilgung von dem Erdboden Gottes, auf welchem das Vorurtheil ihm von jeder Gränze mit gewaffneter Hand zurückweist."
37. Ibid., 103.
38. Altmann, *Moses Mendelssohn*, 467.
39. Hensel, *The Mendelssohn Family*, 3.
40. Randall, *The Career of Philosophy*, vol. 2: *From the German Enlightenment to Darwin*, 56.
41. Arkush, *Moses Mendelsssohn and the Enlightenment*, 242.
42. Altmann, *Moses Mendelssohn*, 28.
43. Mendelssohn, *Gesammelte Schriften*, 8:127.
44. Ibid., 153.
45. Ibid., 154–55.
46. Lessing, *Werke*, 2:315.
47. Mendelssohn, *Gesammelte Schriften*, 8:156.
48. Ibid., 158.
49. Ibid., 59.
50. Ibid., 160.
51. Arkush, *Moses Mendelsohn and the Enlightenment*, 260. Arkush points out that this contradiction was observed in Mendelssohn's day by the Christian thinker Thomas Wizenmann in *Die Resultate der Jacobischer und Mendelssohnischer Philosophie von einem Freywilligen* (1786). Arkush fails to mention, however, that Mendelssohn's fellow Maskil, Saul Ascher, also noticed the contradiction between Mendelssohn's proclamation of Judaism as a Natural Religion and simultaneously maintaining that it was based on revealed legislation. See the discussion of Ascher's *Leviathan* later in this chapter.
52. Mendelssohn, *Gesammelte Schriften*, 8:183.

53. Ibid., 188–89.
54. Ibid., 21.
55. Ibid.
56. Mendelssohn, *Gesammelte Schriften*, 8:23. The text reads: "Hat er nun das Unglück, von der Gemeinde, zu welcher er gehört für dissidentisch gehalten zu werden, und sein Gewissen verbietet ihm, einer andern im Staate herrschenden oder geduldeten Religionspartey beyzutreten; so ist das nützliche und geachteter Bürger ja höchst unglücklich, wenn seiner Gemeinde erlaubt wird, ihn auszustoßen, und er bei ihren gottesdienstlichen Versammlungen verschloßene Thüren findet."
57. Ibid., 25.
58. Horkheimer and Adorno, *Dialektik der Aufklärung*, 202–03.
59. Mendelssohn, *Gesammelte Schriften*, 8:25: "Alle Völker der Erde schienen bisher von dem Wahne bethört zu sein, daß sich Religion nur durch eisene Macht erhalten, Lehren der Seeligkeit nur durch unseeliges Verfolgen ausbereiten, und wahre Begriffe von Gott, der nach unser aller Geständniss, die Liebe ist, nur durch Wirkung des Hasses mittheilen lassen."
60. Wolf, *Von den Krankheiten der Juden*, 3.
61. Arenhof, *Einige jüdische Familienscenen bey Erblicken des Patents über die Freyheiten welche die Juden in den kaiserlichen Staaten erhalten haben*, 5–6.
62. Ibid., 6–7.
63. Ibid., 7.
64. Ibid., 7–8.
65. Ibid., 13–14.
66. Ibid.
67. See Stern, *Der preußische Staat und die Juden*, 3:406.
68. Wessely, *Worte der Wahrheit und des Friedens*, 8.
69. Ibid., 14.
70. Stern, *Der preußische Staat und die Juden*, 3:407–8.
71. Breuer, "Das Bild der Aufklärung bei der deutsch-jüdischen Orthodoxie," 133.
72. Lowenstein, "Two Silent Minorities: Orthodox Jews and Poor Jews in Berlin," 3.
73. Ibid.
74. Grab, "Saul Ascher: Ein jüdisch-deutscher Spätaufklärer zwischen Revolution und Restauration," 136. See also Littmann, "Saul Ascher: First Theorist of Progressive Judaism," 107–21.
75. Meyer, *The Origins of the Modern Jew*, 124.
76. Low, *Jews in the Eyes of the Germans*, 178.
77. Ibid.
78. See Sorkin, *The Transformation of German Jewry*, 74.
79. Low, *Jews in the Eyes of the Germans*, 178.
80. Friedländer, *Sendschreiben*, 10.
81. See Sorkin, *The Transformation of German Jewry*, 74.
82. Friedländer, *Sendschreiben*, 15.

83. Hayoun, "Rabbi Ja'akov Emdens Autobiographie oder der Kämpfer wider die sabbatianische Häresie," 223.
84. Wiesemann, "Jewish Burials in Germany—Between Tradition, the Enlightenment, and the Authorities," 20.
85. Hertz, "The Literary Salon in Berlin, 1780–1806," 194–95.
86. Katz, *Emancipation and Assimilation*, 102, 222.
87. Gilman, *Jewish Self-Hatred*, 2.
88. Ibid.
89. See Arendt, *Rahel Varnhagen*, 7.
90. Weissberg, "Stepping Out: The Writing of Difference in Rahel Varnhagen's Letters," 146.
91. Lowenstein, *The Berlin Jewish Community: Enlightenment, Family and Crisis, 1770–1830*, 107.
92. Rahel Levin Varnhagen, Letter to David Veit, March 22, 1795, in *Rahel Varnhagen im Umgang mit ihren Freunden: Briefe, 1793–1833*, 54.
93. Arendt, *Rahel Varnhagen*, 7–8.
94. Rahel Levin Varnhagen, Diary entry, April 1831, *Rahel: Ein Buch des Andenkens für ihre Freunde*, 564.
95. Arendt, *Rahel Varnhagen*, 216: "The central idea of . . . [Rahel Varnhagen's] life had been the desire to escape from Jewishness, and this desire proved unfulfillable because of the anti-Semitism of her milieu, because of the ban, imposed from the outside, against a Jew's becoming a normal human being."
96. See Katz, *Emancipation and Assimilation*, 222.
97. Reminiscence of Karl August Varnhagen, in *Rahel: Ein Buch des Andenkens für ihre Freunde*, 43.
98. Claussen, *Grenzen der Aufklärung: Zur gesellschaftlichen Geschichte des modernen Antisemitismus*, 19.
99. Ibid., 100.

Chapter 4

1. Claussen, *Grenzen der Aufklärung: Zur gesellschaftlichen Geschichte des modernen Antisemitismus*, 55.
2. Foucault, *The Order of Things*, 23–24.
3. See Habermas, *The Structural Transformation of the Public Sphere: An Inquiry into a Category of Bourgeois Society*, 87.
4. See Sørensen, *Herrschaft und Zärtlichkeit*, 59–61.
5. Carrington, "Die Figur des Juden in der dramatischen Litteratur des 18. Jahrhunderts," 4–5.
6. Szondi, *Die Theorie des bürgerlichen Trauerspiels*, 16.
7. Ibid., 28.
8. Ibid., 30.
9. Ibid., 31.

10. Albert, *Der melancholische Bürger: Ausbildung bürgerlicher Deutungsmuster im Trauerspiel Diderots und Lessings*, 63.
11. See Szondi, *Die Theorie des bürgerlichen Trauerspiels*, 68.
12. Søorensen, *Herrschaft und Zärtlichkeit*, 13.
13. Ibid., 15–19.
14. Glaser, *Das bürgerliche Rührstück*, 7–9.
15. Ibid., 9.
16. Ibid., 10.
17. See Van Cleve, *The Merchant in German Literature of the Enlightenment*, 3–41.
18. Glaser, *Das bürgerliche Rührstück*, 31.
19. Ibid., 38.
20. See Glaser, *Das bürgerliche Rührstück*.
21. Wessels, *Lessing's "Nathan der Weise,"* 361, and Jenzsch, "Jüdische Figuren in deutschen Bühnentexten des 18. Jahrhunderts," 145.
22. Reinicke, *Nathan der Deutsche*, 42.
23. Walach, *Der aufrechte Bürger*, 9.
24. Reinicke, *Nathan der Deutsche*, 64.
25. Schaer, *Die Gesellschaft im deutschen bürgerlichen Drama*, 23.
26. Kant, "Beantwortung der Frage: Was ist Aufklärung?" 35.
27. Bischof, *Dina*, 7.
28. Lotich, *Wer war wohl mehr Jude?*, 25–26.
29. Wessels, *Lessings "Nathan der Weise,"* 360.
30. Ziegelhauser, *Die Juden*, 12.
31. Ibid., 22.
32. Levenson, "Jewish Reactions to Intermarriage in Nineteenth-Century Germany," 5.
33. Steinberg, *Menschen und Menschensituationen*, 41.
34. Lotich, *Wer war wohl mehr Jude?*, 92.
35. *Vorurtheil und Liebe*, 19.
36. Steinberg, *Menschen und Menschensituationen*, 123.
37. Bischof, *Dina*, 75–76.
38. I am here borrowing from the terminology and methodology used by Edward W. Said in *Orientalism*, his classic study of Western perception of ethnic otherness. See especially pp. 3, 12, 21, 44, 153.
39. Katz, *Emancipation and Assimilation*, 102.
40. Ibid., 222.

Chapter 5

1. Rose, *Revolutionary Antisemitism in Germany: From Kant to Wagner*, 41.
2. Ibid., 13.
3. Ibid.
4. Ibid., 42.

5. Sterling, *Judenhaß*, 15.
6. Ibid., 18.
7. Ibid., 18-19.
8. Ellul, *Propaganda*, 6.
9. Ibid., 7.
10. Horkheimer and Adorno, *Dialektik der Aufklärung*, 162.
11. Ellul, *Propaganda*, 39.
12. Ibid., 40.
13. Ibid., 49.
14. See ibid., 50.
15. Ibid., 51.
16. Ibid., 162.
17. Ibid.
18. Ibid.
19. Ibid., 162-63.
20. Ibid., 163.
21. Ibid., 165-66.
22. Fein, "Explanations of the Origin and Evolution of Antisemitism," 4.
23. Arendt, *Antisemitism*, 61.
24. Grattenauer, *Wider die Juden*, 6: "Aber den Juden gebt volles Bürgerrecht, grenzenlose Privilegien, unbeschränke Konzessionen, Frabik-Prämien, Generalpächte und freies Eigenthum eures Grund und Boden. Sie werden euch königlich belohnen denn 'ihr werdet stehen und die Heerden der Juden weiden; eure Söhne und Töchter werden der Juden Knechte und Mägde seyn—Ihr werdet im Schweiße eurers Angesichts arbeiten, aber das erwählte Volk Gottes wird die Früchte genießen und herrlich loben.'"
25. See Horkheimer and Adorno, *Dialektik der Aufklärung*, 167.
26. Grattenauer, *Wider die Juden*, 17.
27. Fenichel, "Elements of a Psychoanalytic Theory of Anti-Semitism," 13-14.
28. Horkheimer and Adorno, *Dialektik der Aufklärung*, 167.
29. Grattenauer, *Wider die Juden*, 52.
30. Ibid., 20.
31. Ibid., 24.
32. Ibid., 34-35.
33. Ibid., 48.
34. Ibid., 32.
35. Ibid., 67.
36. Poliakov, *The History of Anti-Semitism*, 3:188.
37. Buchholz, *Moses und Jesus oder über das intellektuelle und moralische Verhältniß der Juden und Christen: Eine historisch-politische Abhandlung*, 64-65.
38. Ibid., 86.
39. Ibid., 163.
40. Ibid., 182-83.

41. Ironically, Buchholz was a frequent guest at the Jewish salons in Berlin and was a good friend of Rahel Levin's lover, Friedrich Gentz. See Hertz, *Jewish High Society in Old Regime Berlin*, 49–50. Hertz attributes liberal attitudes to Buchholz, which place his vitriolic anti-Semitism in a puzzling light.
42. See Pinson, *Pietism as a Factor in the Rise of German Nationalism*, 105.
43. See Ott, *Ernst Moritz Arndt*, 7.
44. Ibid., 146–47.
45. Ibid., 103.
46. See ibid., 160.
47. Ibid., 210.
48. Ibid., 217.
49. Ibid., 235.
50. Poliakov, *The History of Anti-Semitism*, 3:300.
51. Ibid., 380.
52. Ibid., 383.
53. Ibid.
54. Arndt, *Blick aus der Zeit auf die Zeit*, 183.
55. Ibid., 188.
56. Ibid.
57. Ibid.
58. Ibid., 189.
59. Ott, *Ernst Moritz Arndt*, 119.
60. Arndt, *Blick aus der Zeit auf die Zeit*, 191.
61. Ibid., 192.
62. Ibid., 188.
63. Ott, *Ernst Moritz Arndt*, 133.
64. Poliakov, *The History of Anti-Semitism*, 3:381.
65. Rühs, *Ueber die Ansprüche der Juden an das deutsche Bürgerrecht*, 39.
66. Ibid., 38–39.
67. Ibid., 6.
68. Ascher, *Die Germanomanie: Skizze zu einem Zeitgemälde*, 65.
69. Ibid., 13: "Christenthum und Deutschtum war bald in eines verschmolzen, dies ist für den transzendentalen Idealisten und Identitäts-Philosophen ein leichter Prozeß. Es ward von ihnen so gefolgert. Deutschland's Rettung von dem Joche der fremden Tyrannei kann nur vorbereitet werden, durch Einheit und Einigkeit des Volkes in der Idee. Die Einheit und Einigkeit in der Religion spricht dies Erfordernis ganz aus; dies soll nun durch den zum Katholizismus gesteigerten Protestantismus hergestellt werden, und so bestand daher für diese Denker ein deutsches Christenthum oder eine christliche Deutschheit, die sie zu gründen und zu verbreiten sich versetzten."
70. Ibid., 26.
71. Ibid., 27–28.
72. Littmann, "Saul Ascher: First Theorist of Progressive Judaism," 107.
73. Grab, "Saul Ascher," 169.
74. Saul Ascher, *Die Wartburg Feier*, 1818, quoted in Poliakov, *The History of Anti-Semitism*, 3:390.

75. Landa, *The Jew in Drama*, 9: "In no department of human activity has Jew-baiting been more persistent and more popular than in the realm of the drama. From time immemorial the Jew has either either been libelled or ruthlessly travestied on the stage.... Each generation has carried on the tradition and has handed it down to its successor with an unscrupulous disregard of truth and disdain of human feelings that makes the convention unique in the sphere of artistic endeavor."
76. Freud, *Jokes and Their Relation to the Unconscious*, 143.
77. Ibid., 151.
78. See Jurzik, *Der Stoff des Lachens*, 38.
79. Wilson, *Jokes: Form, Content, Use, and Function*, 132.
80. Ibid., 138.
81. Ibid., 148.
82. Ibid., 140.
83. Berghahn, "Comedy without Laughter," 4.
84. G. E. Lessing, quoted in Berghahn, "Comedy without Laughter," 12.
85. Berghahn, "Comedy without Laughter," 12–13.
86. Jurzik, *Der Stoff des Lachens*, 38.
87. Ibid., 44.
88. Claussen, *Grenzen der Aufklärung*, 39.
89. *Der wuchernde Jude am Pranger*, 5.
90. Ekmann, "Wieso und zu welchem Ende wir lachen," 16.
91. See Bettelheim and Janowitz, *Social Change and Prejudice*, 106.
92. *Der wuchernde Jude am Pranger*, 5.
93. Ibid., 7.
94. Ibid., 8.
95. Ibid., 9.
96. Ibid., 38.
97. Wilson, *Jokes: Form, Content, Use, and Function*, 136.
98. *Der wuchernde Jude am Pranger*, 26.
99. Ibid., 46.
100. Ibid., 45.
101. Baum, "Charakter und Inhalt des Komischen," 236.
102. Ibid., 242.
103. For a discussion of Luther's Judeophobia, see Gilman's *Jewish Self-hatred*, 57–67.
104. Sachs, *Der Teufel nahm ein altes Weib*, 30.
105. *Der wuchernde Jude am Pranger*, 49–50.
106. Ibid., 50.
107. See Karrer, *Parodie, Travestie, Pastiche*, 25.
108. Ibid., 31–32.
109. Ibid., 34.
110. Ibid., 43–44.
111. Ibid., 165.
112. *Nathan der Weise travestiert und modernisiert*, 88.
113. Ibid., 92.

114. Wessels, *Lessings "Nathan der Weise,"* 394.
115. Bakhtin, *Problems of Dostoevsky's Poetics*, 288.
116. *Nathan der Weise travestiert und modernisiert*, 103.
117. Ibid.
118. Ibid., 110.
119. Ibid.
120. Ibid., 118.
121. Ibid., 87.
122. Ibid., 93.
123. Wessels, *Lessings "Nathan der Weise,"* 401.
124. Voss, "Der travestierte Nathan der Weise," 179.
125. Ibid., 179.
126. See Wightman, "The Changing Image of the Jew As Reflected in German Drama in the Time of Lessing and Heine," 72: "On the one hand, the way the uneducated Jew talks is ridiculed and used as a cheap and vicious means of creating humor. On the other hand, if a Jew tries to speak German (as Recha does rather well) this is also ridiculed. So the Jew cannot win either way. If he is to assimilate, he is forced to deny his Jewishness, a reaction which, provoked by the Germans, is nonetheless ridiculed by them."
127. Grossman, "The Space of Yiddish in the German and German-Jewish Discourse," 150.
128. Voss's ideas about Jewish nature find expression in his later play, *Die Emporkömmlinge, oder Harlekin als Gespenst* (1811). One of his characters makes the following statement against converted Jews: "Getauft oder nicht, die jüdische Natur legt sich nicht ab," (14). Voss also has the same character explain how the Wars of Liberation fanned the flames of anti-Semitism: "Grade was uns ruinierte, half ihnen [den Juden] auf, der Krieg," (13). Voss was against attempts by Jews to acculturate themselves into the dominant society.
129. Stümcke, *Die Fortsetzungen, Nachahmungen und Travestien von Lessings "Nathan der Weise,"* XLIII.
130. Wessels, *Lessings "Nathan der Weise,"* 408.
131. Voss, "Der travestierte Nathan der Weise," 167–68.
132. Julius von Voss, quoted in Stümcke, *Die Fortsetzungen, Nachahmungen und Travestien von Lessings "Nathan der Weise,"* XLIII.
133. Gilman, in *Jewish Self-hatred*, 140, calls this pseudo-Yiddish dialect *mauscheln*: "His [Voss's] *mauscheln* is broken German spoken with a stage Yiddish accent, with bits of Hebrew thrown in for effect." See also Grossman, "The Space of Yiddish in the German and German-Jewish Discourse," 145.
134. Albertsen, "Der Jude in der deutschen Literatur, 1750–1850," 27.
135. Jenzsch, "Jüdische Figuren in deutschen Bühnentexten des 18. Jahrhunderts," 107.
136. Krüger, *Berliner Romantik und Berliner Judentum*, 50.
137. Hertz, *Jewish High Society in Old Regime Berlin*, 276.
138. Low, *Jews in the Eyes of Germans*, 191.
139. Brentano, *Der Philister vor, in und nach der Geschichte*, 3.
140. Arnim, *Halle*, 80.

141. Ibid., 78.
142. Ibid., 77.
143. Lea, *Emancipation, Assimilation, and Stereotype*, 11.
144. Arnim, *Halle*, 88.
145. Ibid., 77.
146. Rose, *Revolutionary Antisemitism in Germany*, 26.
147. However, Sessa seems to have gone too far even for Voss. Voss wrote a play attacking Sessa entitled *Euer Verkehr* in 1816.
148. Sessa, *Unser Verkehr: Eine Posse in einem Aufzuge*, 10–11.
149. Ibid., 11.
150. Ibid., 41.
151. Ibid.
152. Ibid., 48.
153. Ibid., 53.
154. Ibid., 54.
155. Ibid., 72.
156. Grossman, in "The Space of Yiddish in the German and German-Jewish Discourse," 155, also feels that the figure of Isidorus Morgenländer is a parody of the Haskalah. He points to the similarity between the names "Morgenländer" and "Friedländer." The name "Morgenländer" is meant to imply that the Jewish civic leader David Friedländer (still active at the time this play was written) was an unwanted Oriental with no place in Western society.
157. Low, *Jews in the Eyes of the Germans*, 109.
158. Neubauer, "*Auf Begehr: Unser Verkehr*, 313.
159. Ibid., 314.
160. Prince Karl August von Hardenberg, August 19, 1815, quoted in ibid., 316.
161. Neubauer, "*Auf Begehr: Unser Verkehr*," 315. See also Lea, *Emancipation, Assimilation, and Stereotype*, 80–84.
162. *Der Morgenblatt*, August 19, 1815, quoted in Neubauer, "*Auf Begehr: Unser Verkehr*," 316.
163. Lea, *Emancipation, Assimilation, and Stereotype*, 84.
164. Neubauer, "*Auf Begehr: Unser Verkehr*," 319.
165. Ibid., 318.
166. Ibid.
167. Schütz, "Über die Posse *Unser Verkehr* und ihren Verfasser," 1747.
168. Ibid.
169. "Ueber Sessa's Posse: Unser Verkehr" *Agrippina*, Nos. 56–57 (1824), 224.
170. Ibid.
171. Rose, *Revolutionary Antisemitism in Germany*, 140.
172. Börne, "Unser Verkehr: Posse," 362.
173. Ibid., 365: "Man pflegt einzuwenden: es werde so oft auf der Bühne dieser oder jeder Stand der Gesellschaft mit Spott behandelt. . . . Warum sollten also die Juden dies nicht auch gefallen lassen wollen! Jedoch sind die Fälle, die man hier zur Vergleichung stellt durchaus verschieden. Dort werden nicht die Stände, sondern den Gliedern dieser Stände zuweilen anhängende

Schwächen und Fehler—es wird der Adelstolz, die Rabulisterei, das pfäffische Wesen belacht, und es weder von dem Schriftsteller gemeint, jene Klassen der Gesellschaft herabzuwürdigen, noch auch tritt die Gefahr daß eine solche Meinung bei den Zuhörern veranlaßt werde.

174. Ibid.

Chapter 6

1. The major twentieth-century thinkers discussed in this chapter have been themselves the subjects of critical inquiry and indeed, controversy. To have delved into the critical reception of these figures, interesting as it is, would have unduly broadened the scope of this study. It is my hope that my brief discussion of their work will spur further discussion and debate.

2. See *Webster's Third New International Dictionary* (Springfield, Mass.: Merriam. 1976), 2405; Brugger, *Philosophical Dictionary*, 421; and *Lexikon für Theologie und Kirche*, 239–46.

3. Horkheimer and Adorno, *Dialektik der Aufklärung*, 151.

4. Arendt, *Antisemitism*, 57.

5. Scholem, "Once More: The German-Jewish Dialogue," 66.

6. Sartre, *Anti-Semite and Jew*, 55–56.

7. Ibid., 44–49: "It is not by chance that the great outbursts of anti-Semitic rage conceal a basic optimism. . . . The more one is absorbed in fighting Evil, the less one is tempted to place the Good in question . . . the anti-Semite has his conscience on his side: he is a criminal in a good cause . . . his mission is to extirpate evil by doing evil . . . he looks at himself as a sanctified evildoer."

8. Ibid., 13.

9. See Said, *Orientalism*, 43.

10. Ibid., 67.

11. Sartre, *Anti-Semite and Jew*, 57.

12. Kristeva, *Strangers to Ourselves*, 2.

13. Ibid., 57.

14. Ibid., 95.

15. See Sartre, *Anti-Semite and Jew*, 100.

16. Kristeva, *Strangers to Ourselves*, 194–95.

17. Arendt, *The Jew As Pariah*, 68.

18. Ibid., 72.

19. See Young-Bruehl, *Hannah Arendt: For Love of the World*, 121.

20. Ibid.

21. Lazare, *Antisemitism: Its History and Causes*, 162.

References

Primary Literature

Arenhof. *Einige jüdische Familienscenen bey Erblicken des Patents über die Freyheiten welche die Juden in den kaiserlichen Staaten erhalten haben.* Vienna: Rudolph Grässer, 1782.
Arndt, Ernst Moritz. *Blick aus der Zeit auf die Zeit.* Frankfurt: Germanien, 1814.
Arnim, Achim von. *Halle: Ein Studentenspiel* (1809). In *Arnims Werke*, edited by Alfred Schier, 3:15–188. Leipzig: Bibliographisches Institut, 1920.
Ascher, Saul. *Bemerkungen über die bürgerliche Verbesserung der Juden veranlaßt, bei der Frage: Soll der Jude Soldat werden?* Frankfurt a.O., 1788.
———. *Die Germanomanie: Skizze zu einem Zeitgemälde.* Berlin: Achenwall, 1815.
———. *Leviathan oder ueber Religion in Rücksicht des Judenthums.* Berlin: Frankesche Buchhandlung, 1792.
Bischof, Jakob. *Dina, das Judenmädchen aus Franken: Ein tragisches Familiengemälde.* Fürth: Im Bureau für Literatur, 1802.
Börne, Ludwig. "Unser Verkehr: Posse." In *Börnes Werke*, vol. 1: *Jugendschriften*, edited by Ludwig Geiger and Leon Zeitlin, 361–66. Berlin: Bong, 1911.
Brentano, Clemens. *Der Philister vor, in und nach der Geschichte* (1811). Berlin: Ernst Frensdorff, 1905.
Buchholz, Friedrich. *Moses und Jesus oder über das intellektuelle und moralische Verhältniß der Juden und Christen: Eine historisch-politische Abhandlung.* Berlin: Johann Friedrich Unger, 1803.
Diez, Heinrich Friedrich von. *Ueber Juden: An Herrn Kriegsrath Dohm in Berlin.* Dessau and Leipzig: Buchhandlung der Gelehrten, 1783.
Dohm, Christian Konrad Wilhelm von. *Über die bürgerliche Verbesserung der Juden* (1781–83). Hildesheim: Olms, 1973.
Friedländer, David. *Sendschreiben an Seinen Hochwürden Herrn Oberconsistorialrath und Probst Teller zu Berlin von einigen Hausvätern jüdischer Religion* (1799). Jerusalem: Zalman Shazar Center, 1975.
Grattenauer, Carl Wilhelm Friedrich. *Erklärung an das Publikum über meine Schrift: "Wider die Juden."* 4th ed. Berlin: Johann Wilhelm Schmidt, 1803.
———. *Wider die Juden: Ein Wort der Warnung an alle unsere christliche Mitbürger.* 5th ed. Berlin: Johann Wilhelm Schmidt, 1803.
Herz, Marcus. *Über die frühe Beerdigung der Juden.* Berlin: Christian Friedrich Voß, 1788.
Kant, Immanuel. "Beantwortung der Frage: Was ist Aufklärung?" In *Immanuel Kant, Schriften zur Religion*, edited by Martina Thom, 37–48. Berlin: Union, 1981.

Lessing, Gotthold Ephraim. *Werke*. Vols. 2 and 7. Edited by H. G. Göpfert. Munich: Hanser, 1976.
Lotich, Karl. *Wer war wohl mehr Jude?* Leipzig: Friedrich Gotthold Jacobäer, 1783.
Mendelssohn, Moses. *Gesammelte Schriften*. Jubiläumausgabe. Edited by Alexander Altmann et al. 14 volumes. Stuttgart-Bad Cannstatt: Fromann, 1983.
Nathan der Weise travestiert und modernisiert (1804). In *Die Fortsetzungen, Nachahmungen, und Travestien von Lessings "Nathan der Weise,"* edited by Heinrich Stümcke, 85–129. Berlin: Selbstverlag für Theatergeschichte, 1904.
Pfranger, Johann Georg. *Der Mönch vom Libanon: Ein Nachtrag zu "Nathan der Weise."* Dessau: In der Buchhandlung der Gelehrten, 1782.
Reinicke, Heinrich. *Nathan der Deutsche* (1784). In *Die Forsetzungen, Nachahmungen, und Travestien von Lessings "Nathan der Weise,"* edited by Heinrich Stümcke, 37–83. Berlin: Selbstverlag für Theatergeschichte, 1904.
Rühs, Friedrich. *Ueber die Ansprüche der Juden an das deutsche Bürgerrecht*. 2nd ed. Berlin: In der Realschulbuchhandlung, 1816.
Sachs, Hans. *Der Teufel nahm ein altes Weib: Ein Fastnachtspiel* (1545). Leipzig and Hartenstein: Erich Matthes, n.d.
Schütz, Friedrich K. Julius. "Über die Posse *Unser Verkehr* und ihren Verfasser." *Zeitung für die elegante Welt* no. 218, 1737–40, and no. 219, 1745–49. Leipzig, 1815.
Sessa, Karl Borromäus Alexander. *Unser Verkehr: Eine Posse in einem Aufzuge* (1815). Berlin: Otto Janke, n.d.
Steinberg, Karl. *Menschen und Menschensituationen*. In *Deutsche Schaubühne*, 4:1–180. Augsburg, 1792.
Tralles, Balthasar Ludwig. *Zufällige altdeutsche und christliche Betrachtungen über Herrn Gotthold Ephraim Lessings neues dramatisches Gedicht "Nathan der Weise."* Breslau: Wilhelm Gottlieb Korn, 1779.
"Ueber Sessas Posse Unser Verkehr." *Agrippina* nos. 56–57 (1824): 224, 227–28.
Varnhagen, Rahel Levin. *Rahel: Ein Buch des Andenkens für ihre Freunde*. Edited by Karl August Varnhagen von Ense. Berlin: Trowisch und Sohn, 1833.
———. *Rahel Varnhagen im Umgang mit ihren Freunden: Briefe, 1793–1833*. Edited by Friedhelm Kemp. Munich: Kösel, 1967.
Vorurtheil und Liebe: Ein Sittengemälde in drei Aufzügen. Basel: Johann Schweighauser, 1792.
Voss, Julius von. *Die Empörkommlinge, oder Harlekin als Gespenst*. In *Lustspiele*, 4–153. Berlin, 1811.
———. *Der travestirte Nathan der Weise* (1804). In *Die Fortsetzungen, Nachahmungen und Travestien von Lessings "Nathan der Weise,"* edited by Heinrich Stümcke, 131–218. Berlin: Selbstverlag für Theatergeschichte, 1904.
Wessely, Naphthali Hartwig Herz. *Worte der Wahrheit und des Friedens an die gesammte jüdische Nation*. Translated by David Friedländer. Breslau, 1798.
Wolf, Elcan Isaac. *Von den Krankheiten der Juden*. Mannheim: C. F. Schwan, 1777.
Der wuchernde Jude am Pranger: Ein Drama in Versen. Berlin: G. Hayn, 1804.
Ziegelhauser, Gottfried Julius. *Die Juden: Eine bürgerliche Scene in einem Aufzuge*. Vienna: Johann Baptist Wallishauser, 1807.

Secondary Literature

Adorno, Theodor W., Else Frenkel-Brunswik, Daniel J. Levinson, and R. Nevitt Sanford. *The Authoritarian Personality*. New York: Norton, 1950.
Albert, Claudia. *Der melancholische Bürger: Ausbildung bürgerlicher Deutungsmuster im Trauerspiel Diderots und Lessings*. Frankfurt: Peter Lang, 1983.
Albertsen, Leif Ludwig. "Der Jude in der deutschen Literatur, 1750–1850." *Arcadia: Zeitschrift für Vergleichende Literaturwissenschaft* 19, no. 1 (1984): 20–33.
Altmann, Alexander. *Moses Mendelssohn: A Biographical Study*. London: Routledge and Kegan Paul, 1973.
Arendt, Hannah. *The Jew As Pariah: Jewish Identity and Politics in the Modern Age*. Edited by Ron H. Feldman. New York: Grove, 1978.
———. *The Origins of Totalitarianism. Vol. 1: Antisemitism*. New York: Harcourt, Brace, Jovanovitch, 1951.
———. *Rahel Varnhagen: The Life of a Jewish Woman*. Rev. ed. Translated by Richard Winston and Clara Winston. New York: Harcourt, Brace, Jovanovitch, 1974.
Arkush, Allan. *Moses Mendelssohn and the Enlightenment*. Albany: State University of New York Press, 1994.
Atkins, Stuart. "Die Ringparabel in Lessings 'Nathan der Weise.'" In *Lessings "Nathan der Weise,"* edited by Klaus Bohnen, 155–67. Darmstadt: Wissenschaftliche Buchgesellschaft, 1984.
Bakhtin, Mikhail. *Problems of Dostoevsky's Poetics*. Edited and translated by Caryl Emerson. Minneapolis: University of Minnesota Press, 1989.
Barner, Wilfried, Gunter Grimm, Helmuth Kiesel, and Martin Kramer. *Lessing: Epoche, Werk, Wirkung*. 4th ed. Munich: Beck, 1981.
Baron, Salo W., et al. *Economic History of the Jews*. Jerusalem: Keter, 1975.
Barton, Peter F. "Der lange Weg zur Toleranz." In *Im Lichte der Toleranz*, edited by Peter F. Barton, 11–33. Vienna: Institut für protestantische Kirchengeschichte, 1981.
Bauer, Ferdinand Christian. *Kirchengeschichte der neueren Zeit*. Tübingen: Fues, 1863.
Baum, Georgina. "Charakter und Inhalt des Komischen." In *Wesen und Form des Komischen im Drama*, edited by Reinhold Grimm and Klaus L. Berghahn, 206–53. Darmstadt: Wissenschaftliche Buchgesellschaft, 1975.
Bennett, Benjamin. *Modern Drama and German Classicism: Renaissance from Lessing to Brecht*. Ithaca, N. Y.: Cornell University Press, 1979.
Berding, Helmut. *Moderner Antisemitismus in Deutschland*. Frankfurt: Suhrkamp, 1988.
Berghahn, Klaus L. "Comedy without Laughter: Jewish Characters in Comedies from Shylock to Nathan." In *Laughter Unlimited: Essays on Humor, Satire, and the Comic*, edited by Reinhold Grimm and Jost Hermand, 3–27. Madison: University of Wisconsin Press, 1991.
———. "Der Jude als der Andere: Das Zeitalter der Toleranz und die Ju-

denfrage." In *Jüdische Intelligenz in Deutschland*, edited by Jost Hermand and Gert Mattenklott, 7–33. Hamburg: Argument Verlag, 1988.

Bergmann, Werner. "Group Theory and Ethnic Relations." In *Error without Trial: Psychological Research on Antisemitism*, edited by Werner Bergmann, 2:139–61. Berlin: de Gruyter, 1988.

Bettelheim, Bruno, and Morris Janowitz. *Social Change and Prejudice*. New York: Free Press, 1964. Enlarged version of *Dynamics of Prejudice* (1950).

Bizet, J. A. "Die Weisheit Nathans." In *Gotthold Ephraim Lessing*, edited by Gerhard Bauer and Sybille Bauer, 302–11. Darmstadt: Wissenschaftliche Buchgesellschaft, 1968.

Borgius, Eugen. *Lessings "Nathan" und "Der Mönch vom Libanon": Zum hundertjährigen Gedächtnis beider Dichtungen*. Barmen: Hugo Klein, 1881.

Bragg, Marvin. *From Gottsched to Goethe: Changes in the Social Function of the Poet and Poetry*. New York: Peter Lang, 1984.

Breuer, Mordechai. "Das Bild der Aufklärung bei der deutsch-jüdischen Orthodoxie." In *Aufklärung und Haskala in jüdischer und nichtjüdischer Sicht*, edited by Karlfried Gründer and Nathan Rotenstreich, 131–42. Heidelberg: Lambert Schneider, 1990.

Brugger, Walter. *Philosophical Dictionary*. Translated by Kenneth Baker (1967). Spokane: Gonzaga University Press, 1972.

Carrington, Herbert. "Die Figur des Juden in der dramatischen Litteratur des 18. Jahrhunderts." Dissertation, Heidelberg, 1897.

Cases, Cesare. "Lessings 'Nathan der Weise.'" In *Lessings "Nathan der Weise,"* edited by Klaus Bohnen, 331–40. Darmstadt: Wissenschaftliche Buchgesellschaft, 1984.

Claussen, Detlev. *Grenzen der Aufklärung: Zur gesellschaftlichen Geschichte des modernen Antisemitismus*. Frankfurt a.M.: Fischer, 1987.

Dambacher, Ilsegret. *Christian Wilhelm von Dohm: Ein Beitrag zur Geschichte des preußischen aufgeklärten Beamtentums und seiner Reformbestrebungen am Ausgang des 18. Jahrhunderts*. Frankfurt a.M.: Peter Lang, 1974.

De Man, Paul. *Blindness and Insight: Essays in the Rhetoric of Contemporary Criticism*. Rev. ed. Minneapolis: University of Minnesota Press, 1983.

Demetz, Peter. "Lessings 'Nathan der Weise': Wirklichkeiten und Wirklichkeit." In *Lessings "Nathan der Weise,"* edited by Klaus Bohnen, 168–218. Darmstadt: Wissenschaftliche Buchgesellschaft, 1984.

Dubnow, Simon. *Geschichte des jüdischen Volkes*. Vol. 8. Berlin: Jüdischer Verlag, 1928.

Eckardt, Jo-Jacqueline. *Lessing's "Nathan the Wise" and the Critics, 1779–1991*. Columbia: Camden House, 1993.

Ekmann, Bjørn. "Wieso und zu welchem Ende wir lachen." *Text und Kontext* 9, no. 1 (1981): 7–46.

Ellul, Jacques. *Propaganda: The Formation of Men's Attitudes*. Translated by Konrad Kellen and Jean Lerner. New York: Knopf, 1968.

Encyclopedia Judaica. 10 vols. New York: Macmillan, 1972.

Erspamer, Peter R. "Framing the 'Jewish Question' during the Enlightenment

and Early Anti-Semitism in Its Aftermath." In *The Yale Handbook of Jewish Culture in Germany*, edited by Sander L. Gilman and Jack Zipes. New Haven: Yale University Press, forthcoming.
Fein, Helen. "Explanations of the Origin and Evolution of Antisemitism." In *The Persisting Question: Sociological Perspectives and Social Contexts of Modern Antisemitism*, edited by Helen Fein, 3–22. Berlin: de Gruyter, 1987.
Fenichel, Otto. "Elements of a Psychoanalytic Theory of Anti-Semitism." In *Anti-Semitism: A Social Disease*, edited by Ernst Simmel, 11–33. New York: International Universities Press, 1947.
Fischer, Kuno. *G. E. Lessing als Reformator der deutschen Literatur.* Vol. 2: *Lessings "Nathan der Weise": Die Idee und die Charaktere der Dichtung.* 5th ed. Stuttgart: Cotta, 1905.
Fischer-Gardner, Karin Barbara. "Der obskure Traum der Toleranz: Zur jüdischen Rezeption von Gotthold Ephraim Lessings *Nathan der Weise*." Ph.D. dissertation, University of California–San Diego, 1991.
Foucault, Michel. *The Archaeology of Knowledge and the Discourse on Languages.* Translated by A. M. Sheridan Smith. New York: Pantheon, 1972.
———. *The Order of Things.* Translated by Alan Sheridan. New York: Random House, 1970.
———. "Polemics, Politics, and Problematizations." In *The Foucault Reader*, edited by Paul Rabinow, 381–89. New York: Pantheon, 1984.
Frank, Manfred. *What is Neostructuralism?* Translated by Sabine Wilke and Richard Grey. Minneapolis: University of Minnesota Press, 1989.
Frenzel, Elisabeth. *Judengestalten auf der deutschen Bühne: Ein notwendiger Querschnitt durch 700 Jahre Rollengeschichte.* Munich: Deutscher Volksverlag, 1942. Originally, "Die Gestalt des Juden auf der neueren deutschen Bühne," dissertation, Berlin, 1940.
Freud, Sigmund. *Jokes and Their Relation to the Unconscious.* Translated by James Strachey. New York: Norton, 1960.
———. "Repression" (1915). In *The Major Works of Sigmund Freud*, edited by Robert Maynard Hutchins, 422–28. Chicago: Britannica, 1952.
Gilman, Sander L. *Jewish Self-hatred: Anti-Semitism and the Hidden Language of the Jews.* Baltimore: Johns Hopkins University Press, 1986.
Glaser, Horst Albert. *Das bürgerliche Rührstück.* Stuttgart: Metzler, 1969.
Glock, Charles Y. and Rodney Stark. *Christian Beliefs and Anti-Semitism.* New York: Harper and Row, 1966.
Grab, Walter. "Saul Ascher: Ein jüdisch-deutscher Spätaufklärer zwischen Revolution und Restauration." *Jahrbuch des Instituts für Deutsche Geschichte* 6 (1977): 131–79. Tel Aviv: Institut für Deutsche Geschichte.
Grab, Walter, ed. *Deutsche Aufklärung und Judenemanzipation.* Tel Aviv: Institut für deutsche Geschichte, 1979.
Grossman, Jeffrey Alan. "The Space of Yiddish in the German and German-Jewish Discourse." Ph.D. dissertation, University of Texas–Austin, 1992.
Habermas, Jürgen. *The Structural Transformation of the Public Sphere.* Translated by Thomas Burger. Cambridge, Mass.: MIT Press, 1991.

Hayoun, Maurice R. "Rabbi Ja'akov Emdens Autobiographie oder der Kämpfer wider die sabbatianische Häresie." In *Judentum im deutschen Sprachraum*, edited by Karl E. Grözinger, 222–36. Frankfurt a.M.: Suhrkamp, 1991.
Heinze, Hartmut. *Das deutsche Märtyrerdrama der Moderne*. Frankfurt a.M.: Peter Lang, 1985.
Hensel, Sebastian. *The Mendelssohn Family*. Translated by Carl Klingemann. New York: Harper and Brothers, 1882.
Hernadi, Paul. "Nathan der Bürger: Lessings Mythos vom aufgeklärten Kaufmann." In *Lessings "Nathan der Weise,"*, edited by Klaus Bohnen, 341–49. Darmstadt: Wissenschaftliche Buchgesellschaft, 1984.
Hertz, Deborah Sadie. *Jewish High Society in Old Regime Berlin*. New Haven: Yale University Press, 1988.
———. "The Literary Salon in Berlin, 1780–1806: The Social History of an Intellectual Institution." Ph.D. dissertation, University of Minnesota–Twin Cities, 1979.
Holquist, Michael. *Dialogism: Bakhtin and His World*. London: Routledge, 1990.
Horkheimer, Max, and Theodor W. Adorno. *Dialektik der Aufklärung* (1947). Frankfurt a.M.: Suhrkamp, 1969.
Jenzsch, Helmut. "Jüdische Figuren in deutschen Bühnentexten des 18. Jahrhunderts." Dissertation, Hamburg, 1974.
Johnson, Paul. *A History of the Jews*. New York: Harper and Row, 1987.
Jurzik, Renate. *Der Stoff des Lachens: Studien über Komik*. Frankfurt a.M.: Campus, 1985.
Karrer, Wolfgang. *Parodie, Travestie, Pastiche*. Munich: Wilhelm Fink, 1977.
Katz, Jacob. *Aus dem Ghetto in die bürgerliche Gesellschaft: Jüdische Emanzipation, 1770–1870*. Frankfurt a.M.: Jüdischer Verlag, 1986.
———. *Emancipation and Assimilation: Studies in Modern Jewish History*. Westmead: Gregg, 1972.
———. *From Prejudice to Destruction: Anti-Semitism, 1700–1933*. Cambridge, Mass.: Harvard University Press, 1980.
———. *Zur Assimilation und Emanzipation der Juden*. Darmstadt: Wissenschaftliche Buchgesellschaft, 1982.
Kettner, Gustav. *Lessings Dramen im Lichte ihrer und unserer Zeit*. Berlin: Weidmannische Buchhandlung, 1904.
Klüger, Ruth. "Kreuzzug und Kinderträume in Lessings *Nathan der Weise*." In *Katastrophen: Über deutsche Literatur*, 189–227. Göttingen: Wallstein, 1994.
König, Dominik von. *Natürlichkeit und Wirklichkeit: Studien zu Lessings "Nathan der Weise."* Bonn: Bouvier, 1976.
Kristeva, Julia. *Strangers to Ourselves*. Translated by Leon S. Roudiez. New York: Columbia University Press, 1991.
Krüger, Hans Karl. *Berliner Romantik und Berliner Judentum*. Bonn: Rohrscheid, 1939.
Landa, M. J. *The Jew in Drama*. London: King, 1926.
Lazare, Bernard. *Antisemitism: Its History and Causes* (1894). London: Britons, 1967.

Lea, Charlene A. *Emancipation, Assimilation and Stereotype: The Image of the Jew in German and Austrian Drama, 1800–1850.* Bonn: Bouvier, 1978.

———. "Tolerance Unlimited: The 'Noble Jew' on the German and Austrian Stage, 1750–1805." *German Quarterly* (Spring 1991): 166–77.

Léon, Abram. *The Jewish Question: A Marxist Interpretation.* New York: Pathfinder Press, 1970.

Levenson, Alan T. "Jewish Reactions to Intermarriage in Nineteenth-Century Germany." Ph.D. dissertation, Ohio State University, 1990.

Leventhal, Robert S. "The Parable as Performance: Interpretation, Cultural Transmission and Political Strategy in Lessing's *Nathan der Weise*." *German Quarterly* (Fall 1988): 503–27.

Lexikon für Theologie und Kirche. Edited by Josef Höfer and Karl Rahner. Freiburg: Herder, 1965.

Liberles, Robert. "Dohm's Treatise on the Jews: A Defence of the Enlightenment." *Leo Baeck Institute Yearbook* 33 (1988): 29–42.

Littmann, Ellen. "Saul Ascher: First Theorist of Progressive Judaism." *Leo Baeck Institute Yearbook* 5 (1960): 107–21.

Low, Alfred D. *Jews in the Eyes of the Germans.* Philadelphia: Institute for the Study of Human Issues, 1979.

Lowenstein, Steven M. *The Berlin Jewish Community: Enlightenment, Family, and Crisis, 1770–1830.* New York: Oxford University Press, 1994.

———. "Two Silent Minorities: Orthodox Jews and Poor Jews in Berlin, 1770–1823." *Leo Baeck Institute Yearbook* 36 (1991): 3–25.

Mayer, Hans. *Outsiders: A Study in Life and Letters.* Translated by Denis M. Sweet. Cambridge, Mass.: MIT Press, 1982.

———. "Der weise Nathan und der Rauber Spiegelberg." In *Lessings "Nathan der Weise,"* edited by Klaus Bohnen, 350–73. Darmstadt: Wissenschaftliche Buchgesellschaft, 1984.

Mendes-Flohr, Paul R., and Jehuda Reinharz, eds. *The Jew in the Modern World: A Documentary History.* New York: Oxford University Press, 1980.

Meyer, Michael A. *The Origins of the Modern Jew: Jewish Identity and European Culture in Germany, 1749–1824.* Detroit: Wayne State University Press, 1967.

Morais, Vamberto. *A Short History of Anti-Semitism.* New York: W. W. Norton, 1987.

Mosse, George L. *German Jews beyond Judaism.* Bloomington: Indiana University Press, 1985.

Neubauer, Hans Joachim. "*Auf Begehr: Unser Verkehr*: Über eine judenfeindliche Posse im Jahre 1815." In *Antisemitismus und jüdische Geschichte: Studien zu Ehren Herbert A. Strauss,* edited by Reiner Erb and Michael Schmidt, Berlin: Wissenschaftlicher Autorenverlag, 1987.

Orr, Douglas W. "Anti-Semitism and the Psychopathology of Everyday Life." In *Anti-Semitism: A Social Disease,* edited by Ernst Simmel, 85–96. New York: International Universities Press, 1947.

Ott, Günter. *Ernst Moritz Arndt: Religion, Christentum und Kirche in der Entwicklung des deutschen Publizisten und Patrioten.* Düsseldorf: Presseverband der Evangelischen Kirche, 1966.

Pinson, Koppel S. *Pietism as a Factor in the Rise of German Nationalism*. New York: Columbia University Press, 1934.
Poliakov, Léon. *The History of Anti-Semitism*. Vol. 3: *From Voltaire to Wagner*. Translated by Miriam Kochen. New York: Vanguard, 1975.
Politzer, Heinz. "Lessings Parabel von den drei Ringen." In *Gotthold Ephraim Lessing*, edited by Gerhard and Sybille Bauer, 343–61. Darmstadt: Wissenschaftliche Buchgesellschaft, 1984.
Prignitz, Christoph. *Vaterlandsliebe und Freiheit: Deutscher Patriotismus von 1750 bis 1850*. Wiesbaden: Steiner, 1981.
Pütz, Peter. *Die deutsche Aufklärung*. Darmstadt: Wissenschaftliche Buchgesellschaft, 1979.
———. *Die Leistung der Form: Lessings Dramen*. Frankfurt a.M.: Suhrkamp, 1986.
Randall, John Herman. *The Career of Philosophy*. Vol. 2: *From the German Enlightenment to Darwin*. New York: Columbia University Press, 1962.
Reichmann, Eva G. *Hostages of Civilisation: The Social Sources of National Socialist Anti-Semitism*. London: Victor Gollancz, 1950.
Reuss, Franz. *Christian Wilhelm Dohms Schrift "Über die bürgerliche Verbesserung der Juden" und deren Einwirkung auf die gebildeten Stände Deutschlands: Eine kultur- und literaturgeschichtliche Studie*. Kaiserslautern: Blenk, 1891.
Ritzel, Wolfgang. *Gotthold Ephraim Lessing*. Stuttgart: Kohlhammer, 1968.
Rose, Paul Lawrence. *Revolutionary Antisemitism in Germany: From Kant to Wagner*. Princeton: Princeton University Press, 1990.
Rubin, Theodore Isaac. *Anti-Semitism: A Disease of the Mind*. New York: Continuum, 1990.
Ruether, Rosemary R. "The Theological Roots of Anti-Semitism." In *The Persisting Question: Sociological Perspectives and Social Contexts of Modern Anti-semitism*, edited by Helen Fein, 23–45. Berlin: de Gruyter, 1987.
Rürup, Reinhard. *Emanzipation und Antisemitismus: Studien zur "Judenfrage" der bürgerlichen Gesellschaft*. Göttingen: Vandenhoeck & Ruprecht, 1975.
Said, Edward W. *Orientalism*. New York: Vintage, 1979.
Sartre, Jean-Paul. *Anti-Semite and Jew*. Translated by George J. Becker. New York: Schocken Books, 1948.
Schaer, Wolfgang. *Die Gesellschaft im deutschen bürgerlichen Drama des 18. Jahrhunderts*. Bonn: Bouvier, 1963.
Schallück, Paul. "Moses Mendelssohn und die deutsche Aufklärung." In *Porträts deutsch-jüdischer Geistesgeschichte*, edited by Thilo Koch, 17–36. Cologne: DuMont, 1961.
Schmidt, Erich. *Lessing: Geschichte seines Lebens und seiner Schriften* (1923). Hildesheim: Olms, 1983.
Schoeps, Julius H. *Moses Mendelssohn*. Königstein: Jüdischer Verlag, 1979.
Scholem, Gershom. "Jews and Germans." In *On Jews and Judaism in Crisis: Selected Essays*, 71–92. New York: Schocken, 1976.
———. "Once More: The German-Jewish Dialogue." In *On Jews and Judaism in Crisis: Selected Essays*, 65–70. New York: Schocken, 1976.

Simmel, Ernst. "Anti-Semitism and Mass Psychopathology." In *Anti-Semitism: A Social Disease*, edited by Ernst Simmel, 33–79. New York: International Universities Press, 1947.
Sombart, Werner. *The Jews and Modern Capitalism*. Translated by M. Epstein. London: T. Fisher Unwin, 1913.
Sørensen, Bengt Algot. *Herrschaft und Zärtlichkeit: Der Patriarchalismus und das Drama im 18. Jahrhundert*. Munich: Beck, 1984.
Sorkin, David. "Jews, the Enlightenment, and Religious Toleration—Some Reflections." *Leo Baeck Institute Yearbook* 37 (1992): 3–16.
———. *The Transformation of German Jewry, 1780–1840*. New York: Oxford University Press, 1987.
Spiel, Hilde. *Fanny von Arnstein: A Daughter of the Enlightenment, 1758–1818*. Translated by Christine Shuttleworth. New York: Berg, 1991.
Stephan, Horst and Hans Leube. *Handbuch der Kirchengeschichte*. Vol. 4: *Die Neuzeit*. Tübingen: Mohr, 1931.
Sterling, Elenore. *Judenhaß: Die Anfänge des politischen Antisemitismus in Deutschland*. Frankfurt: Europäische Verlagsanstalt, 1969.
Stern, Selma. *Der preußische Staat und die Juden*. Vol. 3: *Die Zeit Friedrichs des Großen*. Tübingen: Mohr, 1971.
Stümcke, Heinrich, ed. *Die Fortsetzungen, Nachahmungen und Travestien von Lessings "Nathan der Weise."* Berlin: Selbstverlag für Theatergeschichte, 1904.
Suesse-Fiedler, Sigrid. *Lessings "Nathan der Weise" und sein Leser: Eine wirkungsästhetische Studie*. Stuttgart: Hans-Dieter Heinz, 1980.
Sumner, William Graham. *Folkways: A Study of the Sociological Importance of Usages, Manners, Customs, Mores and Morals* (1906). New York: New American Library, 1946.
Szarota, Elida Maria. *Künstler, Grübler und Rebellen: Studien zum europäischen Märtyrerdrama des 17. Jahrhunderts*. Bern: Francke, 1967.
Szondi, Peter. *Die Theorie des bürgerlichen Trauerspiels im 18. Jahrhundert*. Frankfurt: Suhrkamp, 1973.
Van Cleve, John W. *The Merchant in German Literature of the Enlightenment*. Chapel Hill: University of North Carolina Press, 1986.
Voloshinov, V.N. *Marxism and the Philosophy of Language*. Translated by Ladislav Matejka and I.R. Titunik. Cambridge, Mass.: Harvard University Press, 1986.
Walach, Dagmar. *Der aufrechte Bürger, seine Welt und sein Theater: Zum bürgerlichen Trauerspiel im 18. Jahrhundert*. Munich: Fink, 1980.
Weissberg, Liliane. "Stepping Out: The Writing of Difference in Rahel Varnhagen's Letters." In *Anti-Semitism in Times of Crisis*, edited by Sander L. Gilman and Steven T. Katz, 140–53. New York: New York University Press, 1991.
Wessels, Hans Friedrich. *Lessings "Nathan der Weise": Seine Wirkungsgeschichte bis zum Ende der Goethezeit*. Königstein: Athenäum, 1979.
Wiesemann, Falk. "Jewish Burials in Germany—Between Tradition, the Enlightenment, and the Authorities." *Leo Baeck Institute Yearbook* 37 (1992): 17–31.

Wightman, Rose Schipper. "The Changing Image of the Jew as Reflected in German Drama in the Time of Lessing and Heine." Ph.D. dissertation, Wayne State University, 1967.

Wilson, W. Daniel. *Humanität und Kreuzzugsideologie um 1780*. New York: Peter Lang, 1984.

Wilson, Christopher P. *Jokes: Form, Content, Use and Function*. London: Academic Press, 1979.

Young-Bruehl, Elisabeth. *Hannah Arendt: For Love of the World*. New Haven: Yale University Press, 1982.

Zymner, Rüdiger. "Kunstapotheose in der Ringparabel." *Lessing Yearbook* 24 (1992): 77–96.

Index

Adorno, Theodor W., 8, 12–13, 16, 69, 117, 151
Anti-Semitism, 1–2, 6–7, 11–19, 32–35, 38, 41–45, 113–50
Arendt, Hannah, 1, 65–66, 154–55
Arenhof (Jewish author), 4, 77–80
Argens, Marquis d', 67
Arndt, Ernst Moritz, 122–24
Arnim, Ludwig Joachim (Achim) von, 140–42
Ascher, Saul, 82–90, 126–27
Assimilation, 3, 36–38, 55–63, 98–112, 151–55

Bakhtin, Mikhail M., 19–20, 134
Bemerkungen über die bürgerliche Verbesserung der Juden (Ascher), 82–84
Bettelheim, Bruno, 13
Bischof, Jakob, 101–12
Blick aus der Zeit auf die Zeit (Arndt), 122–24
Bonaparte, Jerome (brother of Napoleon), 5
Börne, Ludwig, 148–49
Brentano, Clemens von, 140–41
Buchholz, Friedrich, 120–22

Congress of Vienna, 29
Consensus formations, 19, 23
Court Jews, 5, 18
Crusades, 33–34

Defamatory humor, 127–50
Deicide, 120
Deism, 25, 27, 33, 35, 60–63, 76
Derisory humor, 127–50
Diderot, Denis, 128
Diez, Heinrich Friedrich von, 60–63, 90
Dina, das Judenmädchen aus Franken (Bischof), 101–12
Dohm, Christian Wilhelm von, 56–60, 68, 118
Domestic tragedy. *See* Family drama

Double bind (religious), 94
Drama, 32–35, 77–80, 98–112, 127–36

Edict of Toleration, 3, 78–84
Einige jüdische Familienscenen (Arenhof), 4, 77–80
Eisenmenger, Johann Andreas, 115, 137
Ellul, Jacques, 114–15
Emancipation (Jewish), 1, 9, 30, 32–41, 55–63, 64–93, 98–112
Emden, Jacob, 92
Enlightenment, 6, 25–28, 31, 35, 38, 64–93, 113, 126–27, 133, 150
Exogamy, 106–9, 137

False projection, theory of, 13–14
Family drama (eighteenth-century), 77–80, 98–112
Fastnachtspiel, 131–32, 136
Fenichel, Otto, 13–14, 117
Ferber, Friedrich Wilhelm von, 70
Fichte, Johann Gottlieb, 115, 118, 125
Foucault, Michel, 19, 44, 98
Frederick the Great. *See* Friedrich II
French Revolution, 28, 114
Freud, Sigmund, 127–28
Friedländer, David, 80, 90–92, 127
Friedrich II (king of Prussia), 4, 68, 70
Friedrich Wilhelm I (king of Prussia), 25
Friedrich Wilhelm II (king of Prussia), 28

Die Germanomanie (Ascher), 126–27
Goethe, Johann Wolfgang von, 52
Goeze, Johann Melchior, 32–35
Grattenauer, Carl Wilhelm Friedrich, 115–20, 137
Guilds, 18

Halle (Arnim), 141–42
Haskalah, 64–93, 126–27, 145
Herz, Henriette, 5–6
Herz, Marcus, 5, 68, 92–93
Horkheimer, Max, 13, 16, 69, 92–93, 117, 151

188 Index

Ingroups and outgroups, 7–8, 23
Islam, 49–50

Jerusalem (Mendelssohn), 71–76
Joseph II (Austrian emperor), 3, 78–84
Die Juden (Lessing), 34, 137
Die Juden (Ziegelhauser), 101–12
Die Judenschule (Sessa), 142–49

Knittelvers, 132, 136
Kristeva, Julia, 153–54

Lavater, Johann Kaspar, 67–68
Lessing, Gotthold Ephraim, 1, 32–55, 57–59, 71–72, 98, 114, 128, 133–39, 155
Leviathan (Ascher), 84–90
Lotich, Johann Karl, 101–12

Maimon, Salomon, 5, 145
Maimonides, 86
Martyr dramas, 52–53
Maskilim, 64–93
Menasseh ben Israel, 68
Mendelssohn, Moses, 5, 32–33, 65–76, 86, 117, 120–21
Mennonites, 57
Menschen und Menschensituationen (Steinberg), 101–12
Middlemen, 18–19
Der Mönch vom Libanon (Pfranger), 45–55
Money circulation. *See* Moneylenders
Moneylenders, 15–19, 77, 79, 119, 129–33
Moses und Jesus (Buchholz), 120–22
Multiculturalism, 151–55
Mysticism, 28, 48

Napoleon, 5, 113, 135–36
Napoleonic Wars. *See* Wars of Liberation
Nathan der Deutsche (Reinicke), 101–12
Nathan der Weise (Lessing), 1, 32–55, 57–59, 71–72, 133–39
Nathan der Weise travestirt und modernisirt (anonymous), 133–36
Nationalism, 28–31, 113–14, 119, 126–27, 133–36
National Socialism, 1
Natural Religion, 25, 27, 43, 46, 71, 133
Nicolai, Friedrich, 27, 41

Orthodox Jews (eighteenth-century traditionalists), 64–65
Outgroups. *See* Ingroups and outgroups

Particularism, 11–12, 21
Pfranger, Johann Georg, 45–55, 118, 121
Philanthropy, 105–6
Propaganda, 114–15
Psychoanalysis, 12–15

Quakers, 57

Reichmann, Eva G., 1, 10
Reimarus, Hermann Samuel, 32, 134
Reinicke, Heinrich, 101–12
Ring Parable (Lessing), 38–40, 59
Romanticism, 28–30, 93–97, 122–24, 140–42
Rührstück, 98–112
Rühs, Friedrich, 124–26
Rules of exclusion, 19, 42

Sachs, Hans, 131–32, 136
Said, Edward W., 153
Salons (Jewish), 5–6, 93–97, 137, 141
Sartre, Jean-Paul, 8–9, 153
Schiller, Friedrich, 53
Schlegel, Dorothea Mendelssohn, 5–6
Scholem, Gershom, 152
Schütz, Friedrich Julius, 146–47
Secularization, 25, 27, 71
Self-hatred (Jewish), 94, 97
Sessa, Karl Borromäus Alexander, 1, 142–49
Simmel, Ernst, 13–14
Spinoza, Baruch de, 86
Steinberg, Karl, 101–12
Sumner, William Graham, 7

Taufepidemie, 65, 93
Taufjuden, 64, 93–97
Der Teufel nahm ein altes Weib (Sachs), 131–32, 136
Tischgesellschaften, 6, 140
Toledot Yeshu, 33–34
Tolerance, 20–22, 32–63, 105–12, 151–55
Tolerance Patent. *See* Edict of Toleration
Torah, 64
Tralles, Balthasar Ludwig, 41–44
Travesties, 127–50

Der travestirte Nathan der Weise (Voss), 136–39

Über die frühe Beerdigung der Juden (Herz), 92–93
Ueber die Ansprüche der Juden an das deutsche Bürgerrecht (Rühs), 124–26
Ueber Juden (Diez), 60–63
Unser Verkehr (Sessa), 1, 142–49

Varnhagen, Karl August, 96
Varnhagen, Rahel, 5–6, 93–97, 137, 154
Voloshinov, Valentin N., 20
Voltaire, François-Marie-Arouet de, 4, 26
Von den Krankheiten der Juden (Wolf), 76–77
Vorurtheil und Liebe (anonymous), 101–12
Voss, Julius von, 136–39

Wars of Liberation, 29, 112, 113–50
Wer war wohl mehr Jude? (Lotich), 101–12
Wessely, Naphthali Hartwig Herz, 80–82
Wider die Juden (Grattenauer), 115–20
Wolf, Elcan Isaac, 76–77
Wolff, Christian von, 25, 71
Wöllner edicts, 27
Worte der Wahrheit und des Friedens (Wessely), 80–82
Der wuchernde Jude am Pranger (anonymous), 129–33

Yiddish, 14, 80–81, 139, 142–43

Ziegelhauser, Gottfried Julius, 101–12

www.ingramcontent.com/pod-product-compliance
Lightning Source LLC
Chambersburg PA
CBHW020759160426
43192CB00006B/379